C000135667

Purge This Realm

Michael S. Edwards

Purge This Realm

A Life of Joseph Rayner Stephens

EPWORTH PRESS

All rights reserved. No part of this publication
may be reproduced, stored in a retrieval system,
or transmitted, in any form or by any means,
electronic, mechanical, photocopying, recording
or otherwise, without the prior permission of the
publisher, Epworth Press.

Copyright © Michael S. Edwards 1994

0 7162 0497 5

First published 1994
by Epworth Press
1 Central Buildings Westminster
London SW1H 9NR

Typeset at The Spartan Press Ltd
Lymington, Hants
Printed and bound in Great Britain by
Biddles Ltd, Guildford and King's Lynn

Judge Eternal, throned in splendour,
    Lord of lords and King of kings,
With thy living fire of judgment
    Purge this realm of bitter things;
Solace all its wide dominion
    With the healing of thy wings.

Henry Scott Holland (1847–1918)

'He wished to see the institutions of his
country purged from every existing abuse,
but at the same time preserved in all
their pristine beauty, and in all their
majesty and glory. He had sought for no
change.'

Joseph Rayner Stephens
(Manchester 1838)

Contents

List of Illustrations

appearing between pages 78 and 79

Drawing of Stephens, aged 24 (By permission of the Royal Library, National Library of Sweden)

Stephens dinner plate, late 1830s (By permission of Mr David Earle)

Portrait of Stephens in 1839, by James Garside (By permission of the Astley Cheetham Art Gallery, Stalybridge)

The People's School, Brierley Street, Stalybridge, the only surviving Stephenite building (By permission of Tameside Local Studies Library, Stalybridge)

The Stalybridge relief office in the period of the cotton famine (By permission of Tameside Local Studies Library, Stalybridge)

The new Ashton Workhouse, built in 1850 (By permission of Tameside Local Studies Library, Stalybridge)

'Old Greybeard'. A Photograph of Stephens in later life (By permission of the Royal Library, National Library of Sweden)

Stephens silverware, including communion vessels used at King Street, Stalybridge, and the inkstand presented by the Society of Oddfellows in 1866 (By permission of Mrs Diana Stephens-Krook)

Foreword

In the Wesleyan Connexion of which he was briefly a minister, Rayner Stephens was remembered, when he was remembered at all, because in the early 1830s he broke with the majority ministerial tradition and advocated the disestablishment of the Church of England. In this century he reappeared in a secular context as an alleged advocate of 'physical-force' Chartism, who drew back in the late 1830s when violence actually looked likely. In this role he failed to commend himself to Left-wing historians like E. P. Thompson, for whom Methodism was a negative force which helped to frustrate the possibilities of a working-class revolution which Thompson (mistakenly) thought ought to have happened in the 1830s or 1840s.

And yet, as Michael Edwards shows in convincing detail, Stephens was more than a just a man of errors, defeated himself and leading others to defeat. He was a man above all of considerable staying-power and rhetorical talent who, once he had resigned from the Wesleyan ministry in 1834, was able to build up a second career as what we might now call a 'political Priest'. He established an independent congregation in Ashton-under-Lyne, which was only then developing from social chaos into a Lancashire cotton-town. From that time his basic loyalties were to the alleviation of the sufferings of the textile-workers who surrounded him and to whom he could always give a language of protest; to Richard Oastler and the Ten-Hours movement, whose programme, basic but interventionist and therefore deeply resented by the mill-owners, demanded a reduction in the working week; to Chartism as a means to these social ends but never as an end in itself; and to a Tory utopian vision of a distant English Christian past, vaguely identified with Alfred the Great, and neither democratic nor socialist. A Wesleyan in his bones, he rejected both teetotalism and American mass revivalism.

Briefly, at the height of the Chartist period, Stephens became a national figure, notorious for threats of what seemed to be physical violence and bloody revolution: those who read his speeches in their

newspapers did so in the dark light of the French Terror. Michael
Edwards suggests that Stephens hoped to intimidate the government,
not to start a revolution; and that what we also see here is a familiar
weakness of political theology, the futile appeal to eschatology, to a day
of divine judgment which would solve all political problems but which in
practice never comes. Imprisoned for his inflammatory language in
1839, Stephens seemed to repent, but when he saw the suffering of the
Lancashire mill-workers and their families in the Cotton Famine in the
early 1860s he fell back again on the same violent compassion.

And yet, as Michael Edwards so clearly illustrates, there was more to
Stephens' speeches than a confused theology of hope:

> To be justified means in a few plain words, to be set right; to be set
> right with God, to be set right with man . . . If that be the meaning of it
> – and your own ministers will not deny that it is the meaning of it – put
> it to them whether any millowner in their society is justified by
> faith . . . He cannot be justified; he cannot have things set right
> between God and himself . . . all is crooked between him and God, all
> is wrong between him and his people; and so long as he continues a
> millowner in the present state and under the present system of
> trade . . . he must be on the highroad to everlasting damnation. Do
> you ask me why? Because he makes free with that which does not
> belong to him. Your bodies and souls are God's and not your
> masters . . . and as long as the millowner does to them what is likely to
> hurt them . . . he is guilty in the sight of God of blood . . . Is he ever
> told that? Never, never, never. The minister in whose society or
> congregation he belongs would rather have one millowner in his
> congregation than a thousand spinners.

These are easy words to read quickly. But imagine them spoken at the
height of a desperate social crisis to many more than a thousand
spinners by a genuine communicator who passionately believed them
and could say them with a moral conviction that is uncommon in politics
today. Stephens had anchored his politics in his theology, and political
theology is a dangerous tool. There were times when he could talk about
'the Throne, the Altar and the Cottage', a phrase which was innocent in
his mouth, but has a grim resonance in modern European history, for it
comes close to the heart of Vichy's far from innocent Right-wing
Catholic ideology. Nevertheless, Stephens had grasped the essential
issue of his day. Were the Lancashire spinners bound to accept what was
happening – had they no alternative but to exchange a lost and largely

imaginary pre-industiral paradise run on strictly hierarchical lines, for a thrusting, individualistic commercialized society in which religion was relegated to the private sphere? This was not just an argument about the place of the 'church' in politics, but an argument, which is far from finished, about the kind of England one would choose to live in. Was there no chance of another kind of Englishness, either more fraternal in the revolutionary tradition, or more religious in terms of the Jesus of the Gospels? His actions in the 1830s and his angry pity in the 1860s, helped to foster those links between some middle-class Christians and some trade-unionists which formed part of the background of the Labour Party.

After 1918 English Nonconformity, including Methodism, found itself in unaccustomed decline. Methodism responded by cutting itself off from its nineteenth-century history and therefore from people like Rayner Stephens. There was a break in continuity for which the intensive study of John Wesley and eighteenth-century Methodism offered little compensation. Michael Edwards' important study of Stephens, which I am delighted to commend, reminds us that the question of England is still unanswered, and that the English churches have still not made up their minds what their answer should be.

John Kent

Preface

He is forgotten now. The dynamic orator who once attracted the adoration or execration of thousands is known today mainly to students of social or Methodist history. Joseph Rayner Stephens remains a distant memory in Ashton and Stalybridge, but although his monument in Stamford Park Tameside and his People's School survive, his chapels have disappeared, and the Dukinfield grave has been vandalized. The voice of the ex-Wesleyan Methodist minister that roused vast northern crowds to revivalist fervour for Christian social justice has been long stilled. Like many of his kind, he was consigned to oblivion while he still lived, for in the more relaxed years of late Victorian prosperity it was embarrassing to remember too much of the recent past. His opposition to the emerging spirit of the age and the violence of his language had discredited him, and he was unfortunate in his only Victorian biographer. Yet his ministry amid the 'dark, satanic mills' marked him out as a pioneer of a Christian social gospel in an industrial age. It was a gospel that he and others preached before the coming of Maurice and the Christian Socialists, and before the Communist Manifesto was written. As his gravestone says, he did what he could; and this is his story.

This book derives from a longer, more detailed study which has taken many years to complete. In the last thirty-five years social historians have showed considerable interest in Stephens' agitations; but apart from the late Dr J. T. Ward's biographical article of 1958, no modern biographies of Stephens (by contrast with most of his fellow leaders in the factory, anti-Poor Law and Chartist movements) have appeared. Usually Methodist historians have referred to him in passing, limiting their interest to his Wesleyan years. Above all, his career as minister and agitator has not been presented as a convincing unity; hence the need for a new biography.

Primary source material for many aspects and periods of Stephens' life is difficult to find. Much has been lost, and inevitably this affects the shape of the book. Other material is still unpublished, and one can only hope that eventually it will be made available. For his public life, however, enough evidence survives, and in gathering it I am indebted to many.

I acknowledge my debt to many libraries for permission to reproduce material, especially to the British Library's Newspaper Library at Colindale, the Tameside Local Studies Library at Stalybridge, and the Manchester Public Libraries Local Studies Unit; also for material reproduced by courtesy of the Director and University Librarian from collections held in the Methodist Archives and Research Centre, the John Rylands University Library of Manchester. The Tameside and Manchester local studies libraries kindly supplied illustrations as well as source material. In addition there is material from the archives of the Methodist Church, Overseas Division (Methodist Missionary Society), which is at the library of the School of Oriental and African Studies, and from the Oldham Local Studies Library archives.

At various times over many years I have used the Bodleian library at Oxford, and the libraries of the British Museum, the University of Nairobi, the London School of Economics and Political Science, the Bishopsgate Institute, Wesley College Bristol, the Northern College (United Reformed and Congregational) in Manchester and the Wesley Historical Society, and Penzance's Morrab and Public Libraries. I must also thank the Butler Library of Columbia University in the United States for making available microfilm of the *People's Magazine*, and the Royal Library of Stockholm for allowing the inclusion of hitherto unpublished illustrations. I am grateful for the use of Crown copyright material held at the Public Records Office at Kew, and reproduced with the permission of the Controller of Her Majesty's Stationery Office. Similar thanks are given to the Records Offices of Greater London, Cheshire and Lancashire, and the General Registry Office. I thank the Chief Executives of the Tameside Borough Council for allowing me to use the deeds of the People's School.

With regard to the many direct quotations in this book, I have tried to trace the holders of copyright material, but if I have unwittingly infringed anyone's copyright, I would be willing to make acknowledgment in any future edition.

I would like to thank Mrs Diana Stephens-Krook, Mr James and Mr David Earle, Mr Rayner Stephens Unwin and Mr David Unwin, descendents of the Revd John and Rebecca Stephens, the parents of Joseph Rayner Stephens, all of whom expressed considerable interest in this book, and most kindly provided family material for it. I am grateful too for the help given by Professors W. R. Ward and Dale A. Johnson, Dr D. A. Farnie, Dr C. D. Field, the Revds Tom Shaw, Kenneth Bounds, Dr Oliver Beckerlegge, Dr J. C. Bowmer, and Dr Janos Pasztor, Mr Bernard Aspinwall, Mr Anthony Ashton, Mr Martin Jolly and the late Mr Eric Youngs, all of whom discussed the issues, offered advice or loaned material.

My special thanks are due to the Revd Professor John Kent for writing the Foreword. As the former Professor of Theology and Religious Studies at the University of Bristol, he was a most stimulating superviser of my M.Litt thesis.

I am much indebted to Mrs Joyce Pook of Reigate, who in recent years has been a most conscientious and resourceful research assistant. I am even more indebted to another friend, Mr Alan Rose of Mottram, the editor of the *Proceedings* of the Methodist Historical Society. He has been a constant source of sound advice and freely offered help for over twenty-five years, and has compiled the index of the book. Between the two of them, they have greatly enriched this work. Also I wish to thank the Revd Graham Slater and the Revd Dr Cyril Rodd, both of the Epworth Press, for the care and trouble they have taken over the manuscript.

Finally, my grateful thanks to my wife, who has suffered a Stephens-haunted husband in many manses, given her support throughout, and even supplied the title of the book.

None of the above are responsible for the views I express in this book.

Michael Edwards

June 1994

I

The Methodist Minister

Joseph Rayner Stephens was the sixth child of a Cornish Wesleyan Methodist minister and an Essex farmer's daughter. He was born on 8 March 1805 in Edinburgh, where his father was a circuit minister. There were twelve children altogether, of whom three others were to distinguish themselves – John as a newspaper editor, Edward as a banker, and George as a university professor. The Revd John Stephens gave affection, but laid down firm principles in the home. On scriptural grounds, wives were strictly subordinate to husbands, and children were to be brought up as Methodists and Tories. He passed on to them the identity he had found for himself, and which meant everything to him.[1]

In his youth, John Stephens had been a lead miner in the obscure village of St Dennis. His father died when he was sixteen, but he was converted, and joined the Methodist society. Poverty was transcended by grace, and his talents were nurtured within the Methodist fellowship. In 1791 he entered the itinerancy – the developing ministry. A wider world beyond the Celtic fringe was opening before him, and he responded with Methodist and patriotic spirit. During the wars with France, he served in leading circuits from Dover to Dundee. A gifted and successful preacher and an able administrator, he was an ally of the rising man in the Wesleyan body, Jabez Bunting. Methodist reformers and Jacobin sympathizers in his circuits got short shrift. Like Wesley and many others, he held that Protestantism was the essential ingredient of an all-British national consciousness: ' . . . our civil constitution and our religious privileges have one common interest; they will stand or fall . . . together'. His pronounced patriotic sentiment was fully recognized in his official Methodist obituary.[2]

Joseph's mother, Rebecca Elizabeth Rayner of Stanford Rivers, had married John Stephens at Wethersfield in 1796. Stephens' biographer Holyoake said she 'came of an Essex yeoman family of the old school'. (Her son thought so highly of the status of yeoman that during the sixties he so described himself on official documents). She was generous, determined, active and courageous, all of which qualities were passed on to Joseph.[3]

His early years were spent in the rapid changes and the domestic austerity of the itinerancy. From the age of eight, he spent two years at Woodhouse Grove Methodist boarding school near Leeds, and later attended Leeds and Manchester Grammar schools. He acquired a lifelong interest in languages and literature, especially of British dialects. He took part in amateur theatricals, and in Manchester at the age of fourteen he witnessed the notorious Peterloo massacre of August 1819, when unarmed, peaceful demonstrators for Parliamentary reform were killed by yeomanry cavalry. In 1821 his parents thought of making him a doctor. Two years later he refused his father's offer of a college education, on the grounds that his brothers and sisters could never complain that more money was spent on his education than theirs. He became a teacher at Cottingham, studying far into the night to keep ahead of his pupils.[4]

The young teacher became a local preacher in the Beverley circuit, and in 1825 offered himself for the Wesleyan ministry. The Beverley superintendent Thomas Galland called him 'a truly valuable young man, and likely to prove both as regards depth of piety, superior abilities and assiduity in their cultivation a very efficient servant of the Connexion'. The Hull district warmly recommended him as a probationer, alluding to his 'personal piety, knowledge of Methodism and cordial attachment to it'. He was accepted, and served for a year in the Beverley circuit itself.[5]

In March 1826 he accepted the Wesleyan Missionary Society's invitation to begin work in Sweden. An English Methodist shipbuilder in Stockholm, Samuel Owen, had requested Methodist provision for his family, and a ministry among the English residents. He offered to support a single missionary, and he had a large room in his house for preaching. With his linguistic ability, the opening was attractive to Stephens. Following current Wesleyan practice, he was ordained so that he could administer the sacraments and gain legal recognition in the field; the service was conducted on 29 May by his father and two assisting ministers. He sailed from London in July 1826.[6]

Sweden was to mould Stephens, but in many ways, it frustrated him. There were few English residents, and fewer who were sympathetic to Methodism. The Missionary Society's policy in 1826 on converting Swedes remains a mystery, but as it sought a linguist who saw it as his first duty to learn Swedish in order to preach, it is probable that it had

Swedish converts in mind. If so, the implications were not faced. Swedish law was more complex than had been thought, and there was a strange inability to foresee the likely hostility of the established Lutheran Church to foreign Protestant missionary work. Was the Swedish mission to minister to English residents (as allowed by the law), to create a Swedish Methodism (which was not), or to revive the Lutheran Church through its existing pietist tradition? Stephens realized quickly that laws against other Protestant traditions were enforced more effectively than the crumbling English penal codes against Dissent, and that the Swedish Church was more formidable than its English counterpart. The dilemma appears in many of his surviving letters to the Missionary Society; either he received impractical answers, or it was left for him to decide policy for himself. Either way, the unresolved ambiguity at the heart of the Stockholm mission led him in the end to quit Sweden.[7]

His initial enthusiasm met with success in unexpected quarters. At once he began learning Swedish. He obtained permission to build a Methodist chapel, and held the first service in Owen's house on 18 November, with about twenty persons present. Rebuffed by the other foreign churches, he approached the Marshal of the Swedish Diet, Count de Geer, and obtained the free use of his large summer house as a chapel. It was opened on 3 December, and Stephens wrote: 'Methodism is now admitted and legally sanctioned, and I hope will not be a lifeless name.' He committed himself by forming a Methodist class meeting; soon it contained five English and two Swedes.[8]

Throughout life, Stephens had a gift for making unlikely friendships. The Count's goodwill encouraged other highly-placed Swedes to take an interest. A Swedish royal chaplain had introduced Countess von Schwerin to the young preacher; she described him as 'this estimable and most excellent man'. She and her son-in-law came regularly to the services and she was impatient for him to preach in Swedish. Stephens was encouraged by his remarkable congregation:

> At almost every service we have clergymen – students, and different members of his Majesty's govt. – some of the privy council &c, the Crown Princess' Father confessor has twice attended preaching – for though a Catholic (he) is a very liberal-minded man.

Owen was delighted, and informed London that Stephens was very much liked, 'and indeed is quite a wonder to all that hear him, and in my opinion you could not have sent a more suitable young man for this station'. Although he did not preach in Swedish until December 1827, Stephens found that he could hold a highly unusual congregation in a foreign capital.[9]

His was the only English-speaking worship in the country, but it was difficult to convince the English residents ('churchmen, dissenters, presbyterians, worldlings'), that Methodism was not sectarian or illiberal. Even the British envoy Lord Bloomfield, a devout Evangelical, did not attend at first because of his official position and Anglican loyalties, though his family came. In October 1828 Stephens consoled him after a double bereavement. Bloomfield thanked him 'for the services you have rendered me, and for the peace which under God, you have administered to my wounded heart'. Stephens became an unofficial chaplain at the embassy, and read prayers in Bloomfield's house twice a day. After the young minister's departure, Bloomfield wrote in November 1829 to assure him that their meeting was 'the most important of my life'. John Scott, who succeeded Stephens in 1830, found among the crowded congregation the United States Consul, the American plenipotentiary, the British Consul-general, the British Representative and his suite, and most of the English speaking community.[10]

Yet his problems were multiplying. His stipend had not been paid, his health was deteriorating, and he was lonely. He was 'young – single – and by no means furnished with native buoyancy and cheerfulness'. He hinted at the temptations he faced without a 'bosom counsellor' or a friend. He began an inner withdrawal by suggesting to the missionary secretary that he visit other lands on the society's behalf. By August 1828 he was 'sinking under the influence of melancholy thought'.[11]

The cause was the massive presence of the Lutheran Church. Although critical of its 'deadness' and supportive of its pietists, he could not deny its potential:

> But of this I am almost convinced, that it will be impossible to establish Methodism as a form or system among them. Neither perhaps is it desirable to do so. The institutions of the Swedish church are so excellent – its system of discipline, were it acted upon, so efficient, whilst its doctrines (those of Luther) differ nothing from our own, except in one or two almost obsolete and surrendered points, but I earnestly hope and believe . . . that a revival will commence in the bosom of the church itself, led by its own ministers and spreading amongst its own members. No sectarian in principle, I

have never yet, I candidly confess it, attempted to bring over the members of the Lutheran Church to the outward forms of Methodism – the spirit – the life is one.

He admitted that 'my own mind wavers much and is often ill at ease on this subject'. It was one thing to preach successfully to Swedes of high rank, but quite another to establish a Swedish Methodist society.[12]

By 1829, he befriended the young son of the French ambassador, the future Liberal Catholic leader Count Charles de Montalembert. Like Stephens, he was lonely and unhappy, for his father disliked his liberalism and he was frustrated in love. Finding no one to celebrate his birthday with him, he read 'poor Stephens', who had been ill, some fragment of Quinet. In July, he confided in Stephens as though he were a Catholic priest. Almost thirty years later when Montalembert was imprisoned by Napoleon III, Stephens remembered their old friendship.[13]

He decided to leave Sweden. The English were marrying into Swedish families, and any children had to be brought up as Lutherans. He was sick, and the class meeting had ceased. In late May he was permitted to return home. Owen was dismayed, and hurried to London to ask for his reappointment for a year, or for his delay until a successor arrived; but he left in November, with the goodwill of Bloomfield and Owen, and according to Scott, to the tears of many Swedes. These sentiments soon died through Stephens' subsequent neglect, and his mounting notoriety at home was contrasted with the temporary success of Scott's evangelism; but Stephens was right about the Swedish mission. The founding of a Swedish Methodism from Scott's labours aroused the ire of the Lutheran Church, and a riot ended the mission in 1842.[14]

Returning missionaries are subject to culture shock, and he re-entered an England undergoing unprecedented convulsions. In Wesleyan Methodism, a venomous controversy in Leeds in 1827 over the installation of an organ had challenged the authority of the all-ministerial Conference over the societies. John Stephens as President of Conference with Bunting as Secretary had expelled the malcontents, but a new and bitter Protestant Methodist Society was the result. Soon this was dwarfed by national religious controversy. Peaceful repeal of Dissenting disabilities in 1828 was followed by a more heart-searching but successful agitation for Catholic emancipation. The confessional Protestant state was no more, and in 1830 a Whig government took office pledged to political reform. Slavery in the British empire was abolished in 1831, and a Reform Act passed the following year with the nation at the point of revolution.[15]

Although all this profoundly affected Stephens' subsequent career, even his whereabouts from November 1829 to the summer of 1830 is unknown. Then he returned to circuit work, a year in the rural peace of Cheltenham being followed by another amid the urban bustle of Newcastle-on-Tyne. He was one of many sponsors of his brother John's newspaper, which was founded in 1830. The *Christian Advocate* was the first Methodist newspaper, and its gifted editor had an independent outlook and an eye to the main chance. The younger John Stephens angered the Wesleyan Conference by publishing unauthorized accounts of its proceedings, and he stirred up a hornet's nest of mutual recrimination when he attacked Bunting for allegedly voting for a pro-slavery candidate. The Stephens family was divided, for the editor's father repudiated the principles of the paper. Until 1834, Joseph kept out of its controversies, but unlike other ministerial sponsors, he did not withdraw his name in protest.[16]

In 1832, Stephens was appointed to the Ashton-under-Lyne circuit. Ashton was a great centre of the Lancashire cotton industry, on which British prosperity was believed to depend. At first, he was less interested in its economic and social conditions than its turbulent religious and political life. Middle-class radicalism triumphed with the Reform Act, and the public influence of the hard-headed cotton manufacturers was beginning to overshadow that of the lord of the manor, the Earl of Stamford. The disillusioned and unenfranchised factory operatives were radicals of a different kind. Trade unionism, Owenist Socialism and factory reform movements all flourished in Ashton.

The Earl of Stamford's nephew, George Chetwode, was the non-resident, pluralist Rector of St Michael's for fifty-four years. He exploited the mining potential of the parish glebe lands, and enjoyed all the town church rates (despite the existence of a second church, St Peter's, from 1824). St Michael's was served by a series of poorly paid curates while he flourished in his Buckinghamshire retreat. It was not surprising that in the thirties, a survey found that almost half the people of Ashton made no Christian profession.[17]

If Chetwode was no enthusiast, others were. The disciples of Joanna Southcott were active in Ashton. The town was the headquarters of the Christian Israelite Church, with its chapel of silver and bronze fittings built in 1825. Its builder, John Wroe, took ten virgins to comfort him, in obedience to a convenient divine command. Forced to flee following a riot, he returned in 1839, and the church survived his death in 1863. Enthusiasm of a different kind came with the increasing number of Irish immigrants. Roman Catholicism took root, though regular services only began in 1846, and not until 1849 was there a resident priest.[18]

Dissent of a markedly anti-Anglican kind was very strong. It attracted both the manufacturing classes and humbler folk. Just as St Michael's was regarded as the centre of local Toryism, so Dissent was identified with Liberalism. Tribal animosities were fed by the Earl of Stamford, who prohibited the building of dissenting chapels on his land, so helping to polarize Ashton's public life between the forces of church and Dissent for about half a century. When Stephens arrived, the Congregationalists were outstripping the Methodists in numbers and wealth, and their Albion Chapel was being enlarged. Wealthier Methodists tended to become Congregationalists. Hugh Mason, who eventually was the wealthiest of the town's cotton masters, was the Sunday school secretary at Stamford Street Methodist New Connexion Chapel. He joined the Albion Chapel in about 1846. As he was to say years later, 'even in religious matters we are none of us the worse for a little wholesome competition'.[19]

Ashton Methodism had a chequered life almost from the beginning. The first chapel was opened in 1781, and there were two more by the time Alexander Kilham's Methodist New Connexion seceded from the parent body in 1797. All three chapels and all but twenty-five of the members joined the new body. Kilham's radicalism and his reformed Methodism made a strong local appeal. In 1799 when Stamford Street chapel was opened in the town's main thoroughfare, the New Connexion's pre-eminence among Ashton Methodists was demonstrated. Despite a recovery, the Wesleyan Methodists never became as strong as the New Connexion circuit; this was unusual, and it produced some untypical local Methodist reactions. Nevertheless, by 1833 the re-established Wesleyan circuit had 1,100 members, just 20 short of the New Connexion number. There were also Independent and Primitive Methodists, but both were weaker than the other two. The Church of England's reaction to them all was summarized by the Ashton curate, John Hutchinson, in 1811. He reported to his bishop:

> We abound with Dissenters . . . the Methodists here are very numerous – and in my opinion are by far the most inveterate enemies of the established church . . . their Teachers are most unremitting in

their exertions to gain proselytes to their party in a way truly intolerant . . . This they do by artful insinuations disseminated among the vulgar and undiscerning class of society that the regular Clergy do not preach the Gospel.[20]

Such was the contentious world that Stephens entered in 1832. He was soon part of it, for by Christmas he was dismissing charges against ministers who neglected their appointments on the grounds that only the District Meeting could hear charges against ministers. 'Mr Crompton (the superintendent minister) is Conference, and you must submit to him.' Dissatisfied with his lodgings,he moved to a more expensive address, where his name appeared on a brass plate on the door. The following March he tried unsuccessfully at the circuit Quarterly Meeting to persuade it to make up a financial deficiency. In August, he declined to take the anniversary services at the Ridgeway Gates Sunday school in Bolton because he disapproved of its discipline and management. Like his father, Stephens was no Wesleyan reformer; but he gave a series of lectures on the Mind of Man which caused friction with his superintendent.[21]

He did not confine himself to Methodist affairs. The first elections for the reformed Parliament were held in December 1832. Many Methodists were among the newly enfranchized, and Wesleyan ministers on both sides of politics were less inhibited in involving themselves than on previous occasions. Ashton was a new constituency, and it was won by a Liberal, Lieutenant-Colonel Williams. At a dinner for a defeated candidate, the Liberal-Radical cotton manufacturer Charles Hindley, Stephens extolled the virtues of freedom in an eloquent speech, which was sourly noted by a Wesleyan reform publication.[22]

His friendship with Hindley opened the door to a wider world than that of Wesleyan Methodism. Through Hindley he became a lecturer at the Ashton Mechanics Institute, and was to be led to the movements for disestablishment and factory reform. Hindley was an ambivalent figure whose humanitarian instincts were constantly at odds with his business interests. Intended for the Moravian ministry, he became a cotton manufacturer. Founder of the Ashton Mechanics Institute, president of a peace society and a factory reformer who sought to regulate labour conditions by foreign treaty, he was one of fifty masters who reduced the wages of cotton spinners during a trade depression; the resulting strike collapsed through fear of starvation. Like an Israelite under the conflicting pressures of Elijah and the prophets of Baal, he constantly halted between two opinions. He had helped to draft the existing but ineffective Hobhouse factory bill, but doubted the prospect of legislation for a ten hour day, which had become an article of faith to his fellow factory reformers. Both reformers and masters increasingly mistrusted him. Later Stephens and other reformers were to attack him publicly, while his nephew Hugh Mason would one day write to the Home Secretary: 'He panders I regret to say to the Chartist leaders and to any man who can influence the lower orders.' Such was the man who played a crucial role in influencing the radically-inclined Stephens to his life's work.[23]

In December 1833, the prospects of Whig reform and the Irish Church Act encouraged Dissenters to go beyond demands for the abolition of church rates, and press for disestablishment. In London, the only body who could claim to represent the policy of the three Dissenting denominations, the Protestant Dissenting Deputies, pronounced religious establishments to be unscriptural, and encouraged petitions for abolition. In the north agitation became militant, as political radicals and Scottish voluntaryists sided with Dissenters. In Ashton, already aroused by the refusal of the Earl of Stamford to allow town centre land for the new Congregational chapel, a public meeting was called to petition for the removal of Dissenting grievances. It was clear that disestablishment would also be advanced but the cautious Hindley, a Moravian wholly identified with the cause of Dissent, was careful to hold it out as an ultimate aim rather than an immedite measure. Yet his Wesleyan friend Stephens was prepared to demand it. Although Wesleyans were expected to be neutral, he agreed to advocate disestablishment at the meeting called for 27 January 1834 in the Congregational chapel.[24]

Stephens knew that he was opposing Connexional sentiment. The Church of John Wesley continued to arouse a lingering affection, even though Methodists were regarded by the Established Church as no different from Dissenters. Politics reinforced sentiment, for the leadership believed that the Establishment was a declaration of state support for Christian values; a movement that united what Bunting was to call 'fierce, formal Dissent' with secular idealism was hardly likely to commend itself to the Wesleyan leadership. Disestablishment was one of the few common strands of a radicalism that it disliked. Conference in 1833 warned against 'too warm an interest' in popular debates which 'do not immediately concern our Connexion', for God's triumph would not come 'by breaking down the several and unessential forms of ecclesiast-

ical government . . . ' Furthermore, the Conference expected that its
collective judgment would be accepted without question by the entire
ministry.[25]

Stephens believed that until Conference had pronounced formally on
the issue, he was free to comment. (Nevertheless he tried to protect
himself by claiming to act as a citizen and a townsman rather than as a
Wesleyan minister.) Later he defined his attitude as 'the way in which a
man, being a Methodist Preacher, may exercise his social and Christian
right publicly to express his opinions on any great religious question
which may come under general consideration'. Sweden had left him
with no love of church establishments, and the Ashton scene merely
confirmed him in this. Most of his congregations felt themselves to be
Dissenters, and agreed with him. Like other Dissenters, they paid
church rate, and were excluded from the universities; their baptisms
were not registered by the state, marriages could not be performed in
their chapels, and their ministers could not officiate at Wesleyan burials
in parochial church grounds. In the light of the removal of their civil
disabilities in 1828, these surviving grievances could not be tolerated.[26]

Thus Stephens' challenge to the wisdom of his superiors was not
simply an act of irresponsible folly; but the militant Dissenting campaign
of 1834 exactly caught his mood. He had praised freedom in 1832, and
now he came forward to put it into practice. 'I am a liberty man – I mean
to hold my own opinion and allow every man, every congregation and
every society to hold their own . . . I am on principle a Dissenter.' The
sunshine of his non-sectarianism had been hidden temporarily behind a
Dissenting thundercloud, and the outlook was stormy for his Wesleyan
future.[27]

At the meeting, he presented about a hundred Wesleyan signatures to
be added to the memorial, and he proposed that the name of the
Wesleyan Methodists be inserted into the preamble. The memorial
itself denounced the union of church and state in strong terms, but it
was matched by the powerful and humorous speech the hitherto
unknown Stephens delivered. No one who heard his blazing peroration
was in any doubt that Dissent had found a new champion, and he was
applauded. The *Manchester Times* published a long account, and an
editorial declared: 'On the CHURCH QUESTION, the administration
would do well to peruse the report of the meeting at ASHTON UNDER
LINE, and especially the eloquent and argumentative speech of the Rev.
Mr. STEPHEN'. Brother John's *Christian Advocate* carried it into many a
Methodist home. In Ashton, the speech committed Dissenters to

disestablishment, and on 3 March a Church Separation Society was formed with Stephens as one of two secretaries. On the 6th Hindley told a meeting of Manchester Dissenters that the Rubicon had been crossed and urged them to co-operate. The *Manchester Times* too hoped that Ashton's example would be followed.[28]

Elsewhere the reaction was equally warm, though different. On 11 March Jabez Bunting wrote to Edmund Grindrod at Manchester: 'Joseph Stephens' Ashton doings fill me with indignation. It is plain that he wants us to exclude him. The thing cannot be tolerated.' He wanted immediate disciplinary measures to make Stephens resign from his secretaryship. A Sheffield speech led to other invitations being withdrawn, and the Sheffield superintendent Richard Reece wrote of his erring brother's 'unprincipled folly and rashness'. There was no friendship between Stephens and George Marsland, the Ashton superintendent, and it is not clear if Marsland cautioned him. He continued to denounce church establishments at Hyde, Oldham and Stalybridge. On 31 March, Robert Newton, Chairman of the Manchester District, notified him that he would face charges at the District Meeting on 28 April; he had implicated his brethren by his speeches, and was secretary of 'a Society or Union alien to Methodism'. The diligent way Stephens began to prepare his defence suggests that he was not seeking exclusion.[29]

The intervention of the *Christian Advocate* changed everything. His brother sensed that he was ripe for conversion to the wider cause of Wesleyan reform, and on 16 April he wrote to offer him the editorial column, and to ask for details of his case before the District Meeting met. Prudently Stephens refrained, but events played into his brother's hands. Further charges of introducing vestry petitions for signature and inserting the words 'and of the Wesleyan Methodists' into the Ashton petition unsettled him. They emphasized his conduct as a minister and he had prepared his defence on the issue. His impeachment was assured, as his brother had foreseen in his letter when he called him 'the first martyr' in his just cause.[30]

His worst fear was confirmed at the District Meeting when Newton declared: 'We are not here to pronounce upon the abstract question of Church and state, but to express a judgment on Mr. Stephens's public acts as a Wesleyan minister.' Conference alone could decide the former. The trial was over before it started, for the five charges were all factual. He *had* spoken at four meetings in favour of disestablishment, added the Wesleyan Methodist name to a Dissenting memorial, announced from

the pulpit that a town petition could be signed in the vestry, and accepted
office in a church separation society; he contested only that he had acted
without consulting his superintendent. He did not deny the facts, only
that they constituted an offence; his brethren acted as though an offence
had been committed, and were concerned only to prove the facts. The
deadlock was complete. Asked by the chairman what defence he offered
for these violations of Methodist law, he replied: 'None, until the facts
he had admitted were shown to be violations of law.' Since it was
contended that the meeting was not required to do this, he 'resolutely
refused to say one word'. After Dr Warren, a senior Manchester
superintendent, insisted that the meeting must produce the law that had
been violated, it was attempted, but Stephens still refused to defend
himself.[31]

Seven resolutions were drawn up and debated after his withdrawal
from the meeting. The resolutions declared that Stephens had
'flagrantly violated the peaceable and anti-sectarian spirit of Wesleyan
Methodism'. His speeches were 'directly at variance with the general
sentiments of Mr Wesley and the Conference'. They were 'distinguished by a spirit highly unbecoming a Wesleyan Minister'. He had
'manifested a great want of deference to the recorded opinions of his
Fathers and Brethren in the ministry'. He had violated the previous
Conference's pastoral address to the societies, accepted office in a
church separation society and had refused to consult his superintendent. His resignation from the secretaryship was demanded on pain
of suspension from the ministry. Dr Warren withdrew his amendment
to substitute a general enquiry into Stephens' conduct when it was seen
to be against the feeling of the meeting.[32]

When the resolutions were read to Stephens, he broke down and
wept. His carefully prepared defence was irrelevant to the charges; thus
it could not be given. His principles were declared anti-Wesleyan
without debate, and he was to be suspended unheard. He never
understood that since Wesleyan agitation for disestablishment was
unknown, his behaviour was bound to be judged anti-Wesleyan; there
was no need for his opponents to produce a written law that had been
violated. Despite lengthy and repeated attempts urging him to submit,
he refused. The next day in a somewhat chastened mood, he offered to
give up his secretaryship if the second and third resolutions dealing with
the general issue were withdrawn. He thought that Dr Warren's
abortive amendment would have allowed the forthcoming Conference
to deal with the issue of church and state without the prejudging of the

District meeting. The meeting was in no mood to agree. It wanted compliance. Despite the pleasing circumstance that it was urged on him by two future leaders of Wesleyan schism – Dr Warren and James Everett – he refused either to surrender his secretaryship or to abstain from future agitation. He was suspended from his ministry until the Conference, and required to move out of the Ashton circuit. Only Dr Warren 'demurred' from this judgment.[33]

Nothing was more calculated to drive Stephens into the arms of the Wesleyan reformers. His suspension by his fellow ministers awoke him to the virtues of lay delegation, and the half-hearted support of Dr Warren made him a fellow opponent of the theological institution for ministerial training. His brother in a militant editorial trumpeted: 'THE RIGHT OF PRIVATE JUDGMENT HAS BEEN AUDACIOUSLY TRAMPLED UPON.' Although he intended to appeal to Conference against his suspension, Stephens wrote in mid-May long letters to the *Christian Advocate* and the *Manchester Times* giving details of the District Meeting. From then on, he became the Advocate's latest David-like hero in its ceaseless conflict with the Connexional Goliath, Jabez Bunting. Yet he was no more a wholesale Wesleyan reformer than was Dr Warren; both were ministerial malcontents who for the time being were being carried along on the rising tide of lay Methodist reform.[34]

Stephens became an instant hero in the Ashton circuit. On 30 April a battery of leading reformers declared that their minister had voiced the principles of the vast majority of Wesleyans. A committee was set up to withold financial contributions – to 'stop the supplies', in reforming parlance. The rafters rang with denunciation at a further gathering in the Mill Lane Sunday School. The sentence was 'ungodly and tyrannical', passed by 'an ungodly priesthood', 'opposite to the voice of the church which is the voice of God'. Above all, 'their motto should be, "Methodism Reformed"'. Whatever their other differences, they all favoured disestablishment, and their agitation was given the oxygen of publicity. The District Meeting had published the minutes of the Stephens case and distributed it throughout the Connexion; reform agitation broke out in a number of widely scattered circuits. Pro-Stephens agitation in the remotest place was reported by the *Advocate*. It also publicized Dr Warren's fight against the Theological Institution, which potentially was a bigger threat to the Connexional leadership. So promising was the prospect that in June, John Stephens launched *Stephens's Methodist Magazine*. It linked the causes of Stephens and Warren in a common demand for Wesleyan reform.[35]

Marsland tried in vain to quieten the growing uproar in the Ashton circuit. He expelled the leading Stephens sympathizers, and the *Advocate* reported the progress of the 'holy inquisition' in the town. The continued publicity and secessions in Bolton and Oldham made Marsland's task impossible. Many members and whole classes 'stopped the supplies', and excluded themselves from membership. Newton came to chair the June circuit Quarterly Meeting, but Bunting was later informed that 'the preachers could not get on' and were 'in a wretched state'. Stephens' ministerial allowance was reduced to enable the circuit to qualify for a grant from the Wesleyan contingency fund. Circuit membership fell dramatically from 1,100 to 450. At Ashton, the seceders occupied the Mill Lane schoolroom, while at Stalybridge only 7 members remained.[36]

Stephens himself was not involved in these events. He had left the circuit intending to go to the continent until Conference, but in the event he retired to Hull. While his brother continued to bring pressure on Conference through his newspaper, their father sought to influence events differently. There is a remarkable account of the distressed father in Jabez Bunting's waiting room confiding his troubles to Jane Davis, a friend of the transported Wesleyan agricultural labourers of Tolpuddle. Bunting was an old friend, and his influence with the Conference was weighty; despite his earlier indignation and the malice of the *Advocate*, Bunting was to do all he could consistent with his beliefs to save Stephens for the Connexion.[37]

The Wesleyan Conference assembled at Wesley's Chapel in the City Road, London on 30 July 1834. Stephens was prepared to give his original defence based on Wesley's condemnation of Constantine's establishment of Christianity in the late Roman Empire. He was well primed by the August issue of *Stephens's Methodist Magazine*, which argued lengthily with a wealth of quotation that Wesley was a churchman by profession and a Dissenter in practice. Such a view from such a source was unlikely to influence 'the living Wesley', as Bunting liked to call the Conference. Richard Reece, a member of the stationing committee which met before it began, confided to his diary a more representative view: 'the case of Jos. Stephens has excited some interest in and out of doors. I trust the Lord will enable us to maintain the principles of old Methodism, against the fancies of a few young men'. As for the Revd John Stephens, he retired from the active ministry after forty-two years' service. Too staunch an upholder of Wesleyan discipline to agree with his son, he was too hurt a parent to witness his humiliation by the Conference.[38]

The case came before the Conference on 4 August. Stephens dismissed any hope that he might submit to the Manchester findings, and made a constantly interrupted appeal against them. He agreed with Dr Warren (hardly tactful in view of the doctor's opposition to the Theological Institution) in trying in his abortive amendment to separate ministerial conduct from the issue of disestablishment. His was an entirely new case. It was not a question of destroying the Church of England, for those who sought its separation from the state held it would promote its prosperity. Wesley's attack on Constantine's establishment showed that while their Father in God wished his societies to remain within the church, he condemned the union of church and state. Thus the District Meeting had no right to demand a pledge:

> The question was – were his opinions anti-Wesleyan or not? Let it be fairly discussed. The separation of the church from the state was a great national question. It had already come under the serious consideration of the country, and would soon be the absorbing question. All classes in the community, religious and political, would enter upon it. It would shake the kingdom. How then could any District Meeting presume to decide upon it – and place him and those who thought with him, under the ban of the Wesleyan Connexion. It must not be. It could never be. He had refused to acknowledge its authority in such a matter. Against its judgment he appealed to this Conference. Should the second and third resolutions become the law of Methodism in this place, he could no longer subscribe to it . . .

The challenge was made, and his youthful defiance of his seniors was clear. According to the only account of his speech, 'occasionally he rose to a height of impassioned eloquence, which brought down the applause of the Conference'. After much questioning, he admitted that he would have relinquished his secretaryship if the two offending resolutions had not been passed. About half-past-two he retired.[39]

Bunting then rose to make what an eye-witness described as 'a glorious speech'. Ater paying tribute to old John Stephens, he argued that a young preacher should have submitted to the District Meeting. As for Wesley:

> Our question is, not whether at the beginning it was best to unite church and state, nor whether if the house had to be constructed now it should be just as it is; our point is: Must Wesleyan Methodist ministers arm themselves with pickaxes and pull down the house in which our father was born, and in which he thought he died . . . For

the Conference to join the agitation against church and state would require a new constitution; and *we have no right to alter the constitution without calling a Convention*. But what would we gain by so doing?

He resumed his speech the next day, and he effectively rebutted Stephens' arguments. On the question of law, 'the memory of the man in the tomb behind is law for us'. Stephens had broken the Conference resolutions on pastoral work. Wesley's sermon on Constantine objected only to a particular establishment:

> I maintain that it is the most unjust thing in the world to cull out a passage not in our standards and say, 'This is Mr Wesley'. The point is, what did he do? Did he attend meetings to agitate against the Established Church? Would not Mr Wesley have sent home any man who did this? . . . Our principle is, *'Dissent when we must*, but be on friendly terms when we can'. Mr Wesley would never have signed a petition against the Establishment.

This was the crux of the matter. Bunting understood the Methodist past better than Stephens. He knew that Stephens had offended against the intimate family bond between Wesley and his preachers that constituted the governing conception of the ministerial brotherhood. When he declared that 'in a District Meeting young ministers as well as old must defer to the collective judgment of the brethren', there was a general cry 'He ought to have submitted'. Bunting moved the confirmation of the District Meeting's action, and demanded a pledge from Stephens that he confine himself to his proper work. If he refused, he was not to be expelled, but suspended for a further year; on giving the pledge, he could be appointed to a circuit.[40]

The discussion that followed revealed that the small opposition could make no headway against Bunting's magnanimity. An amendment that Stephens' suspension be lifted gained only six votes. Bunting's four resolutions were carried. When Stephens reappeared to hear the resolutions and the demand for a pledge, he quibbled about their interpretation. He was given two hours and six ministers to clarify their meaning. The six promptly disagreed among themselves. The following day, Stephens refused the pledge and requested to withdraw from the Connexion. He expressed his satisfaction at his brethren's conduct. Bunting commented: 'I wish to save him, but he seems decided.' Old John Stephens said he was an obedient son, 'but I have no hope of bringing him to acknowledge his error in this'.[41]

Time was to bring about an ironic reversal of roles, for Stephens came to uphold the Established Church, and he lived to see the Wesleyan Conference allow freedom for its ministers to advocate disestablishment. Later controversies clouded what happened in 1834. Stephens resigned under charges; he was not expelled. The charges related solely to disestablishment; he was not victimized for sympathy with working-class radicalism. There is no hint of this in the contemporary evidence, and his sole biographer Holyoake misled his readers by inserting an undated Stephens letter written in 1836, and implying an active interest in factory reform, before his account of the Conference trial of 1834. Although Chartists wanted disestablishment, it was a Dissenting cause before Chartism existed.[42]

Bunting was born to trouble as historical sparks fly upwards. His speech in 1834 has been called odd in view of his acceptance of Catholic emancipation in 1829. Then the influence of the representative figure of the Wesleyan ministry ensured Wesleyan neutrality in the crisis, and that helped to undermine the Protestant Establishment; but in 1834 by opposing Stephens, he seemed to uphold what remained of it. This was not his intention, for he said that if Wesleyans and Dissenters kept quiet, 'the time may come when the argument for an establishment will be taken away'. The essence of his policy in 1829 and 1834 was the same: the Connexion should not be involved in controversial national questions in which there was no direct Methodist interest. In 1834 his hand was forced by a minister who refused to accept the collective judgment of his brethren; thus Wesleyan abstention from agitation for disestablishment depended on curbing Stephens.[43]

If Buntings's policy was consistent, his behaviour was not. He virtually admitted it when memorials from circuits about Stephens were considered: 'Some say a strong arm must be laid to the Tory side. They tried to catch me in order to fry me, but they failed. I wish they had not caught one on the Liberal side'. One of his constant critics had said: 'It is very difficult to answer for the conduct of brethren who, whilst gagging others, allow themselves to speak and do what they please.' For Bunting, the traditional 'no politics' rule seemed to apply only in an anti-radical sense. As for the Stephens pledge, Bunting saw nothing odd in allowing ministers to hold controversial views, but not express them; it was not the last time that the Conference would so proceed. It was not surprising that Wesleyan reformers pushed 'the right of private judgment' to the point of freedom from all restraint.[44]

As for Stephens, the clearest sign that he was still bound by broad Methodist horizons was what he did in the remaining months of 1834. If momentarily he considered retiring into private life, he soon decided to continue the struggle. In late August he returned to Ashton to a welcome from his followers. A commmittee was established and a delegate meeting arranged at Manchester for the following month. The many letters in the columns of the *Advocate* suggested that he enjoyed support in different parts of the country. He preached and lectured to sympathetic Dissenting gatherings from Rochdale to Birmingham. No longer satisfied with the conduct of his ex-brethren, he denounced his treatment by the Conference. Although he was expected to join either the Primitive Methodists or the Methodist New Connexion, he knew that his future depended upon the Ashton and Stalybridge separatists. His followers controlled Mill Lane school in Ashton, but there was a spirited fight for the Sunday school premises at Stalybridge. Stephenite control was only ensured by the casting vote of the chairman of the trustees, John Cheetham, a wealthy manufacturer and a founder of the Stalybridge Congregational Church.[45]

Elsewhere support wavered. The Oldham separatists were more numerous than at Stalybridge, and for a time Stephens preached regularly in their Lord Street Chapel. Other pro-Stephens congregations were established at Bolton and Halifax. In far away Cornwall, the Stephens case caused the Camelford circuit to erupt in 1835. None of these became a lasting part of the Stephenite body. On 24 September the delegate meeting met at George Street Baptist chapel in Manchester. Opinion was deeply divided. Some wanted Stephens to embark on a national itinerancy, others urged everyone to join the Methodist New Connexion, and yet others were set on founding a new body. No agreement was reached, despite a rousing speech by Stephens himself, and separatists could only be advised to join an existing church, or to form a new one. There was to be no king in the reformed Israel, and every man was to do what was right in his own sight. Even the *Advocate* called the meeting 'a failure, though not a miserable failure'.[46]

Stephens understood why. He was being forgotten in the rising enthusiasm of Methodist reformers for Dr Warren. Immediately after the Conference, Dr Warren intensified his campaign against the Theological Institution, and his circuit demanded drastic reform. His agitation deprived Stephens of much needed support at a critical moment; Warren was proving to be a competitor as well as an ally. By September, the outcome of the Warrenite dispute was unknown, and reformers were wary of committing themselves prematurely. Warren was a senior minister well-known in the Connexion; Stephens was junior and less well-known, and he had resigned. Most reformers felt that the Wesleyan Warren rather than the separatist Stephens was more likely to carry their cause to victory. Even the Oldham separatists decided between late August and late September that they would become Warrenites, and the Stephenites suffered further such losses until late 1836. In this unintended way, Warren stole Stephens' thunder. Stephens lost the chance to become the leader of a nationwide Wesleyan reform movement, and his Ashton-based cause came to be seen as little more than a local peculiarity.[47]

A chastened Stephens could do little more than watch the Warrenite drama unfold. Publicly he gave his support – 'surely the men of Manchester would not forsake Dr Warren'. In October, Warren refused a Wesleyan trial for violating Connexional principles, and was suspended. He ignored his chapel trustees, and preached amid mounting uproar. In a Birmingham speech, Stephens tried to link the causes of disestablishment and Wesleyan reform. In this rapidly developing situation, did he think fleetingly of linking his small movement on equal terms with Warren's larger one? It was not to be, for on 7 November his followers founded The Grand Central Association; the result was the biggest clamour to date within Wesleyan Methodism. After losing a Chancery suit against the Conference, Warren was expelled in 1835. Conference made no concessions to the Association, which became a separate Methodist body. In 1836 Warren deserted the Association, and took orders in the Church of England.[48]

The die was cast in November 1834, when the *Christian Advocate* announced that 'the Rev. J. R. Stephens has consented to become the stated pastor of the Ashton separationists'. They had no name, but inevitably they were called Stephenites. Although in December their minister was presented with a silver box for 'advocating the HOLY FREEDOM of his fellow men', his prospects seemed depressing. His was now a purely local schism. The principle of disestablishment began to lose its appeal as the Dissenting campaign ground to a halt. The Whig government disliked it, and its own policy of replacing the church rate with a national tax was denounced by the Dissenters. Its bill to admit Dissenters to the universities was rejected by the House of Lords. The government fell on 14 November, and the prospect of further church legislation disappeared. The incoming Tory administration virtually allowed the Church of England to reform itself. When Lord Melbourne resumed office in April 1835, he let this arrangement continue. The tide of Dissenting clamour ebbed, apparently leaving the Stephenites stranded.[49]

2

Transformation

In November 1834, Joseph Rayner Stephens disappeared into deep sectarian obscurity. He re-emerged in January 1836 to begin a lifelong Christian advocacy of working class causes. Within three and a half years, he was a figure of national stature in the factory reform, anti-Poor Law and Chartist movements. The studious translator of continental pietist poetry became the champion of the Lancastrian proletariat, as with the fervour of a minor prophet he called down the wrath of God on an unjust, Mammon-worshipping social order. Disestablishment and Wesleyan reform were all but forgotten, as he conveyed in burning oratory his vision of a restored Christian society. Thousands of northern workers heard him gladly.

The transformation of January 1836 was no Damascus road conversion. It was the culmination of a long reappraisal that stretched far back into the past. He made up his mind late in 1834, when he took up the cause of the industrial poor at the instigation of Hindley, but over a year passed before he became active. He showed no traceable involvement during his Wesleyan years. The only evidence to the contrary is an undated and misplaced letter quoted by Holyoake, in which Stephens told his father of his growing interest in the factory system; on internal evidence, the letter could not have been written before his resignation from the Wesleyan ministry. The most that can be claimed is that his pastoral ministry in Ashton up to 1834 troubled him. An analysis of his growing uneasiness reveals how a minister steeped in Wesleyan tradition discovered himself, and was drawn to his unique ministry.[1]

It began with the Wesleyan tradition itself. John Wesley had combined inspired innovation in religion with a conservative tendency of mind. For him, politics had a religious foundation, and it was biblical conviction as much as Tory upbringing that made him fear God and honour the king. He distrusted popular politics, and believed that duty and obedience brought greater security and happiness than revolutionary change; but he accepted change that led to greater civil and religious liberty, and he defended Methodism from official victimization. He was not a consistent Tory, for his political reactions owed far more to faith reflecting upon experience than to political principle.

His death was followed by prolonged war with revolutionary France. The war greatly strengthened the conservative tradition of the quasi-ministerial Conference, which was the inheritor of Wesley's authority over the Methodist societies. Protestant patriotism equated revolutionary politics with unbelief and the national enemy, whose revoluton *had* in part fuelled British radicalism. Conference imposed a 'no politics' rule upon its preachers, and supported the war. Repeatedly it demanded loyalty from Methodists, especially in industrial areas; it was all the more urgent in view of continuing fears in high places linking Methodism with Jacobinism. The post-war economic depression and radical ferment only stimulated Conference conservatism and confirmed its growing political influence. In this atmosphere, it was easy to recall Wesley's antagonism to popular radicalism, and difficult to remember that he had written *Thoughts on the Present Scarcity of Provisions*. Luddite machine-breakers were denounced, and radicals expelled from the societies; but there was no Wesleyan protest at the Peterloo massacre of 1819, when fifteen unarmed and peaceful demonstrators were killed and hundreds more wounded. In radical memory, Peterloo lived in infamy, and the Wesleyan Conference was identified with Tory repression.[2]

The young Stephens had witnessed Peterloo. It lingered in his memory, for twice in 1836 he referred to it indignantly in early factory speeches. More important was the immediate aftermath. His father saw Peterloo as 'a contest . . . between a vile demogogue and his venerable king'. He expelled 400 Manchester Methodists suspected of radicalism, published a militant sermon and exulted later to Bunting: 'They are down, and we intend to keep them down.' Such excitement seems extreme, but according to his colleague Thomas Jackson, he was sorely tried and his life was in peril. Although branded afresh in radical eyes by his exertions, the Cornish ex-lead miner knew what poverty was. He reminded his fashionable congregation of the poor of Lancashire, 'shut up in factories, or fastened to the loom from their cradle'. He considered wealth and poverty in the light of the Bible:

> The widest extremes of poverty and riches are permitted, but they are not sanctioned by God. That there are some persons in this Christian

land suffering extreme destitution is a fact too plain to be disputed; and that there are others, rolling in luxury and encumbered with wealth, nobody will deny; and standing on Bible-ground . . . we hesitate not to pronounce this to be wrong.

It was not the government ('wise, mild and liberal') that was to blame, but rather the economic effects of war, over-production, and the conduct of 'unprincipled and desperate manufacturers', who to under-cut their rivals reduced wages. The rich should give their superfluities to the relief of the poor, and the poor should regard the rich as their guardians, benefactors and friends. In the advertisement to the printed sermon, John Stephens attacked the current 'daring spirit of insub-ordination', while hoping that charity, commercial justice or par-liamentary power would improve the lot of the cotton weavers, so that agitators would be deprived of a grievance. Superior to all party politics, when the contest involved patriotism, order and faith, Stephens 'would blow the sacred trumpet to call Jehovah's host to battle'. Here on the lips of the most anti-radical of Wesleyan ministers were some of the themes that would one day be re-worked and echoed in the ministry of his son.[3]

As a Wesleyan minister, Joseph Rayner also learned from Richard Watson, the Wesleyan missionary secretary and theologian. He ordered Watson's *Institutes* in Sweden, and wanted it introduced to Swedish universities. Once he spent three weeks with Watson, and called him in 1834 'essentially a liberal man'. Yet Watson taught that the origin of government was paternal, and that subjection and obedience were to be accepted for the sake of conscience; resistance was only justified if the sovereign tried to subvert the constitution, and then only under the people's natural guides and leaders, the nobility and gentry. At the same time, Watson as missionary secretary fought for the end of slavery. In 1830 he went so far as to say publicly:

> . . . all our missionary enterprises, all our attempts to spread Christianity abroad do in point of fact tend to increase our sympathies with the external circumstances of the oppressed and miserable of all lands. It is impossible for men to care for the souls of others without caring for their bodies also . . . We cannot care for the salvation of the negro without caring for his emancipation from bondage.

It was a short step to apply this teaching to the 'factory slaves' of the north, and Stephens in 1836 was conscious of the abolitionist precedent. The ambivalent Wesleyan political tradition – emphatic biblical reverence for authority combined with strenuous campaigning for a carefully defined and equally biblical humanitarianism – was to be reflected in his own career.[4]

Sweden was crucial for his development because it loosened his Wesleyan ties. The twenty-year old missionary in Stockholm was alone, and free from normal pastoral oversight. His considerable talents matured outside the close-knit fellowship of British Methodism, and he exercised them in the exciting context of a foreign capital. Unsupervised for three formative years, he would never again work easily under a superintendent minister. His judgments owed little to existing Wesleyan standards. In 1834 an angry Richard Reece remembered that Stephens had told the missionary committee that he had never been present at family prayer in Sweden because 'it was not the custom of the country'. (It would be over a century before the Methodist missionary society would generally come to value such respect for indigenous custom.) Rees thought him 'a gifted, self-important little man, having little claim to godliness'. Certainly his youthful freedom gave him wider horizons than those of the Connexion, and made him obstinate and self-willed.[5]

He drew a congregation that no contemporary Methodist probationer would have enjoyed, and won praise in circles remote from Methodism. He was accepted by the Swedish and expatriate nobility. Years later he said: 'I was their personal friend and their family friend and domestic chaplain, and I have moved among the aristocracy on terms of gentlemanly equality.' This was in marked contrast to the failure of the English merchants to become Methodists. In retrospect it was easy for him to imagine that he understood the aristocracy, and not surprising that he came to accept the myth of a large-hearted Christian nobility willing to make the interests of the less highly favoured its own.[6]

It is difficult to discover how much he was influenced by friendship. Many years later, the garrulous Wesleyan patriarch Benjamin Gregory thought that Stephens' 'powerful weaknesses' were 'nurtured into revolutionary passion' in Sweden, where he 'formed some very heterogeneous friendships with adventurous men of genius'. Stephens himself told an Oldham audience in 1834:

> When they left this country and trod other climes, the minds of missionaries were expanded and freed from their country's prejudices, and by association with others, they became lovers of freedom.

The only known intimate friendship was with Charles de Montalembert, who wrote to him in 1829:

Our union, our friendship is a debt we owe to the noble cause of *faith*, religious, moral and political, which we have both embraced, which you proclaim from the altar of the Most High, and which I may perhaps also defend in my country's presence.

Almost thirty years later, Stephens wrote of their mutual love of poetry, metaphysics and moral philosophy, and their discussion of government, nationalities and constitutions. 'Ardent lovers of liberty – the very breath of the life of man – we strove to discover its true and proper centre.' He thought they were unconsciously preparing themselves, 'and perhaps in some degree preparing one another', for their respective future public activities. Montalembert was to return to France to become a founder of *L'Avenir*, a journal that demanded liberty and the separation of church and state. The freedom Sweden offered to them both enabled them to imbibe the new ideas of liberalism, which they were to apply later in the different circumstances of their own countries.[7]

Stephens, like his successor Scott, failed in Sweden because of the hostility of the established Lutheran Church to the successful introduction of a foreign Methodist mission. In law, church authority was sweeping; despite its slackness, it was still influential enough to deal with any imagined threat to its interests. By accepting even two Swedes into membership of a Methodist class meeting, Stephens broke the law; it was in Sweden that he learned to do so with a good conscience. He was both impressed and frustrated by the established church, and it is easy to see how the non-sectarian missionary to Stockholm became a secretary of the Ashton church separation society. At Oldham he said that 'he had seen such establishments in other countries, and could bear proof of their abuses, and the injuries they inflicted'. That had come to matter more to him than the view of the British Wesleyan Conference.[8]

His return home radicalized his nebulous liberalism. He welcomed Catholic emancipation and the abolition of slavery, and praised the 'freedom' granted by the reform bill. His friendship with the Liberal-radical Hindley showed him a radical world beyond Wesleyan Methodism. In the new climate of opinion, traditional assumptions were being questioned, and ancient institutions seemed to be imperilled. Disestablishment brought together dissenters and secular idealists, and Stephens had to answer Wesleyan criticisms of consorting with radicals. In his circuit ministry, he tried with growing uneasiness to reconcile his new views with older convictions of Wesleyan pastoral supremacy.

At first he appeared to settle down to familiar ministerial duties under a superintendent minister; but the heady brew of Stockholm continued to ferment within him. Brother John and his *Christian Advocate* tugged him in a radical direction. When it began to oppose the Wesleyan leadership, Stephens prudently kept a low profile. He had nothing to say about lay delegation to Conference, the curbing of pastoral supremacy in the circuits, or freedom from restrictions on revivalism. He did not really believe in these things, and loyalty to his brother had to be weighed against official censure of the newspaper. What mattered to him was the freedom of the church from civil control, which the *Advocate* first urged in April 1832. Only when he was charged with disestablishment agitation did he become a Wesleyan reformer, and then he was swept along by the strength of a lay reforming tide rather than by any deep conviction of his own.[9]

The Christian Advocate under John Stephens' editorship was keenly interested in labour issues. This was very rare in the literature of Wesleyan reform. The *Advocate* reported the activities of the Tory MP Michael Sadler, the first Parliamentary leader of the factory reformers. His speech on the introduction of a poor law in Ireland, and his candidature in the acrimonious Leeds by-election were fully covered. In 1832, the editor wished Sadler success with his proposed bill to limit factory hours to ten a day 'for the sake of humanity, morality and religion'. Articles appeared on the victims of the factory system, one of which quoted the founder of the factory reform movement, Richard Oastler. Although Sadler was defeated in December 1832, the editor hoped that his bill could still be debated. In 1833 and for most of 1834, his main attention was elsewhere, although in February 1834 the paper published an extract of Robert Owen's account of his labours. In 1838 the editor's brother recalled that in former years a 'great and growing evil in society' caused him 'much anxious thought'. He 'pondered over the subject for years', and although his fellow ministers held different views, 'he could not shut out the idea that he was absolutely right'.[10]

His pastoral ministry in the Ashton circuit had opened his eyes to the reality of industrial poverty:

. . . it was not until he came to a district where the manufacture of cotton was carried on to a great extent that his thoughts and opinions began to assume a tangible shape. The change in him was affected by visiting the cottages of the work-people, by seeing them in the mills, in their homes, on their sick-beds – by inquiring how they lived, and by instituting a regular investigation, that he became acquainted, practically acquainted, with the condition of the working classes. Hereupon he took up the question in what he considered the only efficient manner, and by so doing estranged his friends.

Here he compressed a process that lasted over three years. It took time before he understood the meaning of what he found, and in early 1834 he was deflected by the campaign for disestablishment.[11]

By 1825, Ashton had about forty fairly large cotton firms. By the time Stephens arrived, new mills were being installed with steam engines, which encouraged the growth of power loom weaving. By about 1850, hand looms had been largely replaced. In the mid-forties, some 600,000 spindles and 7,000 power looms employed over 10,000 workers. Ashton proclaimed the power of cotton, and cotton was the symbol of British prosperity; but the prosperity was very one-sided. Employment was at the mercy of boom and slump. The wages of cotton spinners had been falling since 1825, declining from 27/1d per week in 1833 to 22/11d in 1839. The handloom weavers, unable to compete with power looms, were losing their livelihood. Factory machinery was often unsafe, the work monotonous and the discipline irksome to those used to the older ways of domestic industry. Conditions of work for adults were largely unregulated. Workers had to submit to fines and sometimes to floggings; sexual immorality was not unknown on factory premises. As mechanical processes became simpler, increasingly men were replaced by cheaper and more docile women and children. Children six or seven years old could work from 6 am to 9 pm as 'piecers' for about 1/6d to 2/6d per week. The Factory Act of 1833 abolished child labour under the age of nine, limited the hours of those under thirteen, and provided inspectors to enforce the law; but false ages were commonly given, and the Act evaded so that desperate parents could benefit from their children's meagre wages.[12]

The Ashton workers were among the most militant in Lancashire. They supplied agitators for all the labour protest movements in the first half of the century. Illegal trade unionism led by the ultra-radical John Doherty flourished. James France, later one of Stephens' most devoted followers, remembered as a child of five the strike of 1830–1 for an increase of '4/2d or swing'. Soldiers were called in to quell the threatened disturbance and protect the millowners. The strike was defeated. Ashton was one of the first towns to produce a short-time committee for Richard Oastler's factory reform movement.[13]

Yet Ashton enjoyed better conditions than some towns of the industrial north. Only 1.25% of its working population lived in cellars, compared to 30% in Liverpool. John Ross Coulthart's investigation of 1844 found that 94% of houses visited were comfortable and well-furnished. Even Engels admitted in the same year that Ashton was more attractive in appearance than most factory towns. Enlightened employers in the forties began to provide better housing and other facilities for their workers. Very different conditions prevailed in the older parts of the town. There the poorest of the rapidly-growing population, mainly immigrant Irish and handloom weavers, existed in back to back houses and cellars. Charlestown in 1849 had filthy streets, unsavoury squares, and neglected houses with little furniture and few necessities. They were breeding grounds of disease. The asiatic cholera and influenza epidemic of 1832 were severe in Ashton. Most of the old town houses were without piped water, and the streets were unsewered; in sewered streets the average duration of life was six years more, and infant mortality 8% less, than in unsewered streets. From 1838 to 1843, 57% of all deaths were of children under five years of age.[14]

Ashton had few public buildings or amenities in the thirties. It had a very necessary barracks, but no public parks, baths, library or hospital. There was no public day school, and only 5.25% of its children went to the dame or common schools. At nearby Stalybridge, the young James France was taken from school to work at a factory though he continued to attend the Wesleyan Sunday school. Later he went to the Cockerhill night school, where after a working day of twelve hours, he took slate and candle to the classes. The town hall was not built until 1840. Transport facilities were better from the forties, for then the turnpike roads and canals were supplemented by railways.[15]

As Stephens gradually absorbed the life of his people, his misgivings grew. The time of the evening service was two hours later than he had known elsewhere because of factory hours. As he prepared a sermon for a Sunday school service on the text 'they grew in wisdom and stature and in favour with God and with men', he realized that local factory children did not grow. Nor was the Ashton circuit without its working-class Radicals, for the New Connexion circuit had creamed off much of the wealthier support enjoyed elsewhere by the Wesleyans. As far back as 1815, the Wesleyans were accused by the New Connexion stewards at Stamford Street of harbouring Luddites, trade unionists and Jacobins.

In 1834 a local preacher at a pro-Stephens protest meeting said that he was called from his loom to preach the gospel, and that he had fallen before in the field of liberty. Another operative had composed the resolutions of Stephens' Manchester meeting in September 1834. What mattered more to him was his pastoral ministry. In 1839, he tried to convey his sense of shock to a London audience:

> It was impossible for anyone who had not lived in or breathed the foul and pestilential atmosphere which surrounds the factories – it was impossible for anyone who had not dwelt with the people, and visited and communed with them in their heart of hearts as he had done, to have the least conception of the heartless and remorseless tyranny to which the victims of the factory system were subjected.[16]

Historians are divided on whether living standards for the majority of the population before 1850 improved or deteriorated. What is undeniable is that suffering of a distinctive and unfamiliar character existed in early industrial towns. The long series of protest movements from the English Jacobins to the Chartists is inexplicable without it. Stephens was to be one of many who were shocked by it and agitated for redress; yet he acted only after his resignation from Wesleyan Methodism. Wesleyan ministers were not unaware of the problem, but the Connexion had no critique of modern industrial society. The Toryism of its leadership was remote from that of Richard Oastler; involvement in the closely-knit, circuit network could easily become a substitute for social action. Circuit duties and disestablishment all but filled Stephens' own ministry before his resignation. Millowners were often influential members of local Methodist or dissenting congregations. Stephens was friendly with John Cheetham, Joseph Ashton, Charles Howard, and Charles Hindley, all of them substantial cotton masters. The fact that one of these led him first to the cause of Dissent and then to the factory question only showed how strong the influence of such men could be on dissenting ministers (though the advice of Hindley on the factory issue was scarcely typical).[17]

Stephens' resignation from the Wesleyan ministry, and his subsequent eclipse by Dr Warren as the standard-bearer of Wesleyan reform, freed him to take up Hindley's challenge. On 20 October 1834, his brother returned to the labour issue in a remarkable editorial. He claimed that he had done his utmost to understand the real condition of the working classes, and that their well-being had long occupied his attention. They were the basis of society. The manufacturing districts presented 'a new and not very well understood phenomenon . . . that *must* be attended to by an enlightened legislature . . . without any further delay'. Neither theory nor party must hinder this. 'We must carry into active operation the great principles of God's word – truth and righteousness between man and man, without respect of persons. We have done little or nothing as yet for the poor of the land.' The Poor Law Amendment Act that had abolished the principles of the Elizabethan poor law was 'either the delusive dream of the theorist or the insidious though specious manoeuvre of the tyrant'. It would 'complete what is lacking in the demoralization and utter degradation of the lower orders'. Men must be given work to earn wages to uphold themselves 'in the honest pride of Christian independence'.[18]

Here, independently of Oastler's Tory radicalism, were some of the basic beliefs that Stephens was to proclaim for the rest of his life – the importance of the working classes for the whole of society, the urgent need for justice through legislation, and Christian, non-party activity to achieve it. Specific rejection of the Poor Law Amendment Act and even his brother's plea for better relationships between masters and men he also accepted. He was convinced, but there were still two last obstacles – he needed time to organize the Stephenites, and he needed to join others who shared his convictions. Also he intended to marry. All this happened in 1835.

In January Charles Hindley was elected the MP for Ashton, and Joseph Rayner Stephens married Elizabeth Henwood of Hull. She was the niece of a well-known Wesleyan layman, James Henwood. The marriage was solemnized on 28 January at Mary's Church, Hull. It was a happy one, despite the privations of the early years and an alleged scandal in 1839. Richard Oastler, who was a frequent visitor to the home, said of his friend that his servants almost adored him, and that he had never seen a more tender and affectionate husband, nor one more beloved. The sanctity of the married state was to become a major theme in Stephens' speeches. For this, women and children must not work in factories, and those whom God had joined together, no Poor Law Commissioner could put asunder in the new workhouses. The poor man in his cottage was to be as happy as the Queen in her palace; the People's Charter was a knife and fork question. Stephens thundered and agitated so that the poor could enjoy the simple blessings of home life.[19]

For much of 1835 he seems to have withdrawn from public life. He was absent on occasions when his presence would have been expected.

In February the *Advocate* complained that his case was 'too much lost sight of'. He was fighting to preserve the independent life of the Stephenites. It was not easy, for the little army of the new Gideon was always likely to be further reduced by too great a readiness to lap the Warrenite waters. At Ashton he continued to use Mill Lane Sunday school, despite a Wesleyan attempt to dislodge him. At Stalybridge he acquired the lease of King Street chapel. Elsewhere other likely separatist causes went over to Warren's Association. He continued to preach at Oldham, and welcomed two deputies of the Scottish United Christian Church to Ashton in August. He 'had long regretted the existence of divisions in the church. He would not exonerate himself . . . ' He spoke of the exclusions of chapel deeds, and denominational confessions which inhibited unity; he was no longer a militant Dissenter, though he still opposed the Anglican establishment. In the future, he would transcend old divisions by uniting with believers and unbelievers to fight for his social objectives. By December, when he conducted the well-attended anniversary services of the Ancient Foresters at King Street, a future for the Stephenites seemed to be assured.[20]

Stephens was a convinced factory reformer before he joined Richard Oastler's movement for the shortening of working hours. This was the logical next step. Oastler was the forty-six-year-old steward of Fixby Hall, a large country estate in Yorkshire. Educated at a Moravian school, a local preacher of the Methodist New Connexion, he had become so redoubtable a churchman that he could describe himself in relation to the Wesleyan Conference as 'an episcopalian of the first water, a greater Tory than any of them'. Such a man was unlikely to approve of the notoriously Radical disestablisher of the previous year, despite his new convictions. They first met in late 1835, and four years later Oastler recalled the moment:

When I first heard that Stephens had joined the ten-hour bill men, I said to several of my friends I was sorry for it. So that my prejudices were against Stephens. The very first time I met him was at a committee on the ten hours bill in Manchester. I sat with him I believe four or five hours. I watched his movements, and I wondered how a man so basely spoken of in the press should be so amiable, so kind-hearted and benevolent in all his words, gestures and actions. I watched him very, very closely; and we sat I believe three days on that occasion. Before we parted, I said to Mr Stephens, 'Stephens, when I met you the first day, I expected I should not be able to work with you; but I find that your character has been entirely misrepresented, and I now give you the right hand of fellowship; let the world say what it will, we will be friends.'

It was to prove the most important friendship of Stephens' life. From the day in August 1836 when he swore allegiance to 'Richard the Factory King', he found a man he could revere as well as follow. They became close friends. Oastler thought Stephens 'a Christian of the first class'. Stephens called Oastler 'the beau-ideal of the old English character', and wrote that he loved him 'more than any other man'. He admired Oastler's fight 'against covetousness and cruelty, under the mask of liberal principles and evangelical religion'. He was 'no metaphysician', but his statement of facts and appeal to 'the warm and generous feelings of unsophisticated nature' was beyond that of 'any living man we ever heard'. Stephens 'was not blind to the natural defects of exuberances of his character', but felt that no one had accomplished what Oastler had.[21]

Richard Oastler was the embodiment of paradox. Traditional Anglican and fervent ex-Methodist Evangelical, upholder of aristocracy and champion of the poor, a constitutionalist who believed in direct action, a lover of the countryside whose life was given to the industrial poor, he was an old fashioned Tory who disliked every manifestation of the capitalist spirit of the age – including democracy. Above all, he was a Christian working out his faith in the context of an increasingly secularized, industrial society. He had few guidelines, for the church itself had almost abandoned the attempt. A disciple of William Wilberforce and a friend of the Tory MP Michael Sadler, he had encountered industrial poverty during a typhoid epidemic in Leeds, and in 1830 his letter to the *Leeds Mercury* entitled *Yorkshire Slavery* is generally recognized as the beginning of the factory movement. An outgoing romantic, he was a superbly gifted orator. A natural leader, he created a wildly improbable alliance of Tory gentry, Christian clergy and secular-minded working-class Radicals. It is not surprising that the Radical Stephens saw something of his own paradoxical inheritance in that of his friend. Among the factory reformers, Radicals far out-numbered Tories; perhaps only Oastler and a handful of others can truly be called Tory Radicals. Although in 1834 Peel's Tamworth manifesto rejected Tory Radicalism as the philosophy of the emerging Conservative party, Oastler's hybrid movement achieved some of the first substantial social reforms of the century.[22]

Oastler's Toryism was remote from the 'real world' inhabited by the party leadership. It was not a theory, for Tories recoiled from the notion that a set of doctrines could be preferred to the values and institutions bequeathed by the past. It sprang from the land, from small, settled communities in which each order and family were mutually dependent. The sum total of these communities constituted the state; centralization was suspected as much as theory. This socially cohesive society was consecrated by the Christian church, which since the Reformation was the Church of England as by law established. Itself a venerable religious and social institution, the established church had been partially revitalized by the Evangelical revival. Oastler, a produce of both church and revival, started from a vision of an idealized English Christian society that he believed had existed in the past, and which could be restored, adjusted to take account of the industrial present. As he said to the Duke of Wellington, Toryism meant 'a place for everything, and everything in its place'[23]

Into this delightful social harmony had come the original sin of industrial capitalism. A vigorous class of manufacturers using the new inventions of science had created vast but ill-distributed wealth. Old patterns of life and traditional restraints had been swept away in a hurricane of social change, as rural workers were drawn into the new, dehumanized industrial towns. The new order was sanctioned by the political economists, who taught that prosperity depended upon untrammeled freedom for the laws of supply and demand. Ancient trade restrictions and social codes that inhibited the pursuit of self-interest must be abolished. After 1832, manufacturers and their allies could bring considerable political pressure on the Whig government for 'rational' reform. Even morality was interpreted as self-interest. Jeremy Bentham wrote: 'To prove that the immoral action is a miscalculation of self-interest is the purpose of the intelligent moralist.' Society was being seen more and more as simply an aggregate of individuals joined only by contractual relationships. Such notions smacked of the Enlightenment rather than of the Bible; yet such was the fatalistic sway of the new science of political economy that there was little protest from the church. It was the Revd Thomas Malthus who had argued that population outstripped growth in subsistence, so that the natural checks of misery and vice were bound to fall on most human beings. The Bishops of London and Chester happily joined moral philosophers and utilitarians on the Royal Commission that preceded the Poor Law Amendment Act of 1834.[24]

All this was monstrous to Oastler. In the winter of 1835, he called for the repeal of the Act in language that his younger contemporary Karl Marx might have envied:

> The demon called Liberalism who is now stalking the land scattering absolute want in the richest corn fields, and the deepest distress among the busy rattling of our looms – assuming first one name and then another; March of Intellect, Political Economy, Free Trade, Liberal Principles, etc, but always destroying the peace of the cottage and the happiness of the palace – this Demon will be found to have been the enemy of true religion and of the prosperity and well-being of man.

There could be no compromise between the teaching of the political economists and the gospel of fellowship. The 'demon' had infested all political parties, so that all things were to be measured by its yardstick rather than by Christianity. To Oastler there was a world of difference between the paternalistic Elizabethan poor law, which despite its shortcomings, accepted the responsibility of a Christian state for its poor, and the Act of 1834, which in the name of fashionable economic theory, had all but repudiated it. Indeed, Lord Althorp had declared that any poor relief was contrary to the principles of political economy, which was even against private charity. Oastler saw modern economic theory as deeply pagan because it was fatalistic. It dismissed the Christian-based social order, exalted selfishness on 'rational' grounds, and could be properly described as demonic. Seeing life in black and white sharpness, conscious that despite the hardships of the domestic economy, the coming of industrial capitalism had added new, severe miseries to the lives of those who sustained it, Oastler appealed to the old values to restore the balance upset by the new.[25]

He was not opposed to industry as such. He wanted a ten-hour working day for adult factory operatives, and regional boards of employers and employees to settle industrial disputes, fix wages and curb over-production. The Poor Law Amendment Act was to be repealed. Land resettlement and peasant proprietorship were to be introduced, with a state-aided scheme for the reclamation of waste lands. There was to be a graduated tax on capital. Above all, the well-being of the working classes was to be the first object of government. Law must be based on the will of God, not on the forces of supply and demand. 'The real cause of our general distress may be found in our entire abandonment of the great principles of the Divine Legislator.'

Thus Oastler was one of the first to relate Christianity to a modern industrial society. Stimulated by reading the Reformation Bishop Latimer's social sermons, he wrote an open letter to the Archbishop of York calling for a purified, transformed church of the people. He was ignored, for his growing reputation as a fanatical mob orator imperilled the very support he most needed; in any case, the church had long ceased to make pronouncements about the general state of society. As the odds against his success lengthened, a desperate Oastler came to believe that the triumph of *laissez-faire* economics meant the dissolution of the social contract and the destruction of the Christian society. If that happened, the inevitable chaos was something to be welcomed.[26]

Karl Marx would call such ideas 'feudal Socialism':

> Half lamentation, half lampoon; half echo of the past, half menace of the future; at times, by its bitter, witty and incisive criticism, striking the bourgeoisie to the very heart's core; but always ludicrous in its effect through total incapacity to comprehend the march of human history.

Although Marx's own understanding of human history is also open to question, Oastler did misunderstand past, present and future. The lost 'golden age' of rural social cohesion had never existed. It is very doubtful if Christian influence since the Reformation had been as potent in English life as Oastler believed. As for the present, the kindly paternalism of the country gentry was hardly vindicated by the brutal suppression of the Swing riots of 1830, or by the treatment of the Tolpuddle martyrs in 1834. The condition of the industrial classes in the eighteen-thirties is a subject of perennial controversy; but if his opponents exaggerated the benefits of industrialism, Oastler exaggerated its evils. Like Marx, he assumed that capitalism would not adapt itself to the results of criticism. Nor would the future show much trace of 'Tory Radicalism' as Oastler conceived it, and by the dawn of the new century the banner of social reform was often carried by the Liberal party.[27]

Nevertheless the legislative achievements of the factory reformers remain. The principle of government interference for social redress had been established, despite entrenched opposition. It is more difficult to know how far the factory reformers influenced the churches. They tried to awaken the slumbering Christian social conscience to the dangers of accepting the spirit of the age. Their leaders proclaimed the primary Christian obligation to the needy and the oppressed, offering hope in the midst of suffering. They told Christian employers not to act as though enlightened selfishness was the noblest aim in life; they urged employees not to act irresponsibly in the quest for human dignity. Less influential in the Church of England than F. D. Maurice and the Christian Socialists of the 1840s, they accomplished more for society as a whole. No one seriously impugned the Christian motivation of the factory reform leaders, nor can it be denied that they were among the first in the industrial age to challenge the church to recover the social dimensions of faith. Yet church historians have paid less attention to them – with the one exception of Lord Shaftesbury – than social historians.[28]

Stephens was to drink deeply from the Oastlerite fount. Some of Oastler's conclusions he had accepted already; but Radical though he was, he borrowed freely from the Tory's thought, without worrying unduly about logical inconsistency. He accepted the myth of the lost golden age, and gloried in the teaching of King Alfred. He rejoiced in Oastler's watchword of the Altar, the Throne and the Cottage and in the social order bequeathed by history. Like Oastler, he came to mistrust political reform, and saw social redress as won for, and not by, the people. He was impressed by the support of the northern Anglican clergy for the factory reformers, and alienated by Dissenting apathy or opposition. His marked anti-Tory stance of 1834 disappeared. Yet it is mistaken to identify him completely with Oastler by calling him a Tory Radical, or even a revolutionary Tory. Oastler did not do this. In 1839 he said publicly that his friend was of 'a different party in politics to himself'. Unlike Oastler, Stephens associated with the Chartists, and stood for Parliament in 1837 not as a Tory but as an independent candidate. As he wrote in 1838, 'A man must be independent of all parties, or he can never be a patriot.' Even in later life when he was associated with the Tories, he never accepted the name, just as he never became an Anglican priest. Despite Oastler, he was still advocating disestablishment in 1841. Stephens had come to value his costly independence too much to surrender it again to anybody.[29]

The factory movement had enjoyed an adventurous five years of life when Stephens joined it. Sadler's ten hours bill was eclipsed by the agitation for Parliamentary reform, and a Royal Commission concluded that there was no case for shortening the working day of adults – that is, those over the age of thirteen. Sadler resigned his bill to the Whig minister Lord Althorp. The resulting Factory Act of 1833 provided for a forty-eight-hour week without night work for the nine to thirteen age group, to be introduced in three stages. Inspectors were to enforce the law, though many legal loopholes for evasion remained. Oastler's hopes were dashed, and worse was to follow. Owenite trade unionism collapsed, and the Tolpuddle martyrs were transported. In August 1834 the Poor Law Amendment Act became law. Peel's Tamworth manifesto marked the break of the Conservative leadership from its Tory past, and its acceptance of industrial capitalism. The following year Michael Sadler died.

In August 1835 the factory movement began to revive. Althorp's Factory Act was widely disliked. Reformers saw it as a masters' bill that could be easily evaded, while masters resented any restrictions on their freedom of action. Children's ages were falsified, and mill owning justices connived at evasions of the law. The Act's provisions for the nine to thirteen age group were due to be enforced on 1 March 1836 but there was marked reluctance to proceed. Lancastrian reformers reacted by demanding restrictions on the working of factory machines – the 'moving power' – rather than relying on hours alone. Unlike the factories of Yorkshire, the Lancashire cotton industry in theory had been regulated since 1819, and experience had shown that a workable law that fell short of the ideal was better than one that conceded everything, but enforced nothing. The factory reform leaders in Lancashire (Hindley, Doherty, George Condy of the *Manchester Advertiser* and two Dissenting mill owners, Joseph Brotherton and John Fielden) were agreed in supporting Hindley's introduction of a bill for a ten-hour working day with restrictions on the moving power. A Preston delegate conference in August accepted this policy, apparently with the approval of Oastler and the Yorkshire reformers. Three Manchester conferences, in October and December 1835 and January 1836, worked on the bill and planned the forthcoming campaign.

At one of these conferences, Oastler and Stephens met. Even then, Stephens still wrestled with lingering reservations, as his first factory meetings were to reveal; but the die was cast, and he stood on the brink of the four most memorable years of his life.[30]

3

The Political Preacher

On 14 January 1836, Joseph Rayner Stephens arrived in Newcastle upon Tyne for a three day visit. He had been invited by a hundred ministers and laymen to lecture on the voluntary principle; but in the Newcastle music hall he also spoke of northern factory conditions, winning his audience's support for reform. It was the beginning of a public ministry to the working classes that was to last for the rest of his life.[1]

It was an end as well as a beginning, for henceforth he would move in a world of proletarian agitation far removed from the genteel proceedings of the Ashton church separation society. The vast crowds and formalized open-air demonstrations complete with slogans, flags, bands, songs and stirring popular oratory, nurtured personality cults on the grand scale. Indoor gatherings were equally contagious, with a battery of speakers competing for the hero-worship of their audiences. Stephens brought to them a romantic disposition, an instinct for self-dramatization, marked oratorical gifts and an affronted pastoral conscience. The ex-Wesleyan minister soon proved himself a master in the art of proletarian revivalism, with crowds hanging on his every word. After his death, his nephew wrote that he was 'not without the consciousness of power, and the love of power over men'. Yet he did not flinch from confronting his audiences with unpalatable truths, and he never compromised his full Christian convictions in the profoundly secular ethos of working-class radicalism.[2]

The first meeting of the new campaign for Hindley's ten hours bill was held on 19 January in Ashton's Mill Lane schoolroom. Stephens was in the chair, and about a thousand workers attended. He was still feeling his way forward, and he asked one of the speakers, the Revd George Bull, vicar of Byerley, if places of worship were desecrated by being used for factory meetings. He told the audience about his Newcastle tour, and the parallel use of chapels in the abolitionist cause. He had tried to mediate between masters and men, but the masters had spurned him. He spoke at further meetings at Hyde, Stalybridge and Bury. He was loudly cheered in his own King Street chapel as he said: 'They might term him an agitator if they chose; he had agitated some questions with effect, and he was now turned agitator for the factory bill.' He demanded speedy justice for the factory children, and advised the operatives to form Methodist-type classes for further agitation, which would include Parliamentary lobbying in London. The Ashton committee appointed him their deputy for the lobbying. After a day's consideration, he accepted, knowing that it meant trouble in his circuit.[3]

At Manchester on 2 March, he made his first telling speech. He caused a sensation by revealing details of the Poor Law Commissioners' factory migration scheme, which supplied rural paupers to industrial areas for money – it was 'the resuscitation of slavery in the British dominions'. He named a Stalybridge firm that summonsed labourers who left their employment without notice, resulting in pregnant women being put on a prison treadmill. 'I impeach these men at the bar of Almighty God.' He opposed repeal of the eight-hour clause in the existing Factory Act. In dialect, he spoke of three Stalybridge children who agreed with a mill owner to falsify their ages to continue working. 'Thus they were taught and obliged to lie; and they admitted that they "told lies monie a toime to get them out of a hobble".' He was bright, breezy and irreverent towards the great. In London, he hoped to see the Duke of Wellington, 'if he were not hunting, or doing something worse', and the Sabbatarian MP Sir Andrew Agnew, 'who wanted the Sabbath to be observed by the poor – the rich were to please themselves'. The blend of well-informed detail, outrage and humour, was to become typical of his speeches; but already the ultra-radical newspaper editor George Condy disliked their potentially libellous and offensive content.[4]

Shortly afterwards, Stephens led the delegation to London to lobby for Hindley's bill. The existing Act's restriction on hours for the under thirteens had not been enforced on 1 March, and when the delegation met their Parliamentary allies Hindley, Fielden and Lord Ashley, it was known that the Whig government intended to repeal the measure. On 15 March Poulett Thomson, President of the Board of Trade, proposed a bill which enabled twelve-year-olds to be classified as 'young persons', and thus liable for a twelve-hour day. The delegates circularized all MPs appealing to the House of Commons not to allow the government to violate a covenant essential to the health and happiness of children.

An indignant Stephens saw that the government was violating its own inadequate Act in the interests of the masters, and his respect for the reformed Parliament declined. In April, while Oastler roused Yorkshire, he addressed protest meetings in Lancashire. In Ashton market place, he told a crowd of five thousand that nine-tenths of MPs were ignorant of the manufacturing districts. At Stockport he spoke of the rottenness of the social system; at Bolton he predicted that Hindley's bill eventually would be carried. He urged workers to save, so that they could be represented in Parliament. For the first time on record, he proposed the drastic remedies of universal suffrage and the ballot.[5]

On 9 May Poulett Thomson won a majority of two for the second reading, and abandoned his bill. The reformers' joy was muted by a scrutiny of the voting lists. They had counted on Irish support, but the votes of Daniel O'Connell and his party were cast for the government. The returning delegation spoke of their victory 'in spite of open foes and rotten friends', and they resolved to carry the ten hours bill 'or something else, a good deal more and a good deal better'. Stephens in Ashton market place attacked O'Connell's 'base and unworthy act', while praising Hindley and 'that good old hearty cock' Fielden, whose pamphlet *The Curse of the Factory System* had just been published.[6]

Stephens by now had realized how many 'open foes and rotten friends' stood in the way of effective reform. Despite his original expectation, the parsons were absent from factory meetings, and this he attributed to sectarian self-interest. The reformed Parliament reflected the power of the mill owners, which was 'a bad swap' for the previous power of the aristocracy. In late June, Hindley withdrew his bill after official assurances that the existing Act would be better enforced. Doubts about Hindley were not new among seasoned reformers, and he was replaced as Parliamentary leader by Lord Ashley. Hindley's break with Oastler, and his firm's second conviction under the Factory Act now alienated Stephens, who never trusted him again. In mid-August, Stephens and Oastler shared a series of meetings in which Stephens attacked Hindley, and Oastler expressed his delight in finding 'a worthy successor to the beloved Sadler'. At the same Oldham meeting on 18 August, Stephens ridiculed the apologist of the mill owners, Dr Ure, who had compared the factory girls in beauty and attire with the women of ancient Greece. 'The people alluded to were the pale, sickly, ghastly plague-spotted population amongst whom he had a ministry.' Another speaker, the rising leader of a national working-class radicalism, one Feargus O'Connor, hastened to identify himself with the movement of northern social protest. Two days later at Ashton, Stephens pledged allegiance to Oastler, and there was a new menace in his attack on lawbreaking millowners; they would face the treadmill, transportation and hanging – 'we dont care for you'.[7]

By now Stephens was a controversial figure, attacked in the House of Commons and in the press. He was dubbed 'the raving, ranting parson', a paid agitator who should 'stick to his Bible'. His intemperate language probably gave less offence to the millowners than his temperately worded advice to their employees to save, organize, agitate and as a last resort, to commence exclusive dealing. John Stephens in *The Christian Advocate* defended his brother, praising his speeches as 'a specimen of *genuine Wesleyanism*', and advising critics of his language to 'read the appalling facts'. Even John Fielden thought he should use moderate language; to this Stephens agreed. At Stockport he declared: 'The factory system, in moderate language, he denounced as bloody and murderous.' It was not surprising that in the early autumn, there was a division in the Ashton Stephenite circuit.[8]

However, it was Oastler who set the pace in promoting fear among the masters. Stung by the flippant refusal of Blackburn magistrates to enforce the law on lawbreaking millowners, he threatened to teach factory children to damage spindles with knitting needles. Bull, Hindley and Ashley broke off relations with him, but Fielden and Stephens stood by him. Oastler and Stephens spoke at Blackburn a week after the 'sabotage' speech. Stephens took the opportunity to answer a recent criticism:

I have been told by these men to stick to the Bible and leave the spindle to them (Laughter). I mean to stick to the Bible: and if anyone wants to know why I am a factory reform agitator, I tell them it is because I know that the system is repugnant to the word of the living God, and that as long as we have his blessed book in our hands and in our hearts, we must live to see the downfall of that tyranny which is now grinding you to the dust.

He gave details of local evasions of the law, and challenged the men of Blackburn to be *jannock*.[9]

In October, a grateful Oastler invited Stephens to a three-week visit of Yorkshire. In Huddersfield they took part in a spectacular torchlight procession and rally, attended by an estimated ten thousand people. Oastler welcomed 'the turned-off parson' who had survived the disruption of the Stephenite circuit. He 'believes what John Wesley and

Jesus Christ have said', and was 'one of the excellent of the earth'. Stephens contrasted the furore over Oastler's knitting needles with the inhumanity of industrial life:

> We never heard anything about it being diabolical to destroy property when that property is made up of the flesh, bone body and sinews . . . We never heard the least syllable of alarm when the cotton masters are but putting thousands and tens of thousands into the fire as an offering to Moloch. Is a spindle worth more than an arm? Is a shuttle of more value than a limb? Are jennies and looms and hundreds of horsepower worth more than that immortal soul of which God has said, 'What shall it profit a man if he shall gain the whole world, and lose his own soul?'[10]

The crowds listened as closely as they did in Lancashire. In Huddersfield, seemingly for the first time, he alluded to Christianity as part of English law. At Keighley, he brushed aside millowning self-justification with the commandment prohibiting murder. At Bradford he called the mills 'little better than common brothels'. He wanted virtue, domestic comfort and respectability – 'he wanted to have the merry homes, and the bonny lasses of merry old England once more'. At Deighton, he enumerated the reformers' difficulties, and struck an apocalyptic note by preaching that God Himself would arise and scatter their enemies.[11]

The final rally of the campaign was held in the Methodist New Connexion chapel at Oldham. Hindley, Stephens, Fielden and Oastler were the main speakers. Stephens attacked the charge that the poor were profligate. Modern inventions had been misused to dispense with the labour of adult men. 'Bring back the good old times, I do not say when we were without machinery, but when the full-grown man by his own labour could maintain his family in comfort: and we shall then hear no more of the extreme poverty, improvidence, and profligacy of the operative classes.' He attacked Hindley to his face, and promised long-term agitation, first for a ten hours bill, and then for eight hours, 'and all that follows'. Oastler made the final speech, and brought the audience in the packed chapel to its feet, cheering to the point of exhaustion.[12]

In eleven months, Stephens had emerged from obscurity to become 'the champion of the factory child', or simply 'the champion'. His message and style were already fixed, and his pastoral concern as well as his sparkling oratorical gifts made him a firm favourite with northern factory operatives. He was as convinced as Oastler that factory reform was a religious agitation – 'this is the work of God, and . . . it shall be accomplished'. He was not 'mealy-mouthed' in his choice of words. His brother likened him to 'some of those fine old prophets whose province it was under the ancient dispensation to rebuke iniquity and teach men their mutual duties'. Like the prophets, he stirred up many opponents, and he found it hard to see any good in millowners. Hindley's convictions for breaches of the Factory Act rankled in his mind for years. According to his current biographer, even John Fielden of Todmorden, the wealthy radical master who eventually was to carry the ten hours act to victory in the House of Commons, was never much of a philanthropist; he did not pay exceptionally high wages, and conditions in his mill were not greatly different from those in others. Stephens always had great respect for Fielden, even when he disagreed with him; but he never understood the economic realities which affected even sympathetic masters. The bleak events which were to come only confirmed him in his relentless opposition to millowners as a class, along with their allies, the political economists and the Whig politicians.[13]

In his Oldham speech, Stephens attacked the Poor Law Amendment Act of 1834: 'the connection between this cursed Poor Law Bill and the factory system is intimate and inseparable. I never omit to inform my countrymen of this fresh – this last invasion of their rights, and to arouse them to resist it.' By late 1836, the time to resist had come, for the Poor Law Commissioners were poised to introduce the Act into the industrial north.[14]

The verbal violence of the campaign to repeal the Act of 1834 was a gut rejection of one of the most hated Acts ever passed by a British Parliament. There were solid reasons for this hatred. The Act replaced an Act of 1601, the famous 43rd Elizabeth, which implicitly accepted that the relief of the poor was a community responsibility exercised at parish level. Overseers of the Poor collected a compulsory poor rate, and administered relief in a number of ways to applicants known by them. Relief could be in aid of wages, or to assist large families, or to provide children with apprenticeships. In times of exceptional hardship, a large part of the labouring population was relieved, especially in the north, where unemployment was endemic. Relief in aid of wages was an essential element in the budget of the handloom weavers. There was little abuse of the traditional system in the north. Even the coercive side of the old Poor Law – the settlement laws, the punishment of vagrants, the denial of relief to those refusing to enter a workhouse, where one existed – was moderated in practice through local incompetence, expediency or humanitarian concern. Whatever its defects, the law's attempt to meet need, its flexibility of operation, and its personalized relief process gave the old Poor Law widespread community support. English labourers assumed that they had a right to relief in exchange for their labour. Their champion William Cobbett had argued that the mediaeval church had held its lands in trust for the poor, and that their rights were recognized in the Tudor poor law; any violation of those rights called into question the rights of property.

Rising costs, bad harvests, the Swing riots, and the opposition of the political economists, discredited the old poor law. Jeremy Bentham thought that there were no natural rights to relief, but he was prepared to accept it at a level just above starvation, through a centralized system in strictly controlled workhouses. The Revd Thomas Malthus recommended the abolition of the old poor law. Sumner, the Bishop of Chester, taught that poverty and inequality were the best conditions for moral development. A Royal Commission condemned the traditional system, and proposed a new one. Its basic principle was the abolition of outdoor relief for the able-bodied. Relief in the new-style workhouses was to be less than any living commanded by a labour wage.

The resulting Act created a centralized Poor Law Commission, with power to appoint Assistant Commissioners, regulate relief and lay down conditions. Parishes were grouped into Unions administered by elected boards of guardians, each maintaining a workhouse. In practice, they were to be run on stringent lines, with the sexes separated within their unwelcoming walls. Rights of settlement within parishes – which involved entitlement to maintenance – were limited to birth and marriage; the full costs of illegitimacy were to be borne by the mother. Insensitive comments on the new workhouse conditions by assistant Commissioners increased the fear and alarm of those who felt that their ancient rights had been denied. No self-sacrifice could save them from the workhouse. Such was the bleak regime to be introduced in a trade depression to the industrial north, where outdoor relief could be essential to survival.

Radicals opposed the Act as a further degradation of the labouring poor; traditionalists hated it because it contradicted the old paternal society, not least in its novel, centralized bureaucracy. Christian factory reformers who combined both sentiments erupted in anger. If mill-owners chastised with whips, Poor Law Commissioners were chastising with scorpions. Oastler set the pace in condemning 'the three stinking commissioned funguses' with their 'Act of Treason' and 'Cathechism of Hell'. Stephens shared Oastler's belief that the Christian social contract had been violated, and that it was right to resist the law's introduction. He accepted William Cobbett's theory of a mediaeval Christian origin for English poor relief. He was deeply convinced that the Act and its underlying philosophy was contrary to the law of God revealed in scripture. It was impossible to reconcile God's lavish provision for his world in creation with Malthus' theory of population, and the principle of 'less eligibility'. The separation of families in workhouses was a flagrant violation of Christian marriage. He was suspicious of the proposal for the rural police to enforce the Act. Never to the end of his life did he relent in his opposition to it, and his pastoral experience of its victims only gave him a sharper edge to his denunciations. His tirades were to reach such a pitch that some thought him insane; but only by intensifying popular pressure could there be any hope of repeal.[15]

In January 1837, Assistant Commissioner Alfred Power visited Ashton, and by the end of the month London had grouped twelve communities into an Ashton Poor Law Union. Elections of Guardians were held, and safe supporters elected; but new elections were due in March, and this gave opponents time to organize. Ratepayers objected to the expense of the Act, and petitioned against it; but they allowed the nomination of five Guardians to avoid incurring penalties. At a spirited meeting in February addressed by Stephens and others, it was resolved to refuse to pay rates for the new Union, or to acknowledge the power of the Commissioners; they too would petition against the Act. Precisely what happened in March is obscure, but middle-class opinion was not convinced by the policy of total boycott. The new Union had a majority of pro-Act Guardians, who elected the Dukinfield millowner Samuel Robinson as chairman; but according to the Oldham diarist Edwin Butterworth, Ashton itself returned three Tory and two Radical Guardians. He added that the old select vestry would continue to administer poor relief for a further three months. On 22 April, Stephens harangued about 600 workmen outside the New Inn at Lees. The meeting (under the chairmanship of the Lees tailor Abel Swann, a loyal Stephenite) was called to consider resistance to the law, and support for a South Lancashire Anti-Poor Law Association. By May or June, the Ashton petition of churchwardens, Overseers of the Poor and the select vestry was sent to London, where it was ignored.[16]

Stephens did not neglect the wider struggle. In January he spoke with Oastler and Fielden at Salford. By April, he was involved in a by-election at Huddersfield, which had successfully defied the new Poor Law. Oastler was a candidate, and Stephens toured the constituency urging workers to boycott the shops and taverns of the Whig candidate's supporters; but the middle-class voters elected the Whig by a majority of fifty. On 16 May, he spoke at a huge demonstration at Peep Green, on Hartshead Moor, called by the new West Riding Anti-Poor Law Central Committee. With banners flying and bands playing, over 200,000 workers attended; only a fraction of them could have heard the speeches of O'Connor, Fielden, Oastler, Stephens and Robert Owen, the founding father of British Socialism. Stephens attacked 'that utter disregard of justice to the female sex which the bastardy clauses of the poor law act exhibited'. The Act violated the constitution, and if the rights of Magna Carta were denied, 'blood should not be witheld to obtain them'.[17]

The day after Peep Green, seven of the leaders met at Fixby Hall. They signed a resolution demanding government capital for the starving unemployed to support themselves through agricultural and industrial labour; after repayment, they would remain owners of the property involved. Among the signatories were Oastler, Stephens, Owen and James Bernard, the ultra-Tory initiator of the Central National Association. The next day, Stephens advocated the new policy; state aid for agricultural co-operative societies, with land to be tilled in common, and to remain the property of the workers. Already, Owen had written in *The New Moral World*: 'Although Stephens is a clergyman, he is a most ardent friend of the working classes and a very liberal man.' Elsewhere, press coverage was much less appreciative.[18]

The King's death on 20 June meant a general election. Stephens 'raised a laugh' at Oldham the next day by announcing his candidature for Ashton. His father too thought him 'daft' to stand. He had no chance of winning. Although immensely popular with the unenfranchized workers, his reputation for extremism limited his appeal to the respectable electorate. There was no Tory–Radical alliance at Ashton like that enjoyed by Oastler at Huddersfield. The Tory candidate was the prominent Wesleyan, James Wood, himself a critic of the new poor law. The sitting Liberal–Radical member Charles Hindley was highly esteemed – except by factory reformers – and was also opposed to the Act of 1834. It was not surprising that during the campaign, Stephens was reported to have stated that he hoped the Tory would win. He chose to stand to further his own causes, which he did with great energy. His apocalyptic manifesto was unmistakeably Cobbettite in tone:

> The security of all property has been endangered by withdrawing protection from the property of the poor. In robbing them, we have prepared the way for the destruction of all the other classes of society. The English labourer can no longer earn his bread by the sweat of his brow . . .

The new poor law 'will inevitably pauperize the whole of the labouring population'. It 'treats the poor worse than the felon, . . . makes marriage a mockery and offers brutal violence to the holiest feelings of our nature'. He would never accept 'this wicked law'. Belonging to no political party, he was for repeal of the Act, for 'a fair and effective' factory bill, and for universal manhood suffrage.

He drew huge crowds to his public meetings in the market place and behind his chapel. He preached for two hours and twenty minutes to an estimated Sunday evening congregation of 1,500 people on the opposition of the New Testament to the principles of the new poor law. On nomination day, while his father was confiding to his diary 'I can hardly wish him success', Stephens set a long remembered record of sustained oratory, speaking for four hours and three-quarters on the hustings. 'Upon a show of hands being called for, about four hundred hands were held up for Mr Hindley, thirty for Wood, and a "forest" for Mr Stephens.' After that, the actual result was an anti-climax: Hindley 237, Wood 201, Stephens 19. Undismayed, Stephens addressed the people at considerable length, 'and then went in procession, followed by about seven or eight thousand persons, the latter hooting all persons supposed to be hostile to their candidate'. [19]

Oastler had failed again at Huddersfield, and Whig victory in the country depressed the anti-poor law forces. In Ashton Samuel Robinson, chairman of the poor law Union, published an open letter to Hindley dealing with his objections to the Act, and defending it against 'the current of popular error and prejudice' in which 'even life and property are scarcely safe'. Stephens was in his mind when he criticized those who always had popular grievances on their lips. In October, Alfred Power wrote to the Commissioners that there was no incendiarism in Ashton; Stephens alone was responsible for the excitement there. The Commission's immigration agent, Richard Muggeridge, said that recent radical meetings in Manchester were total failures, and that Stephens and others had complained of the 'apathy and indifference' of the working classes to their "real interests and welfare" '.[20]

In November, Stephens was attacked in a violently abusive pamphlet by John Easby, a Manchester Liberal who had campaigned for Hindley in the election, and who held Stephens responsible for an assault on his father. To this purely personal attack, Stephens made no reply. During the temporary malaise, he had reverted to factory reform. He challenged Daniel O'Connell to a public debate for his vote for Poulett Thomson the previous year. The Irish leader was too slippery to be caught and refused. Stephens was more successful in Leeds, confronting Edward Baines of the *Leeds Mercury* and the factory overseer John Wrigglesworth over a proposed eleven hour bill. He ridiculed Wrigglesworth, and warned Baines of the consequences of the continuance of child labour. In a subsequent Huddersfield meeting Stephens stressed that he did not want a return to pre-industrial conditions, but the application of the principles of British law to the social changes wrought by science and technology. At an Oldham dinner in late November, he again spoke in favour of universal suffrage and the ballot.[21]

The anti-poor law campaign was recovering. The creation of the South Lancashire Anti-Poor Law Association co-ordinated local groups and sent out 'missionaries' to mobilize support. It set an immediate objective by sponsoring a mass petition against the Act, to be presented to the Commons in February 1838, to coincide with the hearing of motions for repeal. Stephens became a leading figure in the new Association. All were greatly helped by the appearance of O'Connor's *Northern Star* newspaper in November. The new Leeds paper was wholly devoted to radical working-class politics, and was totally opposed to the new poor law. Stephens bought twenty one-pound shares in it. His speeches were more extensively reported than ever before, which in turn contributed to the paper's initial success. O'Connor exaggerated when later he wrote that before the advent of the *Star* Stephens 'was not known beyond the limits of a portion of Lancashire, and even there not truly known'; Peep Green had made him a national leader in the anti-poor law struggle. With an efficient organization giving a clear lead, and a paper to sell that fully supported them, the anti-poor law campaigners took new heart.[22]

Radical opinion was ignited by the case of seven Glasgow cotton spinners, who as trade union leaders had led a strike against wage reductions. The shooting of a blackleg spinner led to their arrest on charges of murder and conspiracy to murder. After a long trial, they were convicted in January 1838 of being members of an association engaged in illegal activities, and sentenced to seven years' transportation. The case united trade unionists and radicals, and tended to divide both from middle-class sympathizers of the anti-poor law campaign. Yet Oastler and Stephens were roused. Through the trial, Stephens held that conviction made anarchy and revolution more certain; his own arrest would follow, and confrontation with a repressive government was to be welcomed. His language reached a new pitch of violence. In a dangerously exalted mood fed by Bishop Latimer's denunciation of unjust judges, he championed the Glasgow cotton spinners in the most notorious speeches of his life.[23]

In the first of two Manchester speeches in October, he assailed 'the base and perfidious and bloody Whig administration', demanding a memorial to the Queen for Lord Melbourne's dismissal and a bill of rights. In the second, with Oastler and O'Connor and his fellow speakers, he quoted Blackstone, that when the people's grievances were unredressed, they had the right to take matters into their own hands. The only question was whether the time had come for the shedding of his blood. Those who criticized such violent language in a Christian minister 'do not understand what the Christian ministry is, or what it was appointed for'.[24]

In December he set out for Newcastle and Scotland. On New Year's day on the Newcastle parade ground, he was to speak at an anti-poor law meeting with Oastler, O'Connor and a battery of speakers which included James Paul Cobbett. A local press report reckoned that at no time were 2,500 people present, and only 700 remained to the end. Stephens had been disgusted at Sir John Walsham, the local Assistant Poor Law Commissioner, whom he had seen on his journey north. He was irritated by the preceding speaker, James Cobbett, who wanted the people to understand that he opposed breaches of the law and acts of violence. Stephens called on reporters to carry his words to the people. The new poor law was not law, since it was contrary to God's law revealed in scripture. Referring to banners being carried at the meeting, he shouted:

> It was because he believed in God that he hated the new Poor Law act; and it was because he believed in God that he refused allegiance to that law. If Mr Cobbett could have shewn him it was law, still he would have unfurled his banner and said, 'by the law of God and by the breath of man, for child and wife I will war to the knife! (Tremendous cheers)'.

The new poor law relieved the people of allegiance to the Crown; it must be resisted at all costs. After recalling stories of Sir John Walsham's meanness over outdoor relief, the speaker described his encounter with him, contrasting his opulent appearance with the condition of the wretched victims of his policy. Sooner than they should suffer:

> Newcastle ought to be – and should be – one blaze of fire, with only one way to put it out, and that with the blood of all those who supported this abominable measure. Was that, he would ask, plain speaking? (cheers and cries of 'hear, hear'). He hoped the gentlemen of the press would not only put down his words, but their cheers also; and when Lord John Russell read them, he would say, 'this man shall go' – and when he went, these boys (the people) would go too – and when these boys went, Lord John Russell would go! (renewed shouts).

Whatever his motives, he had abandoned the last shred of verbal restraint, and nothing he said after that would remove the impression thus made. Even so, he denounced the new police force, praised soldiers who refused to fight for the new poor law, and called himself 'a revolutionist by fire . . . by blood, to the knife, to the death'. The English Marat was going to Scotland, and he ended without conscious irony by wishing one and all a happy new year. In the speech, he was moving a resolution that included the statement that the Poor Law Amendment Act 'ought to be resisted to the uttermost in every legal way'.[25]

After speaking with O'Connor in Edinburgh, he attended the trial of the cotton spinners in Glasgow, and made another speech there. The Glasgow case had changed his mind on trade unions. In a well-governed society they were a calamity, as they produced a constant civil war between classes; but he approved of them 'in the present detestable state of society' because 'good men must combine when the wicked conspire'. The soldiers were with them; they would ever point their arms at those struggling in the cause of industrious poverty against idle wealth. The millowners would have the revolution they dreaded:

> We have sworn by our God, by heaven, earth and hell, that from the east, the west, the north and the south we shall wrap in one awful sheet of devouring flame, which no arm can resist, the manufactories of the cotton tyrants, and the places of those who raised them by rapine and murder, and founded them on the wretchedness of the

millions, whom God – our God – Scotland's God, created to be happy (tremendous cheers).

The government did nothing, although for some time agents had been taking notes of Stephens' speeches. The Whig judge Henry Cockburn was dismayed, and wondered why this direct interference in a pending trial was unpunished.[26]

Stephens' enemies were multiplying. Lord Brougham had attacked his Peep Green speech in the House of Lords. It was unholy, irreverent and full of 'abominable profanity'. The working-class leader Francis Place thought him 'a malignant crazy man . . . a fanatic possessing great command of language and great power of declamation . . . His followers were never exhausted with bawling his praises, and never tired of contemplating the mischief he constantly proposed to them'. Place was an anti-clerical opponent of factory reform and poor law repeal; but soon other radical groups would share Place's disgust at appeals to 'physical force' by Stephens, Oastler and O'Connor.[27]

On and on went the seemingly tireless Stephens. At a Stalybridge Radical dinner, he repated the cry for a ten hours bill. In a large Manchester meeting to petition the Queen for the Glasgow cotton spinners, he called for justice rather than mercy. He was expecting imminent arrest, and said that nothing would delight him more. On 24 January at Rochdale, he resumed his attack on the poor law: 'If it were right to confiscate the property of the poor by abrogating the 43rd Elizabeth, it is right for the poor to take a dagger in one hand and a torch in the other, and do the best for themselves.'[28]

His violent speeches preceded the February Parliamentary debate and the presentation of the anti-poor law petition. The petitions of south Lancashire were produced at a major demonstration in Manchester on 5 February. They included three from Ashton with another yet to be presented, totalling 16,368 signatures; from Stalybridge the Radical Association's secretary John Deegan presented a petition signed by 5,420 people, with Stephens promising another from the women of the town. He told his audience that Power and Robinson thought it would be dangerous to introduce the new poor law into Ashton. At Ashton they had decided to refuse to vote for Guardians in the March elections. When the law was operative in Ashton, 'my office as the peoples guide and leader is at an end'. But the government was not to be moved by bravado, debates or petitions, and on 10 February Fielden's motion to repeal the Poor Law Amendment Act was lost by 307 votes to 17. The anti-poor law campaign had failed, and this had profound consequences for the subsequent activities of Oastler and Stephens.[29]

In March the northern leadership decided on a remonstrance. The House of Commons was to be asked to hear representatives of the unenfranchized and unemployed at the bar of the House. Six leaders including Stephens were chosen, subject to endorsement at public meetings; but there was little hope that the Commons would hear them. There were only two real courses left. One was to accept that no social reform was possible until universal suffrage was law; the other was to bring new pressure on the government by recommending that the people acquire arms. The radicals who were to become Chartists were attracted to the first; Oastler and Stephens (who by now thought of universal suffrage as the restoration of what he believed had existed in a remote Anglo-Saxon past), were drawn to the second. As the anti-Poor Law movement declined, this divergence increased.[30]

There was no such problem over the Ashton Guardian elections, but only a united, successful attempt to frustrate the law. No returns were made for Ashton and four other places – a victory against the national trend for the policy of total boycott. Eleven Guardians were elected elsewhere in the Union, including three for Dukinfield, where Stephens lived. His old ally of 1834, the magistrate and millowner John Cheetham, was the new chairman; but since poor relief continued to be administered as before, he could do little. Power thought that the excitable Ashton populace made the town one of the four most difficult in the north. At Dukinfield in late March, Stephens had reduced the ratepayers' meeting to chaos, and won a spectacular verbal triumph over Cheetham and Robinson. When an attempt was made in May by Dukinfield Whig landlords to deprive their tenants of the vote in the select vestry, Stephens frustrated it. Such incidents boosted his local reputation as the people's champion. The remonstrance was adopted at Charlestown, and once more he attacked the new poor law, to 5,000 people assembled in Ashton market place to mark the coronation of Queen Victoria.[31]

He wrote a series of articles for the *Northern Star* on Oastler, and helped him in the continuing anti-poor law struggle at Huddersfield. With O'Connor, Stephens led the crowd that disrupted the Guardians' meetings. In May, he stayed at Fixby Hall when Oastler was ill with exhaustion. He was present when his friend was dismissed by his employer, and he helped to organize a fund for him. Both men thought it was both legal and right for the people to arm in the future struggle against the new poor law; according to O'Connor, they knew that secret arming had begun, and believed that open arming lessened the risk of irresponsible action.[32]

Fielden openly disagreed. At Bradford, Stephens and Fielden shared a platform. Stephens called Fielden 'the Ulysses of our enterprise', but he wanted arming for self-defence, though 'I would not have a drop of blood shed.' As O'Connor had once hastened to unite with the powerful factory reformers, now Stephens, seeing the anti-poor law movement transform itself into one for universal suffrage, decided to ally himself with O'Connor. At Saddleworth on 9 June, mounted on Oastler's pony, accompanied by a brass band and leading a procession of his Stalybridge supporters half-a-mile long, Stephens met the main party of radicals and led them on to the ground with banners flying. He was not going to petition, but 'endeavour to unite all in the accomplishment of the object laid down by Mr O'Connor, namely a good day's wage for a fair day's work, and . . . it mattered not to him the political name of his ally . . . ' At a radical dinner at Keighley in July, he urged arming, since constitutional steps for repeal had met with contempt. 'He warned them not to think of using them, but to have them ready, and then they might rely on having the infernal law repealed.' Prime Minister, Home Secretary and Commissioners deserved impeachment. He thought his words would be brought to the attention of the Attorney-General, and he threatened to impeach the Crown itself.[33]

Stephens was courting arrest, and it was only through the Home Secretary's forbearance that he and Oastler had not been prosecuted. Russell wrote of Oastler's speeches in September 1838: 'So long as mere violence of language is employed without effect, it is better . . . not to add to the importance of these mob orators by prosecutions.' Against this he had to balance the alarm of the Poor Law Commissioners over law enforcement, and the safety of their agents; but this was lessened by the policy of bypassing difficult Unions. For the moment, the issue was left unresolved; but as the dying days of the year were to show, there was a limit to Whig toleration.[34]

By 1838, many radicals were convinced that effective social reform depended upon possession of the vote. Universal suffrage had been the demand of British radicals since 1780, and it was restated in May 1838 in the People's Charter by William Lovett of the London Working Men's Association. Its six points were universal manhood suffrage, payment of MPs, equal electoral districts, abolition of property qualifications for MPs, annual parliaments and the ballot. Working men from all the diverse regions of the United Kingdom were brought together by acceptance of the six-point Charter. A huge, unwieldy radical movement was in the making, composed of those who saw political reform as an end in itself, and those who wanted it for social redress. In August and September 1838, mass meetings adopted the Charter and elected delegates to a proposed National Convention.

The anti-poor law leaders had to decide where they stood. Richard Oastler was a Tory who believed that universal suffrage would produce confusion and despotism; he could never be a Chartist. No such inhibitions moved John Fielden, a radical who joined at once. Unlike Oastler, Stephens had urged the ballot and universal suffrage; unlike Fielden, he was disillusioned with the reformed parliament since its failure to repeal the Poor Law Amendment Act. The threat of direct action, not further petitioning, was his choice. He had admitted reluctantly:

> they had been taught that they were the natural guardians of their own rights and privileges. He acknowledged that it was a true doctrine in the present, unfortunate and anti-Christian state of society, but in the opposite state of society, the opposite doctrine was the true one.

Yet political reform did not guarantee social redress in 1838, just as it had not in 1832. Although O'Connor and others had shared the factory reform and anti-poor law struggles, opponents of both were to be found among the Chartists, and Stephens' first impulse was not to get involved.[35]

He reckoned without Chartist eagerness to recruit him. Asked to represent Ashton in the Convention, he reflected that in its very diversity, the biggest of all radical movements could be used to further his old causes. Many Chartists shared them, and his presence on their platforms would spoil the 'Whig juggles' of the rest. He insisted that they understood his reservations, and would only co-operate on his own terms. He spelt them out to a Chartist meeting in Ashton market place:

> if they were successful, the scheme would prove abortive, for it was in the great question of capital and labour and its proper arrangements that were concentrated the future welfare of the labouring millions. Holding these opinions, he did not wish to embarrass such men as Mr Fielden and the other good men who have taken such a lead in this measure, and because he had taken another course; he was for

physical force and the promoters of this question were for moral force; they were for petitioning, and in that he could not join them. The day had gone by when people ought to petition; it was already proved that their prayers were not listened to; and the parliament they were about to petition he would not recognize as a parliament. They had by the passing of the Poor Law rendered themselves constitutionally defunct; he could not, therefore, or would not sign their petition; but if the people agreed to petition, he would not do anything to paralyse their efforts . . . If they wanted a man to represent them unshackled and independent, he was ready to serve them; but if they wished for a man to agree to all and anything that was proposed, they must find another man to do it.

On a show of hands the vote given to him in his absence was confirmed. In the excitement of later events, it was easy to forget what had happened that day; but in the light of the confirmation following his candid disclaimer, the Chartists had only themselves to blame for the consequences.[36]

He had still to interpret Chartism in a mutually acceptable way. This he did brilliantly at the great rally at Kersal Moor on 24 September. A crowd estimated by the *Manchester Advertiser* as 200,000 gathered to watch a procession arrive. It was led by two mounted trumpeters and a band, and it represented all parts of the kingdom. Fielden was chairman, and the battery of speakers included the two greatest radical orators, O'Connor and Stephens. Stephens made the most memorable speech of his life. He reconciled his hot championship of social justice with his lukewarm attachment to the Charter in a famous definition:

This question – the question of universal suffrage – is a knife and fork question after all. The question is a bread and cheese question after all. If any man asks me what I mean by universal suffrage, I tell him . . . that every working man in the land has a right to a good coat on his back, a good hat upon his head, a good roof for the shelter of his household, a good dinner upon his table, no more work than will keep him in health whilst at it, and as much wages as will keep him in plenty, and in enjoyment of all the pleasures of life that a reasonable man can desire (Hear hear).

He reminded the crowd there would have been no need for the new agitation if the original principles of the constitution had been observed. In advancing universal suffrage, which they knew 'has ever been dear to my heart', he saw himself as a restorer, not an innovator. It was legal to bear arms, and direct action against the new Poor Law was necessary to support their rights. He seconded the resolution adopting the Charter 'in the manner you have heard . . . so far as I can, and so far as you can go with me'. He had struck a chord in the collective mind of the vast crowd, for in Lancashire class conflict and hunger made necessities rather than abstract rights the dominant issue.[37]

He made another impressive speech at a radical dinner in Liverpool's Queen's Theatre the following night. According to the eye witness Robert Lowery

> . . . he exclaimed with a burst of overpowering fervour, 'I am no Chartist, that for your five points', – snapping his fingers – 'I am no O'Connor's man – but while I live and where I live there shall be the law of God and righteousness'.[38]

In October, he began a round of torchlight meetings. They seemed to originate with O'Connor, and Stephens disliked them; but he thought working men had no alternative to night meetings. Torchlight meetings had a sinister, revolutionary reputation, and they alarmed the authorities. Stephens' militancy rose as he became certain that a revolution was coming. At Carlisle, he thought a divine revolution had begun, because the people were demanding the commands of the Bible rather than the provision of an act of parliament. On 29 October he visited Norwich, where he addressed a large radical meeting at St Andrews Hall. He warned of the coming doom:

> England stands on a mine – a volcano is beneath her – you may dance on it – you may pluck flowers from its surface, but it only sleeps – the match is lighted, the train is laid, and unless the misery and distress of the poor be met by good feeling and speedy recovery, no man can tell what day, what an hour may bring forth.

The young zealot George Julian Harney of the London Democratic Association exulted in 'the glorious Stephens', and had the meeting elect him 'the People's Bishop of Norwich'. The *Norfolk Chronicle* published the speech 'with no slight degree of reluctance and with unspeakable feelings of distaste'.[39]

'The people's bishop' left his 'diocese', apparently never to return. His theme of imminent revolution was causing Chartist dissension. The Birmingham Chartist leaders were for 'moral force'; they disliked torchlight meetings and talk of arming. Stephens answered them at

Rochdale on 7 November, where he spoke with O'Connor (who was careful not to commit himself on arming). Braving hostile rocket throwing, Stephens stressed his past constitutional proceedings; their failure meant that the only way left was to arm in self-defence. Those who disagreed knew nothing of God's law or of human nature. The following week at Wigan, he went further. Thoroughly aroused, he called his Chartist critics 'foolish old women'. 'The firelock must come first and then the vote afterwards. Universal suffrage might be a very fine thing, but it was in the moon yet, and they must have a very long pike with a crook at the end of it before they would be able to pull it down.' They must have arms, and use them; the divine revolution had begun. He was back at the extremism of Newcastle, and ended with its very words: 'For child and wife, I will war to the knife'.[40]

The growing Chartist opposition to arming, from Scotland and London as well as from Birmingham, made Stephens realize how little he had in common with Chartism. Even his ally O'Connor was silent on arming, though he had set a date for the end of peaceful struggle. Stephens' priority was his social causes, O'Connor's was Chartism. Thus, O'Connor was absent from Wigan, and went to Birmingham to restore Chartist unity. He succeeded at the price of joining in a denunciation of physical force, though he defended Stephens. Their paths were diverging, and Stephens knew that his days as a 'Chartist' were numbered.[41]

Suddenly, government resolve over torchlight meetings overshadowed Chartist differences. Rioting occurred at Todmorden, and local authorities called for military support. Stephens' supporters began to intimidate local opponents. At Leigh on 13 November, nine sworn depositions were made by eye-witnesses, accusing Stephens of inciting violence against named poor law Guardians while the crowd discharged firearms. The following night at Hyde, other eye-witnesses swore that he asked the people if they were ready, and was answered by further volleys. In November, the Prime Minister Lord Melbourne decided that Stephens had to be prosecuted, though he delayed action until the Attorney-General convinced him early in December that torchlight meetings were illegal. A proclamation was issued at Ashton on 5 December, confirmed by royal proclamation a week later; but despite the ban, torchlight meetings continued. Sir Frederick Roe, the chief of the Bow Street Runners, sent Henry Goddard, one of his best detectives, to the factory towns of Lancashire. He was ordered to investigate quietly and discreetly, and to have assistance at hand without showing it.[42]

On 8 December an Ashton mill was burnt down. It belonged to James Jowett, one of the Ashton magistrates who had issued the proclamation against torchlight meetings. Inevitably Stephens was blamed, though at the time of the fire he and O'Connor were addressing an illegal torchlight meeting at Bury. Goddard and a Home Office reporter attended, and were not disappointed. Stephens attacked Jowett by name for sentencing a boy to hard labour for an accidental factory fire. ' . . . it was a question with him if that Devil's Magistrate's house would not ere long be too hot for him'. The instigator of the Ashton factory fire was never known, but in the rising alarm, Stephens was believed capable of any evil. The next day in an Ashton sermon, the hairdresser Robert Ripley would swear Stephens promised that the Convention would establish a republic, that Ashton would fraternize with the military garrison, and that 'by putting up this little finger, instead of one fire, Dukinfield, Ashton and Stalybridge will be one wide sheet of flame'. Stephens and his followers denied it vehemently, but his Newcastle and Wigan speeches made it seem plausible; the Whig press was quick to accuse him of the Ashton fire. Fox Maule, under secretary at the Home Office, referred to it in a widely reported speech; arrest was only a matter of time. Goddard attended torchlight meetings and Ashton services. In London Roe was told that the government was waiting for sufficient information for a prosecution, but so far only the Leigh magistrates had been helpful.[43]

Still Chartist dissension continued unabated. Stephens was attacked by 'moral force' Chartists from Scotland, London and Birmingham, as well as by Daniel O'Connell. Forced to choose between Stephens and his critics, O'Connor chose Stephens. He would not moderate his own language, and he had renewed doubts about Birmingham. At last he recommended arming, though the arms were not to be used, and he spoke with Stephens at Bury. It was his misfortune that Stephens had decided to withdraw from Chartist meetings. At Bury he had warned: 'I never will be a party man of any kind, having told you that my principles are the principles of England before party existed.' On 13 December he wrote an open letter cancelling a planned visit to Newcastle, and withdrawing from public meetings because of wilful misrepresentation. He was finished with Chartism, but Chartism had not finished with him.[44]

It made no difference to government plans. The very day the letter was written, Goddard reported that Stephens said at Leigh that weapons should be ready, and that a local poor law Guardian should be tarred and feathered. The next day, 500 special constables were sworn in. While the Lord Lieutenant, Lord Francis Egerton, was not unduly worried, the Ashton authorities were less sanguine. Goddard's alarmist information from spies about future mill burnings was at once linked to Stephens. On 22 December the Ashton magistrates took depositions from Robert Ripley, Richard Boardman and others that two Sundays before the fire, Stephens had attacked Jowett from the pulpit. Two days later, copies were sent to the Home Office. At a Christmas day tea party at Charlestown chapel to which Oastler had been invited, Stephens indicated that he was well aware of the moves being made against him. On the 27th, the two Ashton magistrates Sanderson and Kenworthy heard all the reports on Stephens, and signed a warrant for his arrest. They thought that military power would be necessary to carry it out.[45]

Less than ten minutes after the court adjourned, Goddard and his assistant Shackell had a stroke of good fortune. They saw Stephens walking towards them and alone. Following him, Goddard arrested him at the Bush Inn in Stamford Street. On their way by post-chaise to Lord Francis Egerton at Worsley, they stopped at Manchester for refreshment, and a crowd quickly gathered. A stop press notice appeared in the Manchester evening papers – 'the blood-hounds have laid hold on Stephens'. It included the ominous words, 'Gentlemen, the time has come'. At Worsley, a nervous Egerton conveniently remembered that he had not taken the oath to the new Queen, and could not act; the two Ashton magistrates and their clerk had to be found and brought to him. The resourceful Goddard assembled the reluctant party, and returned with them to Worsley, only to find Egerton's houses guarded by two troops of dragoons. Stephens was remanded by the magistrates, and taken by dragoon escort to the New Bailey prison in Manchester, where he was handed over to the Governor at 1.15 am. Goddard discharged a highly dangerous mission without shedding a drop of blood.[46]

Two examinations followed, while Oastler busied himself with legal assistance for his friend. At the second on 3 January, he was released on bail of £2,200 – half from him, and a quarter each from his two sureties, Abel Williamson and J. R. Richardson. He was committed for trial at Liverpool assizes on eighteen charges relating to meetings at Ashton, Pennington (Leigh) and Hyde. The evident uncertainty about the charge, the heavy bail and legal delays were all to be seized upon by Stephens' friends in the months ahead.[47]

Local reaction was mixed. Captain Clarke, a Hyde magistrate, who had denounced Stephens as 'a firebrand – a demon', reported to the Home Office that his arrest had led to 'a great feeling of safety'. The informers did not feel safe. The Stephenites and their radical allies met at the Charlestown chapel on the night of the arrest, and resolved to boycott the fourteen who had given evidence against their minister. Some of the fourteen complained to the magistrates that their lives and property were in danger, and three of them – Ripley, Boardman and Marples – were legally compensated. At King Street chapel in Stalybridge, the trade unionist John Deegan advised the people not to give way to their feelings. The following night, he addressed two further meetings called to celebrate Stephens' release. A committee was apointed to collect money for his defence. On Sunday, an estimated 10,000 people, 'preserving the most reverential silence', heard Stephens preach in Ashton market place on the authority of the Word of God in all matters of faith and practice. He 'solemnly denounced God's curse on the people of Ashton if they ever suffered that law (the Poor Law Amendment Act) to be established among them; and God's blessing would rest upon them if they refused to allow it within their borders'.[48]

National newspapers published detailed accounts of the arrest, and gave biographical sketches. There was widespread press criticism of the government's handling of the case. The diarist Charles Greville thought that a conviction could not be secured, and that 'the magistrates completely lost their heads'. There was a rush of Chartist sympathy for the first 'martyr'. O'Connor suspected the government of provocation, and proclaimed in the *Northern Star* that 'THE TIME FOR FIGHTING HAS NOT YET COME'. He attended the court hearings, advised threatening crowds against violence, and spoke at indignant protest meetings.[49]

Unexpectedly, the trial was delayed. Stephens expected to be indicted for conspiracy against the laws, and he wanted nothing better than to dispute the legality of the Poor Law Amendment Act in court. Government sensed the danger, and decided that the case was to proceed on the January charges, by way of two grand juries to the court of Queen's Bench in London. Without prior knowledge of the indictments, Stephens appeared at the Liverpool grand jury on 28 March. Two bills were found against him, to which a third from Chester was later added. He went to London in late April to obtain copies, and plead not guilty. He hoped that all three charges would be heard at Liverpool, but the Crown was in difficulty with the cases from Ashton and Leigh, and had received fresh evidence from Hyde. Thus the Attorney-General prosecuted only on charges of sedition, riot and unlawful assembly at Hyde, before a special jury at Chester.[50]

These developments unsettled Stephens. This was the second trial in which he expected to defend principles, and was forced to answer unanswerable facts. Since the facts concerned Chartist meetings from which he had since withdrawn, they linked his name to Chartist aims which he had never shared. His friends published a pamphlet by his authority in May, advising him to refuse a defence. He needed sound legal advice, and he had thought of approaching Sir Charles Wetherell (who had appeared for Warren in his case against the Wesleyan Conference in 1835) to represent him at his trial. In the end he yielded to family pressure, and made the disastrous mistake of defending himself against the Attorney-General.[51]

Meanwhile, trouble had arisen over his defence fund. At first, the committee issued an appeal, local committees were formed and meetings were held to raise funds. Soon, differences emerged between those who put Stephens before Chartism, and those who put Chartism before Stephens. The former knew him, and shared his real convictions; they gave gladly and offered their services, Oastler being particularly active. They were outnumbered by the Chartists, whose leaders knew Stephens was not one of them, but supported him as an act of policy. Grassroots Chartists gave because they did believe that Stephens was one of them, but their sympathy waned during 1839 as this grew increasingly doubtful. There were also regional and local cross-currents, for the main Manchester committee refused to support the London pro-Stephens agitation, and in April the Ashton Chartists tried to dissolve the Manchester committee and appoint another. Manchester ignored it, but the seeds of confusion had been sown.[52]

Stephens used his remaining time to preach and publish a series of sermons expounding his unique biblical radicalism. In nearly all of them, he discreetly distanced himself from Chartism, trying to influence Christian opinion without offending Chartist unbelief. Most of them were preached at Ashton and Stalybridge, but three were delivered in London. They were published under the title of *The Political Pulpit*, and were widely circulated by Chartist itinerant speakers. In March, Robert Lowery and Abram Duncan used them with success in the mining and Methodist county of Cornwall. At Penzance, 'had we twice as many of Stephens' sermons they would have sold, so powerful was the feeling in our favour'. At Fraddam, 'they are working wonders'. Duncan sold nearly three thousand, and later told the Convention:

> I am convinced that those sermons have done more good than ten thousand speeches (Cheers). It was the first document which taught the people their religious right to freedom, and well assured am I, that if Stephens was five months in Cornwall, he would rout all the Methodist parsons from the country.

Elsewhere they were read from Ireland to Nottingham Forest and Leicester.[53]

Stephens was forbidden to take his seat at the National Convention which opened on 4 February. He could preach but not agitate, and was allowed to publish letters which enabled him to take part in a new controversy. The notorious Marcus pamphlets appeared late in 1838. They argued that over-population was the cause of current distress, and suggested the drastic remedy of infanticide. Every third infant of poor families was to be killed painlessly at birth. The identity and motives of Marcus remain mysteries. Was he a Malthusian extremist to be taken seriously, or an anti-Malthusian satirist? The literal-minded Stephens was the first to condemn Marcus. According to hostile press reports, he accused one of the Poor Law Commissioners of being the author. They denied it, but Stephens denied that he had made the accusation. In a letter to *The Times*, he called it 'this fresh instance of the inveterate malignity of my enemies'. The author could be any one of a number of new poor law officials and supporters. Stephens taunted the three Poor Law Commissioners with lacking the courage to publish Marcus. An inflamed dispute followed, confirming existing prejudices. Stephens was branded as insane for an accusation he did not make; the Commissioners were suspected of authorship, despite their truthful denials. One result was that Stephens' condemnation brought fame to the Marcus pamphlets; another was that they became a basic theme of his anti-poor law speeches for years to come.[54]

In April, he took a holiday at Dudley, 'in seach of that health that overwork has somewhat broken down'. By the end of the month, he was in London. Although he had resigned his seat in the Convention earlier in the year, he appeared before it, and was received with cheers. He spoke in various London taverns for his defence fund. On 12 May, he delivered three open-air sermons at Islington's Shepherd and Shepherdess Fields in the morning, Primrose Hill in the afternoon, and Kennington Common in the evening. At Primrose Hill, he preached bare-headed in the rain to hundreds of people for an hour and a half. Thousands waited an hour for his arrival on Kennington Common. Despite a sharp easterly wind and frequent showers, they remained until nightfall, 'such was the anxiety to hear this extraordinary man'. The magic that worked in the north was not confined there.[55]

He returned to the heady world of millowners and illegal arming. Late in May, he denounced in sweeping terms the new proclamation against drilling and arms. All authority must go, unless it secured a comfortable maintenance to the poor. He cared nothing about the Charter, a republic or a monarchy unless they did the same. Early in June, he urged Ashton to fraternize with the newly arrived soldiers, who were rumoured to be there to enforce the new poor law. He gloried publicly in the charge of seducing the soldiers; but despite his bravado, there was little prospect of their disaffection. It was not the poor law, but rising tension and illegal arming that brought them to Ashton.[56]

Disaffection was rife among Chartists. On 13 May, the Convention moved to Birmingham, and adjourned until July. Its bluff on physical force had been called, and there was marked reluctance to proceed to violence. Those who were willing were arming, knowing that a rising would spread quickly; they included the Ashton Chartists. Some wanted a national holiday, or general strike; others feared the resulting government repression and popular anger. Stephens caught the drift of such debates when he visited the Convention in May. He was against a planned rising, and feared the consequences of its failure; he still hoped that intimidation would succeed. He was to speak of 'the awful delusions' of the Convention. Chartists were being arrested, and in June O'Connor founded a national defence fund on their behalf. The same month, a quarrel broke out between Stephens and his hardline Chartist successor in the Convention.[57]

Peter Murray M'Douall was his nominee for the Ashton succession. A surgeon and a physical force Chartist who favoured the national holiday, M'Douall had been an ardent supporter of Stephens – 'he knew Mr Stephens so well that he did not think that under any circumstances he could be offended with him'. On 21 June he accused Stephens at an Ashton meeting of an unnamed offence that prevented them from ever meeting again. In the absence of Stephens, a committee of his friends was appointed to examine the charge. On 24 June, M'Douall resigned his Ashton seat in the Convention, as he had been accused of 'factious motives', and a desire to benefit from the Stephens defence fund. Stephens wrote to his trustees renouncing all claim on his fund for 'private reasons'. Two further meetings were called, but Stephens was absent. At the second, held on the 26th behind Charlestown chapel in the presence of a great crowd, M'Douall had to speak. He charged Stephens with an indecent assault on the unmarried sister-in-law of the Chartist leader Bronterre O'Brien; Stephens' written admission had been witnessed by a member of the Convention. The stunned crowd broke into two conflicting parties, and the exciting evening was crowned by the sudden arrest of M'Douall. Released on bail two days later, M'Douall held another meeting in Ashton market place, and continued to represent Ashton in the Convention. Stephens returned to his pulpit on 7 July. Neither church, nor wife, nor O'Brien are recorded as having believed the accusation; ministry, marriage and friendship all survived. His trustees assured him that the defence fund would be used only for its original purpose, and he withdrew his renunciation. The scandal vanished abruptly from the press on the collapse of Chartism in July.

The full truth is unlikely to be known, but the incident damaged Stephens' reputation. True or false, the charge implied an offence against the marriage bond; as minister and agitator, his credibility was at stake. The sanctity of marriage was basic to his opposition to the new poor law, for in the 'bastilles' (as the new workhouses were called) the sexes were separated. His church heard his explanation on 7 July and was content, since he was restored to his ministry; but apparently his words were not published. Those who did not hear them, or who were not inclined to believe them, were far from satisfied. For the first time, local confidence in the 'Champion' was shaken.[58]

Chartism collapsed shortly after the Convention reconvened. The Birmingham Bull Ring riot was suppressed, and four members of the Convention arrested, including M'Douall. The Commons rejected the Chartist petition, as Stephens had prophesied. The Convention adopted a 'sacred month' (yet another name for a general strike), to begin on 12 August; but it was divided and hesitant, and arrests of Chartists continued, the Ashton leader Timothy Higgins among them. O'Connor, still convinced that 'the time for fighting has not yet come', persuaded the Convention to reduce the sacred month to a three-day strike. The Convention steadily lost prestige, and the August strike was ineffective. Even in south Lancashire, there were doubts about readiness for a physical force solution. It all confirmed Stephens' growing contempt for Chartism, and he criticized it sharply. In a farewell sermon, he reminded his congregation that he was neither radical nor Chartist:

Why, when your brethren at Ashton chose me to be their representative in the Convention . . . did not I tell you then again and again, that I did not care two straws about the five points; that if I went to London I would not present a petition that I had not signed . . . I told you that I was only a one-point man, and that point was a good prayer and a long spear . . . Is it any news to you to be told that Stephens does not recommend a national holiday? Is there any man alive . . . that ever heard me recommend a national holiday . . . ?

In a rare admission, he added: 'I have a great deal of nonsense to answer for, but I have not that rubbish on my hands. That is Attwood's humbug, not mine.' (Attwood was the radical banker who led the Birmingham Political Union.) The service ended with a sung doxology and the blessing; after his disgruntled flock had departed, Stephens, again complaining of poor health, prepared to leave for Chester for the trial that was now imminent.[59]

O'Connor's apologists have presented Stephens as an irresponsible, charismatic demagogue who undermined O'Connor's strategy of intimidation, by frightening middle-class opinion through the unqualified language of civil war. Thus Stephens is made partly responsible for O'Connor's failure. Yet Stephens was not the only man associated with Chartism who opposed O'Connorite intimidation; O'Connor's own divisive character and that of Chartism itself cannot be overlooked in assessing his failure. Whether either man had anything that can be called a strategy in these wild, unpredictable months is doubtful. They reacted to events rather than moulded them. Their language was different in degree rather than in kind; middle-class opinion alienated by Stephens was unlikely to be reassured by O'Connor. Stephens' violent language was not without qualification, for he always drew a distinction between a planned, man-made revolution which he opposed, and a spontaneous popular uprising, which was acceptable because it was divine.

In a movement riddled with ambiguity, they operated from two distinct premises. O'Connor was a radical politician intent on building a united national working-class movement; Stephens was an independent minister exercising a prophetic Christian ministry from the platforms of that movement. At no time was Stephens a Chartist, and O'Connor knew it. However much policy dictated that the difference should not be stressed, Stephens between September 1838 and August 1839 made it clear when necessary. He would never accept the claims of party, and he had been elected to the Convention on his own terms; he acted accordingly. He was never at ease with a movement with purely secular aims, being a man of the Bible rather than of the Charter. His association with Chartism was based on mutual convenience. They accepted him despite his misgivings, in order to gain his unique oratorical gifts; he spoke at their meetings to advance social reforms that many of them wanted. Neither could blame the other for the unforeseen and unwelcome consequences of the bargain. For O'Connor, it created dilemmas for Chartist unity, and for Stephens it involved 'a great deal of nonsense to answer for'. Ironically, in the eyes of contemporaries and posterity, his trial was about to confirm the misleading Chartist image he thought he had discarded.[60]

4

The Question of Physical Force

In 1907, the local artist Samuel Lees drew a bespectacled, mild looking lady sitting by a kitchen range, with a black cat at her feet and simple home comforts at her side. On her lap, she sharpens a battleaxe on a stone. The drawing purports to be a follower of Joseph Rayner Stephens preparing for an attack on the cotton masters. It is a reminder that Stephens' talk of physical force had its ludicrous side; but it also bears witness to the lasting impression that Stephens made. The advocacy of violence will always be associated with his name.[1]

From the beginning, it awakened powerful misgivings. He was not the only man in public life during the eighteen-thirties to use violent language, but no one else carried it so far, or could urge it with such talent. Moreover, he was a minister of the gospel, which as the friendly critic Abram Duncan reminded him in 1838, should have made him a man of peace. It was natural for the government to single him out as the first 'Chartist' to be arrested. In the century between Waterloo and the first world war, what are now called liberation struggles took place elsewhere, not in 'this land of liberty'. He was widely regarded as either a dangerous fanatic, or an irresponsible fool; either way his character was flawed, and he was not to be trusted. If he had 'a great deal of nonsense to answer for', it was this above all else that needed an answer.[2]

Stephens did not behave violently. He boasted of his brace of loaded pistols and polished silver dagger, but there is no record that he ever used them, despite his claim that his own life had often been threatened. He was never accused before a court of grievous bodily harm. By 1839, the limit of his aggression was an unproved accusation of indecent assault, and leading intimidating Huddersfield anti-poor law crowds. Inciting others to violence against named opponents was another matter, but here caution is necessary. The allegations of November and December 1838 rely on the evidence of informers and police spies. The resolve of the Ashton magistrates, and later of the government, to secure any evidence against Stephens must not be under-estimated, and in the widespread alarm following the Ashton fire, the worst could be believed. It is not clear if the named individuals were victimized as a result of Stephens' alleged incitements, and he was never so charged. Naturally, Stephens himself denied it. He claimed in his open letter:

> I have been wilfully misrepresented, and have been most wickedly made to appear as a promoter of strife – an instigator of incendiarism and assassination; although it is notorious and undeniable that from first to last there has never been a single breach of the peace committed or contemplated by any one individual, or any one of the thousand meetings I have attended; many of these meetings held at night, most of them attended by thousands and tens of thousands . . .

If he was right, it was equally notorious and undeniable that during nearly four years of agitation, there had been a gathering crescendo of violent themes in his speeches. Why did this happen, and how did it develop?[3]

Romantic art had created a new, self-conscious image of the noble revolutionary. It was depicted in Delacroix's great painting of 1831, *Liberty Guiding the People*. The people, with arms in their hands, climb over the fallen to victory in a new and higher French revolution, led on by Liberty wearing a Phrygian cap and waving a tricolour flag. Stephens was receptive to such sentiments. In his school days he had enjoyed amateur theatricals, and had befriended Harrison Ainsworth and Samuel Warren, both of whom later became Romantic novelists. He may have caught the Romantic spirit in 1829, during his ardent discussions on liberty with Montalembert. 'We fancied as we dreamed and talked together, that we saw some mighty change about to take place, but we could not tell what that change would be . . . '[4]

He returned home to discover the mighty change of the Reform Act. Although revolution was averted, the threat of it by the Whigs and their allies, including the working classes, had brought powerful pressure on the government. Factory reformers in late years never allowed the respectable Edward Baines of Leeds to forget a certain day in 1832; amid Whig and tricolour banners borne by poles surmounted by pikes, he had presided over a spate of revolutionary oratory, and led a crowd of 30,000 people in execrating Wellington, the bishops and the Queen for their last ditch opposition to the bill. Although the working classes were left without the vote, the factory reformers learned the lesson that in an age of political reform, entrenched opposition could be overcome through revolutionary intimidation.[5]

The language of Romantic revolutionism could be divorced from actual revolution, and used for effect in any current dispute. The hyperbole was meant to inspire resistance; by conveying the popular image of a revolutionary, it might alarm opponents into making concessions. It was not meant to be taken literally. Thus on 12 May 1834, John Stephens issued a rousing call to Weslyan reformers through his newspaper:

> Wesleyans awake! One and all, up and to arms! The fiercest and most crafty of your foes, so long and so warily mining his way, has at length sprung forth into the very heart of the camp. 'Down with the democrats' is the war-cry of the despot and his dupes. It is a war to the knife. Power has challenged principle – might is matched with right; truth, holiness and freedom are all trampled down by the iron heel of the ecclesiastical autocrat. These are fearful odds, but we are not appalled. Nay, we rejoice and exult exceedingly . . .

Here is the very phrase later to be made notorious by the editor's brother at Newcastle – war to the knife. However distasteful Bunting found it, he did not expect an imminent murderous assault by the editor; the Stephens brothers simply used words as weapons.[6]

By 1836, the depth of the opposition to factory reform was self-evident. To a newcomer like Stephens, confident in his powers of persuasion, and unwilling to accept that Christian mill-owners – with whom he had shared missionary platforms – could oppose humanitarian reforms, it was particularly shocking. Nevertheless, in March 1836 he proclaimed himself 'the apostle of a constitutional, legal and scriptural resistance'. Oastler was older and had longer experience of the struggle. Poulett Thomson's amendment and the connivance of mill-owning justices at breaches of the law convinced him that cotton masters could exert undue pressure on a Whig government to weaken its own legislation, and that inconvenient laws would not be enforced. There is evidence that in July, the factory reform leaders agreed that their appeal must be not to the reason, but to the fears of the masters. Fielden's informant wrote to him that to Oastler, 'this was the vantage ground which, if they used it properly, would enable them to carry the day', and Stephens had agreed. This policy explains both Stephens' 'treadmill and hanging' speech in August, and Oastler's 'sabotage' threat the following month.

Once introduced, the appeal to fear had to be maintained and increased if it was to achieve its end, and its consequences were unforeseeable.[7]

Nevertheless, the factory movement followed a constitutional path throughout. The anti-poor law campaign was far more bitter. Here the perceived aim was not to introduce good legislation, but to resist bad; now it was the workers who knew fear, not their masters. Oastler and Stephens believed that the Act of 1834 destroyed an existing Christian-inspired system of poor relief, and replaced it with a demonic one. It was their Christian duty to resist evil laws, and with a good conscience they united with many others to prevent its local introduction. Their language rose to new heights of invective. To Stephens the Act was 'the deadliest exhalation from the pit of hell', 'the law of Devils', bringing God's doom on the country. Since Christianity was part of English law, the Act was unconstitutional, and was not to be obeyed. By destroying the right of the poor to maintenance, it undermined the whole fabric of society, and made anarchy and conflict certain. These were not his aims, but the inevitable consequence of sustained injustice through bad law. God had been affronted, and punishment could only be avoided through speedy repentance. It is in this semi-apocalyptic context, not merely in that of the cotton spinners' trial, that the outrageous words of Newcastle and Glasgow must be seen.[8]

At Newcastle, he did not hide his motive. Since he was moving a resolution that the new poor law should be resisted in every legal way, he needed to justify his fiery rhetoric:

> He was not a blood-thirsty man; he never struck a man, or quarrelled with a man – indeed, he believed himself to be as good natured as most men when not put out of the way – (a laugh) – but he wanted to tell them what they had a right to do when the time came, and it was their duty to do it if this were the best time in which to begin. He talked thus because he hoped – almost against hope – by talking in this way and seeing them thus determined, that those men would be compelled by fear to repeal what it was just and righteous to repeal, and what they would otherwise not repeal.

So he went off to Scotland, to '*preach* (my italics) Glasgow to the ground and Edinburgh into flames unless justice was done to the cotton spinners in Glasgow'. Both cities survived.[9]

At least he realized that total opposition to a demonic law demanded nothing less than self-sacrifice. He told the reporters at Newcastle to be sure to record his plain speaking, so that Lord John Russell would act against him. Naturally, he hoped by so doing to hasten ultimate victory, but he was willing to accept the incidental hardship. From Newcastle onwards, he began to court arrest, in order to challenge the legality of the Poor Law Amendment Act before the world, in one blaze of newsprint.[10]

His language did not deflect him from the constitutional struggle, and he was active in petitioning. The Commons defeat of February 1838 disillusioned him. He and Oastler despaired of parliament. Nor did the solution of universal suffrage satisfy them, since apart from anything else, it involved further petitioning of the same parliament. The alternative was to arm the people, so that parliament would be coerced into the desired action. Since the possession of arms was legal, Oastler and Stephens saw arming as a new phase of an open constitutional struggle; arming in secret was happening already. At Bradford and Saddleworth, Stephens openly urged workers to get arms, but not to use them; but other reformers like Fielden saw the danger in arming, and opposed it.[11]

The danger became clear in Stephens' Chartist period. There was no Chartist unanimity on arming (as on so much else). Chartists cannot be divided into two simple parties of physical and moral force, since the terms were fluid in meaning, and many supported whichever method seemed likely to succeed at any given moment. The Chartists of the Birmingham Political Union were for moral force, but Stephens brushed aside their objections. Northern Chartists had shared the factory and anti-poor law struggles. They were more sympathetic to physical force, which meant anything from intimidation to a planned rising. As has been seen, even O'Connor did not wholly agree with Stephens; their minds moved on different planes. During October, Stephens' expectation of a rising increased; at last he had to face the dilemma that in a rising, arms were bound to be used. Arming was more than a matter of exerting pressure on government through telling words; guidance had to be given to the prospective users.[12]

The key to understanding what followed is the nature of the expected rising. Whatever Chartists envisaged, Stephens thought that the working classes would not rise for mere political reform. There would be a spontaneous, general movement of the people for social redress, in conformity with the revealed will of God in scripture. As he proclaimed excitedly at Carlisle:

> The revolution has begun, and not all the power of the middle class, or Parliament . . . can prevent the progress of this divine revolution

(Loud cheers). He called it divine because the people are not going for 'the bill, the whole bill, and nothing but the bill', but for 'the book, the whole book, and nothing but the book' (Cheers).

This was the divine revolution in which it was a duty to use weapons. In his ferocious speech at Wigan, he went beyond his usual intimidating language. He urged every man

> To have arms in his house, and if need be to have them in his hands; and not only to have them, but to be prepared for their use – (loud and continued cheering) – and not only prepare to use them, but actually to use them for the very purpose for which they were made, for the reason why God gave us cold lead and sharp steel was to put an ounce of the one, and six inches of the other into the bodies and brains of any men . . . having tried all the means he had beforehand, then was the time for the people to prepare for war . . . It was God's insurrection – it was God's rebellion – it was a divine revolution, a revolution in favour of truth and righteousness through the spirit of God and by means of the right arms of men (Loud cheers).

Yet the spontaneous rising did not come; instead, Henry Goddard came, with a warrant for his arrest.[13]

All this was to be contrasted to the secret, contrived revolt of a minority for lesser, political ends. Only gradually was Stephens aware of the existence of this, but his whole approach was against it. At the second Peep Green meeting in October, he said that the people would meet unarmed, unless threatened. At Rochdale in November, he emphasized once more the strictly legal character of his agitation to date. He constantly emphasized the social demands rather than the political; at Wigan, 'he would not give two straws' for universal suffrage, but would 'go and war upon the side of truth against untruth . . . ' He hastened to add that 'when he said before he did not care two straws about universal suffrage, he meant without other things came with it'. As he said truly in his Ashton farewell sermon: 'I have *always* told you that Universal Suffrage, annual Parliaments, Vote by Ballot, and all the rest of the rigmarole, was not worth fighting for.' Chartists could not easily accept that Stephens's searing words did not apply to a planned rising for the Charter; it was precisely this that the extreme physical-force Chartists envisaged. Isolated between the devil of secret conspiracy and the deep blue sea of open misrepresentation, Stephens withdrew from Chartist gatherings to go his own way.[14]

After his visit to the Convention in May 1839, he was impressed by the growing danger of a planned rising. He linked it to the sacred month or national holiday adopted by the Convention in July with the support of O'Connor. In Chester Castle the following year, he told a Home Office inspector: 'I necessarily was acquainted with much that was going forward at the time of the National Holiday, and was the means of it not being generally adopted.' Even if he exaggerated his influence, he had no scruples in discouraging it. He knew that the Ashton Chartists were involved. In May he counselled his Ashton congregation to forbear, because their oppressors were stronger than they were. He urged them 'for a while to stand until God by his providence shall make you fully prepared to go forward'. In a June sermon he said: 'Why, if the hour of God's vengeance and your redemption were fully in . . . twelve legions of troops from heaven would have come to honour it'. When Chartism collapsed, he felt more free to denounce the planned rising. In his farewell sermon on 3 August, he denied he was a Chartist, and attacked the national holiday:

> A National Holiday means universal anarchy and confusion, and the insurrection of one portion of the nation, the weakest, against other portion of the nation that are as one body, guided and directed by one head . . . A National Holiday means a national fight. Are you going to fight?

Liberty did not mean forcing reluctant workers to strike:

> My notion of liberty is that every man should be allowed to think for himself and to act for himself, so long as his conduct is obviously such as not to injure his fellow creatures (Hear hear). I don't like liberty all on one side. Then you would have the public sympathy against you.

A national holiday would mean that the harvest would rot. He advised his disgruntled flock:

> My friends, never put your trust in, and never follow after, men who pretend to be able to manufacture a revolution. A revolution, a rolling away of the whole from evil to good, from wrong to right, from injustice and oppression to righteousness and equal rule, never yet was manufactured. God, who teaches you what your rights are . . . will, in his own good time, if that time should come – God will teach your hands to war, and your fingers to fight.[15]

It was natural for Chartists to feel that 'Stephens has changed'. Yet their leaders were fully aware of the truth. O'Connor had told a defence fund meeting in January 1839: 'Mr Stephens was neither a Whig, a Radical nor a Tory, and that was one of the reasons why they all admired him'. He might have added that he was no Chartist either. Despite Stephens' disclaimers, it was hard for ordinary Chartists to accept that the man who so inspired them was not one of them; many of them had contributed to his defence fund, and they felt bewildered and even betrayed by the one who used the boldest physical force language, and yet who opposed the national holiday. In the thoroughly secular Chartist movement, few had understood that he distinguished two revolutions, one God-inspired, and the other man-contrived.[16]

For his part, Stephens had not been deliberately dishonest, but he does not emerge with credit from the twists and turns of his physical-force language. The appeal to fear is unpredictable in its consequences. The effectiveness of Chartist agitation was in its inherent ambiguity, which kept supporters and opponents alert and guessing. At Wigan he abandoned this for direct encouragement of violence in the cause of God. He was permanently discredited in the eyes of moderate opinion. He made a grievous error of judgment in identifying God's vengeance with the growing revolutionary tension of late 1838. The actual rising when it came was the small, planned and doomed affair at Newport, not the spontaneous, mass revolt of his imagination. Because that never came, his violent advice was never put to the test, and we shall never know if he would have manned a barricade. From his prison cell, he lamented Newport: 'If to have foretold events be to have occasioned them, then I plead guilty to the "insurrection" in Wales.' If previously he had distinguished purpose and consequence so clearly, he would not have alienated so much potential support.[17]

That this happened can be seen from the reaction of his former church. Despite what is too often assumed from the quietist pronouncements of the Wesleyan Conference, Wesleyan Methodists were not indifferent to the plight of the poor. In 1837, the *Wesleyan Methodist Magazine* attacked the Poor Law Amendment Act for treating poverty as a crime, for separating families and restraining the poor from worship; but it was only the Primitive Methodists who lent their chapels and supported the anti- poor law struggle. An editorial in the official Wesleyan newspaper, *The Watchman*, explained why:

The New Poor Law never can, and never ought to be the law of this Christian land so long as it is unpurged of those obnoxious clauses which we have from the first protested . . . The prospect of such a consummation (of a constitutional reform of the law) is now, we fear, indefinitely postponed through the rash and insane opposition of Messrs Oastler and Stephens and others, whose unconstitutional violence has branded the cause with a certain infamy.

Yet in the less violent atmosphere of 1844, the *Magazine* was sympathetic to Ashley's attempt to restrict child labour.[18]

At the time, Stephens did not realize that his words would do permanent damage to his reputation. Similar language had been used in 1832 without that effect, because those who used it had triumphed; but factory reform was to be a continued struggle with varying degrees of success, the Act of 1834 ruled poor law practice for about a century, and Chartist aims only succeeded after Chartism died. Stephens' reputation for violent language pursued him all his days, undermining trust in his judgment in the minds of many who were not his admirers. Among Christians in the settled years of the late nineteenth century, the fact that a minister could use such words was inexplicable and inexcusable.

Yet at the deepest level, it was not politics but the Bible that conditioned the thinking of Stephens. His was the dilemma once faced by the prophets of Israel: what happens when God's people persist in rejecting his judgments? The biblical answer was that stubborn refusal to repent brought violent divine retribution, either in the form of foreign oppression or internal upheaval. God's prophet must declare this, even if like Jeremiah he suffers for it. Christ too 'must have been a most outrageously violent man', for he came not to send peace, but a sword. By 1839, Stephens had come to see his struggle for social justice as part of the eternal battle between God and Mammon. As the God-sanctioned order crumbled before the man-contrived system of enlightened selfishness, the prospect of violence ceased to be a political calculation; in a world created by a just God, it was an inescapable reality. It should not be hidden, but openly proclaimed. The soaring apocalyptic strain in Stephens echoed the great clash between good and evil in the prophets and the Revelation of St John. The choice was still between God's order or universal chaos. He was a voice crying in the wilderness, pointing to the doom drawing ever nearer, preaching the urgent need to repent, to prepare for the wrath to come. Nor was this merely a mood of pretentious self-dramatization that descended on him in his pulpit. In his sober moments, he believed that the Bible required him to preach as he did. Even his closest friend Oastler once gently rebuked him for his language. Stephens smiled at him and replied:

What can I do? How am I to get rid of the Bible? I did not write it. It is put into my hands as the Word of God. I believe it to be so. What can I do? It is a very violent book; when it is found to be a lie, I'll hold my tongue, but not until then.[19]

5

The Man and his Message

At the height of his fame, Stephens was described by *The Times* as 'a little, sharp-featured, dark-complexioned man'. *The Observer* thought him 'a very fine looking man . . . of sedate deportment and benevolent countenance'. The usual bespectacled portrait conveys a studious image. Another, painted by James Garside in 1839, shows him in oratorical pose, and gives him a distinctly hypnotic look. On later prints, the look vanishes, resulting in a more flattering countenance. A Wesleyan Methodist writing years later remembered that 'the Stephens family were remarkably fine-featured'. He was happily married to a wife who thought even less of the hardships of their chosen path than he did. Four children are known to have been born to them, of whom only one, Henrietta, was to survive childhood. They lived in a house on Dukinfield Green.[1]

All acknowledged his private virtues. 'His manners in private are exceedingly pleasing and unassuming', noted one newspaper informant. 'His disposition is playful, particularly when children are present, of which he is very fond', said another. A third called him 'mild and good-humoured'. Even a prison inspector in 1840 commented on his gentlemanly manners. In later life, he himself claimed that he was 'not a public man by nature or by choice', preferring to be at home, with his children, books, and cattle, 'discharging the duties of my profession'. He could move with equal ease among Swedish and expatriate aristocrats, and factory operatives and handloom weavers of Ashton. In his earlier years he had studied British dialects, particularly those of Scotland and north-east England, as well as Anglo-Saxon; all this helped him to master Swedish. His biographer Holyoake compared him to Kossuth in his mastery of languages. Well-informed, studious, and much travelled, he continued to translate continental pietist poetry. He inspired one of his brothers (George) to a lasting love of Scandinavian literature, which resulted in a scholarly career culminating in the chair of English studies at Copenhagen university. Three other brothers,

Samuel, John and Edward, emigrated to Australia; Joseph Rayner had shares in the South Australia company. His ailing father continued to correspond, despite all that had happened.[2]

His pietist example in Sweden had encouraged others to give up swearing, cards, and the theatre. For many years, he was virtually a teetotaller, for until the ten hours' bill was won, he had vowed to abstain to save money for the poor. At the same time, he was not afraid to frequent public houses to further his causes. He was accused by hostile newspapers of drinking alcohol and taking laudanum; his Stalybridge flock denied it, and said he habitually drank lemonade. In 1836 he persuaded scores of men to give up drinking and join the teetotallers. His pastoral concern went deeper than this. Late in 1838, when Stalybridge employers discharged known Stephenites, their minister surrendered his stipend of £50 a year to help them. The hardbitten Feargus O'Connor was impressed:

> He gave up his miserable, voluntary pittance – every farthing of it – for the support of the martyrs. I was sometimes in the habit of dining with him; but during this famine I called upon him, and found that he had no dinner for himself. He never once complained.

Oastler thought no one was kinder than his friend; he was a 'Christian of the first class':

> I have known him when he had just so much in the house as would supply his own wants for the noonday meal, part with it all to a poor object who craved his charity, and go without his dinner to feed them.[3]

Such benevolence made him a hero in the neighbourhood. He was first 'the Champion of the factory child', and then simply 'The Champion'. Songs were composed to 'Our Champion Stephens'. An uneducated Stalybridge factory girl had seventeen of her verses published in the *Northern Star*. One of them was:

> We long have been friendless, distress'd and forlorn,
> But Stephens he has loudly blown the ram's horn,
> These walls of oppression, they shall surely fall,
> Though our tyrants are great, God is greater than all.

Richard Oastler heard him preach with 'hundreds and thousands thronging to get a glimpse of him, to hear his voice, and striving to touch the hem of his garment. I have seen them accompany him both to and

Drawing of Stephens, aged 24

Stephens dinner plate

Portrait of Stephens in 1839 by James Garside

The People's School, Brierley Street, Stalybridge

Stalybridge relief office during the cotton famine

The new Ashton workhouse

'Old Greybeard'.
Stephens in later life

Communion vessels and other Stephens' silverware

from his place of worship, and press so strongly upon him that he has been ready to faint, and I have called them to keep back, but they heeded me not.' The far from sympathetic Henry Goddard found that 'Stephens was so idolized and worship'd by all the operatives, that there is not a family in all Ashton and other places but had not got his Portrait manufactured on all their tea cups, basins, plates and saucers.' (Many were smashed after the M'Douall accusation in July 1839, but a few fortunately survive to this day.)[4]

The beauty, order and harmony of the Christmas day tea party at Charlestown chapel in 1838 moved Oastler to tears. Stephens explained to the thousand of his flock who were present:

> He knew you loved me – he knew I was most esteemed where I have lived longest and was best known; but he was not aware how much you loved me . . . Oastler has said truly that no town in the kingdom could show such a gathering as this. A few years ago and Ashton could not have shown it either.

He thought the change was due to putting aside faction:

> You have come together as men, whom the Father of all has made of one blood – as sinners, whom the Saviour of all came to heal and help alike – as brethren, to bless that one God and Saviour to breathe peace towards all the earth, and show goodwill towards all mankind. I have done my utmost to teach you this by precept and by example also. Oastler has beheld tonight some of the fruits . . . You are the witnesses, living witnesses, of the tone and tenor of my ministrations amongst you.[5]

Beyond the ranks of the faithful, Stephens' influence was through his championing of the cause of working men, women and children. There was no doubt about his commitment to lighten the burden of men and children; and whatever may be thought now about his opposition to female labour, the protective attitude that inspired it was appreciated by radical women at the time. Brighton women presented him with an address in January 1839:

> Our feelings as women have been enlisted by your soul-stirring denunciations of the infamous and truly inhuman New Poor Law Amendment Act – which would cruelly destroy the dearest ties of existence . . . and which would render our sex the victims of consummate villainy. Our hearts, sir, have responded to your fervent

advocacy of the poor, emaciated and oppressed factory child . . . As women, we thank you in all true sincerity, for your eloquent repudiation of the grievous wrongs inflicted upon . . . our unfortunate sisters of more especially the north of England. May you go on and prosper, cheering the weak, arousing the apathetic, and dismaying the oppressor . . . [6]

As this address indicates, it was his oratory that convinced. In the words of *The Times*, he had 'the gift of eloquence to an extraordinary and dangerous degree'. The editor of the *Northern Star* thought that the Newcastle speech was 'one of the most triumphant specimens of human eloquence we ever heard'. Friend and foe alike were impressed by his speeches at Liverpool in September 1838. One reporter who thought him 'a compound of fool and villain' conceded:

His voice is loud, clear and pleasing. His delivery embodies all the grace of art in the apparent absence of art . . . the great charm of his oratory is the pervading earnestness of look, gesture, and word. His soul as it were, discovers itself to his auditors in the abundance of love and sympathy, and he stretches his arms forward as if he would fly into and mingle with them. The perfect orator is further apparent in his language . . . It exactly suited the people and the occasion. There was no effort after metaphor, no clap trap sentiment to bring them, in theatrical language, down; but there was a calculated ingenuity in his inculcation of dangerous, if not wicked counsel . . . I need not add that the object was accomplished. Judging from the enthusiasm he had excited, he appeared to have poured a new intelligence into them, inspiring them at the same time with a crowd of novel and mighty desires.[7]

His speech in Liverpool's Queen's Theatre was heard by the young Chartist Robert Lowery, one of Stephens' admirers:

In his speech at the Queen's Theatre, he described how his attention was first drawn to the evils of the factory system as a minister of the Gospel in Lancashire. He found that certain members could not attend their class meetings on the week day evenings – that any religious service he might have was attended by few of the factory people of his congregation; the children were more ready to sleep than attend to instruction in the Sabbath-school. He described the mere children carried in their father's arms at five in the morning to the mills – the mothers having to leave their younger children at home to work in these places, and their sucking infants being taken to them at the dinner and breakfast hours. He pointed out the ignorance of the masses, the want of provision for the education of that population, and the impossibility of their benefitting by any such provision if opportunity for so doing was not secured to them by law . . . Then he painted the struggle as still going on, and spoke of the hopelessness of law seeking to stifle inquiry and to stem the rising intelligence of the inquiring people – as did the Philistines to old Sampson (sic) – by binding him – and just as Sampson did when they taunted him in triumph and fancied security – so would the people do now, if so fettered and blinded, they would at last, when their oppressors thought themselves safe in their wrongdoing, grasp the pillars of the State and wrench them from their foundations, so that the whole structure would fall, and all be buried beneath its ruins. He had the whole audience spellbound, and thrilling, as it were, in actual view of such a scene.

Lowery added that in the open air, his power over a crowd was even greater. 'I have read of no such power exercised in this country by open air preachers since the time of Whitfield, and he had not such vast concourses of people to address.' Not everyone agreed; Tom Trollope, who with his mother the novelist Fanny Trollope heard both Oastler and Stephens in 1839, was more impressed by Oastler (as was the Wesleyan minister Benjamin Gregory). Nevertheless, while allowing for Lowery's exaggeration, it can be claimed for Stephens that in these fleeting years, no Christian preacher had comparable influence over the industrial operative classes, and none would have anything like as much again.[8]

Throughout his life, Stephens stood in the Evangelical Christian tradition. Both in his lifetime and since, it has been suggested that he was unorthodox. For this many things were responsible. The new science of political economy had all but paralysed the making of Christian social judgments, and the few who made them often *were* unorthodox. The ex-Methodist New Connexion minister Joseph Barker, who was also a Chartist, had denied the sacrament of Baptism, and was later for a time to deny Christianity itself. Chartist churches combined a minimum of Christianity with a maximum of Chartist advocacy. Stephens himself repeatedly stressed practical Christianity rather than metaphysical theology, and criticized those who did the opposite. The notion of a 'political preacher' was open to misunderstanding. He moved easily among those of all persuasions and none. He corresponded with a freethinker like Robert Owen, befriended the young George Holyoake, and shared platforms with secularists such as Feargus O'Connor. He accepted the right to unbelief. Some of his own flock were affected by unbelief in varying degrees; most were Chartists in the week, and Stephenites on Sundays, exposing them to acute dilemmas of faith. The cumulative effect, added to general mistrust of his extremism, made the suspicion of infidelity plausible.[9]

The charge was rebutted by a source which by 1839 was hostile to Stephens. John Stephens relinquished the editorship of the *Christian Advocate* early in 1837. By 1839, an editorial Pharaoh had arisen determined to know not Joseph; his was an evil course, and his arrest was to be welcomed. Yet in January 1839 the editor John Middleton Hare commented on a charge of infidelity: 'We entirely disapprove of Mr Stephens's violence, but we believe him to be orthodox as a divine'. Stephens himself from time to time answered criticisms that he should 'stick to his Bible'. He claimed that the Stephenites were 'Bible politicians, Bible agitators, and Bible love restorers'. The word of God 'had been the sole standard of his agitation'. Though politically startling, his surviving published sermons reveal no hint of unorthodoxy.[10]

In Sweden, he had preached basic Evangelical beliefs:

I have thought it my duty to preach the great truths of our religion, calling sinners to repentance, and exhorting them to faith in a divine Redeemer ... I have every reason to rejoice in the conversation of some, the awakening of many.

In Ashton, he was confronted by millowners long exposed to such beliefs in Anglican, Methodist and Dissenting churches:

When this question first presented itself to my mind, I said to myself – I know some of these millowners. They always behaved well to me. They never thrashed me: they never took the strap or the billy-roller to me (Laughter). They dont whip their horses or drive them hard against the hill. How can they be so gentlemanly to me, and so humane to their horses, and yet be so oppressive, and cruel and tyrannical to their work-people? Some of them, I said to myself, I know to be Churchmen – some Methodists – some Baptists – some Independents: and I have met them on Bible platforms and on missionary platforms, subscribing their money liberally to send the scriptures and missionaries to heathen countries. They were among the foremost in denouncing slavery among the blacks in India, who only work eight hours a day. Yes, I repeated these things and then asked myself – how can these men act thus, and yet be so atrociously cruel in their own mills, and among men whose fathers were richer and better off than their fathers were?[11]

John Stephens recalled 'the profoundly practical character' of Wesley's theology, which never forgot the sermons of Jesus and the epistle of James. 'Hence he denounced sin wherever he found it, and whoever were its perpetrators, without fear, favour or allowance. O that the sect of such Wesleyans were larger than it is!' In a later editorial, John Stephens wrote: 'Solafidianism is carried to such violent extremes, even in professedly Arminian churches, that men are apt to forget the obligation under which they lie to do as well as to believe.' His brother was now to remind them. When the masters opposed his efforts at mediation, he turned to the cause of the operatives. He resolved to preach nothing but factory sermons, and interpreted his Evangelical faith accordingly:

> To be justified means in a few plain words, to be set right; to be set right with God, to be set right with man; God setting us right with himself, with our own heart, and with one another . . . If that be the meaning of it – and your own ministers will not deny that it is the meaning of it – put it to them whether any millowner in their society is justified by faith . . . He cannot be justified; he cannot have things set right between God and himself . . . All is wrong, all is crooked between him and God; all is wrong between him and the people; and so long as he continues a millowner in the present state and under the present system of trade . . . he must be on the highroad to everlasting damnation. Do you ask me why? Because he makes free with that which does not belong to him. Your bodies and souls are God's, and not your masters' . . . and as long as the millowner does to your bodies and to your souls that which is likely to hurt them . . . he is guilty in the sight of God of blood . . . Is he ever told that? Never, never, never. The minister to whose society or congregation he belongs would rather have one millowner in his congregation than a thousand spinners.

As for repentance:

> When they have the millowners before them, do your ministers ever tell them that repentance means a knowledge of the sin of working

men, women and children fifteen hours a day? . . . Your ministers tell
you that repentance leads to faith, and faith to holiness. They tell you
a man cannot believe unless he repent, and that he cannot be saved
unless he believe. That is true. But does he ever tell the millowner
that God will find him a good market for his manufactures, without
the necessity of overworking his own work-people; that God can open
channels . . . for trade and commerce, without the necessity for the
millowner every now and then to work his mills over time, and every
now and then to turn them into the street and say, 'they shall not work
at all?' No . . . [12]

He did not abandon the Evangelical faith of his Methodist years; he
earthed it in Ashton soil. He could appeal, like the Methodist he had
been, to the individual. In his first sermon of the new year in 1839, he
said: 'You know I have always told you . . . that your first business . . . is,
each one for himself to make his peace with God'. Only then could he
turn to the Christian social struggle:

the battle we are fighting from one end of England to the other is not
the battle most men take it to be. It goes much further . . . It is not a
battle of party against party . . . It is not a struggle for power or for
place . . . It is the working of the mystery of iniquity mentioned in holy
scripture – the mystery of ungodliness . . . It is the battle between
God and Mammon – between Christ the prince of peace and
Beelzebub the prince of the devil. The question is, whether God shall
reign in England, or whether Satan shall domineer – the question is
whether the laws of heaven and the institutions of mercy are to be the
laws of a Christian land, and the institutions of a Christian people; or
whether laws begotten below and born here on earth are to be the laws
and institutions to which a once Christian land, and a once Christian
people, are to be compelled to submit. It is the battle, my brethren, of
this book (the Bible) against the earth and against hell. [13]

In the battle, he had enquired not only into the factory system, but into
the Poor Law Amendment Act. He had 'asked whether we are to believe
God, when He says He has filled the whole earth with plenteousness –
or are we to believe the framers of that Act, who tell us that for myriads
of her children, nature has furnished no provision – no place at her
niggard board?' He concluded that 'these "amendments" of God's laws
in the kingdoms of nature, providence and grace are so thoroughly
detestable, so truly diabolical, that I have wondered . . . that there were

men ... who dared ... to come into the homes of Englishmen and into the House of God with this law of devils in their hand'. It was his stress on God's providence that undergirded his social protest. Industrialism had undermined the traditional view that for the great majority of people, pain, hunger and poverty were inevitable elements in God's providence. Industry had created vast, if ill-distributed wealth, and its potential seemed unlimited. Poverty in the midst of poverty had to be accepted; poverty in the midst of plenty could not. The first Christian social protestors of the industrial age could not admit that the suffering of a man-made factory system and the new Poor Law could be attributed to God. It was to be fought as evil, not accepted as providential. Here was the root of Stephens's objection to the Poor Law Amendment Act.[14]

He dismissed the parrot cry of no politics in the pulpit:

> ... unless a priest of the living God be a politician in the pulpit, he has no business there at all. (Several voices: 'No, he has not'). Law and religion can never be separated. If you attempt to disassociate them or to disunite them, it is like attempting to disassociate and disunite the soul from the body of man, and expect after you have done so, to find a living being before you ... Read this book from the beginning to the end, and tell me whether in the whole of its code of laws, you find one law out of them all that does not apply to this world and to this world only. These are the laws of God ... 'Thy will be done on earth, as it is in heaven'.

From Moses to John of Patmos, no biblical figure could be found who 'was not in the strictest sense of the term a political teacher ... a denouncer of God's anger on men politically wicked, and of God's favour in regard to men politically good'.[15]

His three London sermons were typical of his teaching. God's commands must be obeyed in private life and in the social economy. Creeds and systems obscured the Lawgiver's will. Churches were 'diffuse in matters of abstract speculation', but 'silent as regards the weightier subjects of religion, which are judgment, mercy and faith'. As for the state, 'no earthly power that claims domination by virtue of divine authority can decree things contrary to the decrees of heaven'. Violent revolution was 'sinful in the sight of God unless there be just cause for it'. Unjust laws must be resisted. 'I am here ... to blow to the ends of the earth and beyond them the lie ... that a thing called law ... no matter what it is, is therefore to be obeyed.' Since the days of Wesley and Whitfield, 'we have lost the spirit of Christianity in the outward forms of religion'. If the Church of England 'ceases to be the guardian, the defender, the advocate and champion of the poor, it ought to cease to be the national religion of England'. God had created plenty, not poverty, 'but there are those who stand between the plenteousness and those who require it'. The Bible preached contentment to the poor and woes to the rich; it was wrong to preach contentment to those without food or raiment. If many could not earn enough to live, even though they worked every day of the week, society is dissolved into its original elements, and the commandment against stealing is superseded. His politics were simple. 'I am for the cottager being as happy, as secure and as contented under his humble roof as the Queen is on her throne in her palace.' Unless the mighty of the land did justice to the poor, 'then I denounce God's curse upon them, from the Crown downwards'.[16]

Like the Christian socialists, some of whose emphases he anticipated, Stephens knew there was such a thing as society, and that the Bible addressed it directly. The poor constituted the base of the Christian society, and unless they were secure, all else was in jeopardy. It was the task of the Christian ministry to 'stand for ever as a moral breakwater against the swelling surge of pride and oppression'. Since the coming of the Enlightenment and the all-pervading sway of the new science of political economy, the church had not pronounced, and had almost ceased to think, about society as a whole in the light of Biblical revelation. The factory reformers mark the beginning of a recovery. They were not theologians as Maurice was. Their theology (like that of the Christian socialists) can be described as reductionist, but it was not unorthodox. They were pioneers in the proclamation of an Evangelical social gospel.[17]

6

Crisis and Recovery

The long delayed trial of Joseph Rayner Stephens took place at Chester Assizes on 15 August 1839 before Mr Justice Pattison and a special jury of twelve, of whom seven were merchants. Three hundred people attended, and the courtroom was full. The Attorney-General, Sir John Campbell, appeared for the prosecution, and the accused defended himself. He was charged with intending to disturb the public peace on 14 November 1838 by making a seditious speech at Hyde; two other counts charged him with a riot, and being present at an unlawful assembly.[1]

The atmosphere in Chester was tense. Early in August, Lord John Russell had attacked Oastler and Stephens in the Commons as firebrands. Earlier witnesses at Ashton had been intimidated, and Chartist reaction was unpredictable. The prosecution feared a rescue attempt from the court by an armed mob, and a letter written to the Mayor was published on the city walls. These fears proved groundless, and the trial proceeded in peace.[2]

By singling out the Hyde evidence from the other indictments, the prosecution forced Stephens to defend his part in a minor, though threatening Chartist gathering. In his farewell sermon, he had referred sarcastically to 'the Hyde speech, in which I contrived to create a riot and misdemeanour in speaking not five minutes'. It was not a speech, merely a series of disjointed remarks about physical force. However willing he was to suffer for opposition to the new poor law, he was not prepared to become a Chartist martyr; yet the charge linked his name once more to a movement he had repudiated, and to aims he did not share. He had to answer unanswerable facts rather than defend his principles. The dilemma he faced five years earlier at Manchester was repeated at Chester, for if he confined himself to the charge, he had no defence. He half-disclosed this to the special jury, in a parenthesis he attributed to the prosecution:

Gentlemen, if this were a simple case, as the Attorney-General wishes you to believe it to be, of attending that meeting – *a meeting so*

clearly unlawful that he need not to say five words on the subject; if this were
a case so simple, and the mere fact of the meeting having been so
convened and held, the mere fact of my having attended that meeting
and said certain words was all that was requisite to prove on this
occasion, then gentlemen, I ask you what reasonable pretext there is
for your being present in the box on this occasion?

He would not waste time defending the indefensible.[3]

The Attorney-General opened his case by defining an unlawful
assembly. Then he described the torchlight meeting at Hyde, with its
firearms and banners reading 'Tyrants heave and tremble', 'liberty or
death', 'Ashton demands universal suffrage or universal vengeance',
and 'for children and wife, we will war to the knife'. Stephens told the
crowd that he had spoken to the soldiers, and they would not act against
them. Burial club funds had been used to purchase arms. When he
asked the crowd if they were armed, he was answered by a discharge of
firearms. He said, 'I see you are ready', and wished them 'good night'.
The meeting had continued until nearly midnight. Campbell had no
doubt that the defendent was guilty, and that this was an unlawful
assembly. Stephens had incited soldiers to disobey the law, and the
crowd to arm for revolution, and unless he could call witnesses to deny
these facts, he must be found guilty.[4]

In the cross-examination of the seven prosecution witnesses, Stephens' legal inexperience was exposed. Both special constable George
Miller and factory surgeon William Tinker revealed facts damaging to
his case. According to Thomas Dunning, a Chartist present at the trial,
more came out under Campbell's re-examination. Four of the witnesses
were manufacturers, and Stephens did bring out their links to each
other and to the prosecution; but the damage had been done.[5]

Stephens rose to defend himself. His attempt to subpoena Lord John
Russell having failed, he called no witnesses; he intended to spend time
to discredit the prosecution by stressing the hidden political motivation
of the trial. He was determined to restate the basic themes of his
ministry. Hyde was not quite overlooked, but implicit in his lengthy
defence was the realization that he was bound to be found guilty as
charged.[6]

At great length he questioned the fairness of the trial. Irregularities
were taking place because government suspected him of instigating the
Ashton factory fire. He contrasted his beliefs sharply from those of the
Whig Attorney-General. Stephens had shown that 'the principles of

what is now called liberalism and reform are the most dangerous
principles that can be entertained by any'. Power was from God, not the
people, and if God's laws were found anywhere outside the Bible, it was
in the English constitution. With a wealth of quotation, he claimed that
he was the victim of a Whig conspiracy for advocating factory reform and
poor law repeal. The trial 'was a political prosecution from beginning to
end'.[7]

Next he repudiated Chartism:

> I am dragged here . . . as though I were a party to the Convention, and
> to the disturbances of Birmingham, to the Charter . . . and all the rest
> of that rigmarole in which I never had a share. I only came forward to
> the men of Leigh, and there declared my detestation of the doctrines
> of Chartism, declared that if Radicals were in power, my views were
> such that my head would be brought first to the block, and my blood
> would be the first blood that would have to flow for the olden liberties
> of the country. Gentlemen, this is the individual who is now brought
> before you as a Chartist, and his proceedings made to appear as
> though he was identified with all that has taken place in this
> country . . . If I am to be tried, let me be tried in my own person, and
> not in the person of Chartism . . . If I am to be tried, let me be tried
> upon my own opinions – upon my own principles – upon my own
> authorized and published documents.

Although it was no surprise to their leaders that Stephens was no
Chartist, it created revulsion among Chartists in general. They had
applauded his daring words from their platforms, and had contributed
to his defence fund; they felt betrayed. Thomas Dunning was pleased
that M'Douall (who also was being tried) defended Chartist principles,
and got a lighter sentence than Stephens. Despite his continued
devotion to working-class causes, doubts about his trustworthiness
would follow him for the rest of his life. Yet in his own mind, he had been
quite consistent. He had never hidden his views on Chartism. In his trial
he wanted only to show the political motivation of the prosecution,
which by implication was misrepresenting him. It was his misfortune
that his public repudiation of Chartism attracted far more attention than
his subtle attempt to expose the prosecution.[8]

Fitfully, he returned to the events at Hyde. The Attorney-General
had failed to prove anything unlawful about the meeting 'so far as I had
anything to do with it'. The witnesses had not been alarmed, the
procession had been orderly. He made an emotional defence of the

banner inscribed 'for child and wife, we will war to the knife'. On and on he went, until after five and a half hours even he felt exhausted, and he sat down.[9]

Campbell gave a caustic reply. Nine-tenths of the defendant's speech would have been disallowed to any professional advocate. Stephens had praised himself and calumniated others. He had tried to divert attention from the real charge. There had been no delay in the trial. It was not a political prosecution; yet Campbell accused Stephens of hypocrisy in 'trying to shake off the Chartists', and he named leading Tories who supported the Act of 1834. He was just as concerned as Stephens for the poor, but on doctrines of disobedience to laws thought to be wrong, he doubted if civil society could exist. Since he had reminded Stephens of the real charge, it was as well that he returned to it himself; the damaging testimony of Tinker, the Chartist banners carried at Hyde, and the fact that the defendant had entered into the full spirit of the meeting, all proved his case.[10]

The Judge's summing up left little doubt about the verdict:

> The observations which the defendant has made were adduced in very powerful language, with great talent and ability, and with a fluency and power of language which one very seldom saw equalled, and which would undoubtedly make, as they ought to make, a great impression on the minds of the jury, provided that they really bore upon the points in question.

The jury had to take the evidence they had before them:

> If the jury were of opinion that the meeting was an unlawful assembly, and that the defendant was present, it would be their duty to find him guilty, although nothing was done so as to constitute an actual riot.[11]

At twenty to eight, after only a few seconds deliberation, the jury found the defendant guilty. The Judge 'entirely concurred', since 'the evidence is all one way'. He sentenced Stephens to eighteen months imprisonment in the Knutsford House of Correction, followed by a five-year period in which he had to find sureties for himself of £500, and for two others of £250 each. Campbell said he would not proceed on the other indictments, and supported Stephens' plea for the use of pen, paper and ink in prison; the Judge thought they would not be denied him. The prisoner was removed, and was allowed to write to his wife. Later he wrote again to tell her that the Judge had promised to allow him to remain at Chester Castle, which was better than Knutsford. He added: 'to my thinking my defence was not a good speech. I was not myself – fatigued with the previous business – and exhausted from reading so many quotations'.[12]

Chartism collapsed with the rejection of the petition, the arrest of its leaders and the failure of the national holiday. In late October, just before the Newport rising, Campbell proudly declared at Edinburgh that Chartism had been put down by the government without any blood being shed. Oastler was awaiting trial for debt, and O'Connor and Stephens were allies no more.

Chester Castle in October 1840 held fifteen Chartist prisoners, twelve of them for collecting arms. Among them were Timothy Higgins of Ashton, the veteran radical William Benbow, and the Stephenite John Broadbent; until August, Peter M'Douall had been another. Although Stephens called it 'a moderately good jail', all political prisoners were treated as criminals. Their few privileges were resented by visiting magistrates, who tried to restrict them. All had a meagre, unpalatable diet, and endured the humiliation and boredom inseparable from imprisonment. Correspondence could be confiscated, and only *The Times* could be read. Some prisoners were in cells below ground with water running down the walls, but Stephens was spared this.[13]

Stephens was not harshly treated. He rose between 6 and 6.30 a.m. from a straw bed. He could supplement the prison diet at his own expense. His cell was damp, but he could use a private room to study and eat. Like other prisoners, he exercised in the yard, and was not allowed to sit up after 7 p.m. With others, he complained, since he found it hard to spend twelve or thirteen hours a day in bed. Despite colds and rheumatism, his health had never been better. His wife and child now lived in Chester, and since he had promised not to abuse the privilege, he was allowed to see them unsupervised. He wrote to a friend that he was treated with respect and kindess. Even the Governor enjoyed conversing with him. He thought that nearly all the staff were 'kind men carrying out a harsh and inhuman system'.[14]

Although forbidden to write for publication, he arranged for his letters to churches and individuals to be collected by friends and published in the new *Stephens's Monthly Magazine*. The visiting magistrates objected to the first issue, in which Stephens drew attention to their power to reduce diet, enforce prison dress and impose solitary confinement. They insisted on inspecting his future correspondence; but as he had said in the offending letter, he had 'a sturdy mind that only grows the stronger and the stubborner for all such attempts to break it down'. He was again in trouble in June, when his contributions to the magazine were restricted, though many continued to appear.[15]

In response to public concern over the treatment of Chartist prisoners, three Home Office inspectors were appointed to investigate. At Chester Castle, Major Williams interviewed Stephens in October 1840. He reported that the notorious offender was 'a very astute, clever individual' who apparently aimed at power through his 'new sect':

> I suspect that he has little or no feeling about religion. I asked him if he attended the prison chapel. He said 'he had no objection, but that it was breakfast time' – a trifle, but showing the little respect he entertains even for appearances. I assume his agitation is assumed for temporal purposes . . . He has the power and ability of much mischief in him – is of gentlemanly manners and habits . . .

In general, the three inspectors' reports were seldom fair to imprisoned Chartist leaders. The Stephenites were never regarded by their minister as a political power base, and he constantly warned them against the evils of party in politics and religion. Nor was attendance at the prison chapel a reliable guide to religious sincerity. Williams reported that the prisoner Benbow attended, but although a nominal Baptist, he 'really is of no religion', and he 'showed the most marked disrespect'. Stephens held that clergy and magistrates alike were responsible for subjecting thousands to a brutalized prison discipline, and he had taxed the Chester chaplain with it:

> I have spoken my mind very fully on all these points to Mr Eaton our chaplain. I told him he ought not to wonder if men pulled down gaols or burned down workhouses right 'lawlessly' when they were so 'lawfully' starved, degraded and tortured, as he himself well knew them to be.

Knowing Williams for what he was, Stephens did not waste time arguing about chapel attendance, but was content to put him off with a flippant remark.[16]

The Newport rising filled him with grief. He wrote:

> I have said over and over again that 'the revolution has begun'. It is going on. Nothing can now stop it. I, and those with whom I acted in my opposition to the 'factory system', the 'new poor law' and other practical oppressions, assisted the people in giving constitutional

expression to their just complaints . . . We were spurned – spit upon – and trampled under foot. It was made a crime to meet openly – to speak as our fathers spake. And what was left? Why, nothing but the dark – the secret – the dread 'conspiracy,' nothing but that, which always leads to burning and blood. I am now in a dungeon for trying to prevent this. I would have given my own blood to have prevented it . . . Nothing but a wet and cloudy night saved Wales from falling into the hands of a people goaded into an actual – an organized – an armed rebellion!

Such was his answer to those who blamed him and Oastler for the rising. Later he warned Williams that one single success through able military advice would inspire the masses to revolt. He had prevented the adoption of the national holiday among the working classes. 'I repeat again, if ever they meet with the slightest success there will be a general rise.' He remained convinced that it would come, even if it was delayed.[17]

Williams thought that Stephens was a focal point of trouble in the jail. His enmity with M'Douall had resulted in the Chartist prisoners being split into two camps; on one occasion it led to open violence and a broken jaw. Stephens told Williams: 'I have been insulted by one set of Chartists here, who sided with M'Douall, although I have in frequent instances given them both money and food.' Williams reported that Stephens and M'Douall had eaten their meals in rooms adjoining the turnkey's lodgings, and M'Douall had taken advantage of this to seduce one of the turnkey's daughters. This had added to Stephens's indignation, which 'had no bounds' (understandably so in the light of M'Douall's accusations against him in July 1839). He thought that when M'Douall's immorality was known, it would have a very serious effect upon his influence among the working classes.[18]

Despite this, Williams believed that Stephens' greater privileges were to blame. Williams noted of Stephens, 'he is an object of suspicion to Mr M'Douall and his followers, who call him Traitor, and are indignant at his pocketting the whole of the money raised by subscription for his defence by Counsel, when he defended himself and employed none'. Neither man had employed a barrister, but in prison Stephens had both his defence fund, and the contributions of his churches for his support; M'Douall had only a little over £25 from Chartist sources to pay for the costs of his defence. Stephens was generous with his money – years later, it was revealed that he supported five or six of his fellow-prisoners

– but he was hardly likely to pay M'Douall's legal expenses. In any case, he wrote in October 1839:

> It is the unanimous opinion of all my fellow-prisoners here, in which I fully concur, that every farthing spent in 'law' is money thrown away. Whatever can be raised for your friends ought to be given for themselves, their wives and families: they will want it all. I advise every man to defend himself, to tell the best and most straightforward tale he can, without going to the expense even for a single witness.

As for M'Douall, he attacked Stephens through the press as a traitor who should be treated with 'dignified contempt' throughout his life. Before his release, M'Douall dwelt in writing on all he had sacrificed for the cause. Pressed by his solicitor to settle his account, he appealed for help through the *Northern Star*. He reacted angrily after his release to a further reminder of the still unpaid bill. In his attitude to the 'traitor', M'Douall attracted a good deal of Chartist sympathy; yet two leading fellow-prisoners at Chester Castle took a different view. Timothy Higgins differed from Stephens in politics and religion; he had suffered for criticizing the 'Champion'. Nevertheless, Higgins wrote that M'Douall shared the privileges enjoyed by Stephens, who in any case had only what the printed rules allowed. Stephens 'is a man who as a fellow prisoner will ever be endeared to me'. The ultra-radical William Benbow was dismissive of M'Douall. 'As a surgeon I would not trust him with a dog's leg to cure – and as a Chartist his only principle is money'.[19]

Outside Chester Castle, the Stephens defence fund caused trouble between Stephens and O'Connor. There was widespread confusion about this fund. It was founded in January 1839 for the defence of Stephens, when he was the only 'Chartist' facing prosecution, and it was administered by pro-Stephens trustees. Some of its contributors were not Chartists; Oastler was active in raising funds for it. Among those who were Chartists were many who did not accept that Stephens' loyalty was still to the earlier movements of social protest. They wanted the surplus of the fund to be used for the defence of other Chartists awaiting trial. The trustees refused; yet Stephens defended himself. In November 1839, the overriding need to raise funds for the defence of John Frost, the Chartist leader of the Newport rising, brought new pressure on the Stephens fund from O'Connor himself.[20]

Since the trial, Stephens' name had all but vanished from the pages of O'Connor's *Northern Star*. For opposing the national holiday, Stephens had 'endured a torrent of abuse and animosity' for which he held O'Connor largely responsible. O'Connor's first reaction to the Newport rising was to call on all friendly organizations to release funds for Frost's defence. On 7 November, he ingratiated himself with the Stephenites at Charlestown. Two days later, the *Star* published a letter from Stephens to the Leigh radicals, in which he said that it was up to his trustees to decide if the fund was to be used for others, though he opposed it; Chartists should apply to the Convention instead. Before the Stephens fund delegates met on 9 December to dispose of the surplus for 'the object for which it was collected', M'Douall's 'traitor' letter appeared in the *Star*, and Yorkshire Chartists urged that the surplus should be used for Frost. On the 5th, O'Connor spoke to the Hyde and Stalybridge Stephenites. On 10 December, the Manchester committee of the Chartist defence fund resolved to appropriate the Stephens surplus, and sent two of its number to the Stephens fund treasurer, Thomas Fielden; they were refused the money. Late in December, O'Connor pressed for a loan, saying that Fielden would be responsible if Frost was convicted for want of a good defence; he was rebuffed. Frost was not executed, but the dispute smouldered on until July 1840; then the Chartists tried again, only to be told that the surplus had been paid to Stephens some months earlier.[21]

Stephens in prison was indignant, and blamed O'Connor for bullying the Fieldens. It had opened the eyes of one of his correspondents to 'the character of that disinterested patriot and his patriotic paper'. 'If Mr John Fielden will not become security for Mr O'Connor at one time, and if at another Mr Thomas Fielden will not be a party to a more barefaced act of robbery at Mr O'Connor's bidding, they are both of them held up to public ignominy and execration.' The manoeuvres over the fund provoked Stephens into revealing policy differences. Four days after O'Connor's meeting at Charlestown, Stephens wrote:

> That a man should openly tell the people how heartily he hated the ballot and all such sneaking, cowardly, new-fangled 'reforms' of our old English hold-up-the-head institutions, and yet be a favourite with them, was too much for a 'five-point' Radical to endure. So Stephens must be denounced, and he was denounced accordingly.

In May, Timothy Higgins compared the behaviour of Stephens favourably with what he had heard of the now imprisoned O'Connor.

Again Stephens commented on the abuse he had endured earlier for opposing his policies, but 'I bear no ill will against Mr O'Connor or anyone else who has basely and treacherously attacked me'. The publicly revealed policy differences confirmed the alienation of the two men; thus their open break was a by-product of O'Connor's concern for Frost's defence.[22]

Late in October 1840 Stephens received a letter from his ailing father. He declined to help with his son's proposed *People's Magazine* – 'your political views and mine are as wide as the poles asunder'. He thought it was 'visionary' to expect agitation to revolutionize the country in a short time – 'national changes are slow in their progress'. This letter from a devoted father had a great effect on him; but within a few months it was overshadowed by death. John Stephens died at Brixton hill on 29 January 1841. His son was expecting release within a fortnight. An angel of mercy in the unlikely form of Home Secretary Lord Normanby remitted the last few days of his sentence, and he was set free on 1 February, 'to attend to the last, sad duties to the deceased'. The ex-miner from St Denis was buried close to John Wesley in the hallowed ground behind Wesley's Chapel in London's City Road.[23]

After his release, Stephens faced an uphill struggle to survive. For five years, he was subject to legal restrictions for good behaviour. Politically, he was discredited with large sections of middle-class and working-class opinion; as a minister, he faced serious problems through Stephenite debt and emigration. At a modest welcome meeting at Stalybridge in February 1841, he reaffirmed all his old causes and his repudiation of Chartism. He hoped that his new *People's Magazine* would prove successful in furthering his objectives; but in this he was disappointed. Local affairs claimed much of his time, even though he lived at Chorlton on Medlock – which doubtless was due to the needs of his Manchester-based magazine. He was isolated as never before. There was still John Fielden, whom he called 'the only honest man in the House (of Commons)'. His great friend Richard Oastler was in the Fleet debtor's prison; Stephens visited him, and afterwards commended his friend's Tory radical *Fleet Papers*. Doubtless this was significant, since all the signs indicated the need for a reappraisal in the light of the failure of physical force; God's revolution was no longer to be identified with current radical agitation.[24]

His isolation was soon brought home to him. In May 1841, the veteran Staffordshire Chartist John Richards tried in vain to obtain a building in which Stephens could preach for an Oastler defence fund meeting. In August, he held two debates for the same fund at the Manchester Hall of Science with the Owenite Socialist lecturer Robert Buchanan. At the first he was oddly ineffective, though he opposed the deterministic philosophy of Owenism; but at the second he did better, attacking the Owenite view of man as inadequate. Unlike other contemporary Christian anti-socialist lecturers, he thought the responsibility for Socialist error rested with Christians, whose practical infidelity drove the people 'into the arms of the deceiver and the destroyer'. Although he retained the respect of Socialists, he rejected their creed, as he did that of the Chartists; they were 'the two points, spiritual and political, at which the dark genius of revolution has planted his advanced posts in this fearful struggle between the old and the new . . . ' He had shunned both radical causes.[25]

Nor did conventional politics inspire him. Although the Tories under Sir Robert Peel came to power in September, they had come to terms with *laissez-faire* economics long before, and within two months Stephens called for a third party to be led by Lord Ashley. Apart from the radical Fielden, only with a few traditional Tories would he find any common ground. He was intensely suspicious of the new Anti-Corn Law League, with its remedy of free trade for the hunger of the people. He thought free trade would ruin British agriculture and reduce wages, and he called for government-financed schemes to reclaim and develop land. He continued to attack the Poor Law Amendment Act. All this went against the grain of current politics, and Stephens made little headway. In 1843, Edwin Butterworth heard him preach in an obscure part of Oldham. He dubbed Stephens 'that singularly eloquent, eccentric political and religious agitator'. His followers were 'half chartists and half socialists . . . on a better distribution of land occupancy, and tories as regards their views on the political economy of the factory system'. Stephens was out of fashion.[26]

Severe economic depression rekindled the fires of Chartism. Although Parliament rejected a second petition, a strike in Ashton developed into a riot when plugs were knocked out of mill boilers. The strike developed into a renewed demand for the Charter. Despite the return of militancy and stormy meetings in the Charlestown meeting room, Stephens kept aloof. In August 1842 he helped the Tory candidate John Walter in a disorderly Nottingham by-election. Walter, Oastler's friend and the editor of *The Times*, was an opponent of the new poor law, and in 1841 he had enjoyed the support of Oastler and

O'Connor. In 1842 the Whig candidate was the Quaker Joseph Sturge, who accepted the six points of the Charter; thus Stephens and Doherty helped Walter, while O'Connor, M'Douall and others supported Sturge. In the market place, Stephens mounted the Tory wagon, and the Chartists led by O'Connor charged, and captured it after a fight. Stephens fled. O'Connor exulted in the *Northern Star*: 'We smashed the renegade Stephens and the Tory bloodhounds.' It was small compensation for Walter's subsequent victory.[27]

In 1843 the factory issue revived through Home Secretary Sir James Graham's abortive bill to give children in the eight to thirteen age group six and a half hours work and three hours education a day. Since the bill provided for virtual Anglican control of the necessary schools, it aroused Dissenting and Wesleyan Methodist hostility, and petitions poured into Parliament. (Stephens too denounced the bill.) It was withdrawn, but the promise of further government legislation revived the factory reform movement. Its new campaign was coupled with agitation for Oastler's release, and for protection in opposition to free trade. Stephens took part in a meeting at the Manchester Corn Exchange on 14 December, but only on the plea of Fielden would the meeting consent to hear Stephens. His dialogue on the legality of the Poor Law Amendment Act with Busfeild Ferrand, a pugnacious Tory protectionist MP, brought the condemnation of Anti-Corn Law League publicists. The notorious Glasgow speech was recalled, and Ferrand's Tory radical group was 'the very alpha and omega of revolution, spoilation of property, levelling of ranks and destruction of all existing institutions'.[28]

The years from 1844 to 1847 saw the triumph of the revived factory movement. After complex political manoeuvres, Graham's revised bill became law. It limited the working hours of women to twelve per day, without nightwork, and those of the eight to thirteen group to six and a half; there was to be more rigorous inspection. The reformers were twice defeated on ten hours amendments moved by Ashley, but the conversion of old opponents like Lord John Russell was a hopeful sign. A newly liberated Oastler joined the struggle, and in 1846 Ashley introduced a new ten hours bill. Fielden replaced Ashley as Parliamentary leader, but the bill was narrowly defeated. Salvation came from an unlikely quarter. The free trade campaign peaked with the conversion of the prime minster, Sir Robert Peel. In June, the corn laws were abolished, Peel resigned, and Russell formed a Whig government. For the first time, a Prime Minister pledged to factory reform was in power. A new ten hours' agitation swept the north. A cry for an eleven hours compromise brought out the inevitable Hindley with a suitable bill, but it came to nothing. Principle triumphed over compromise when Fielden carried the ten hours' bill in June 1847 – an achievement for which he has never received the full credit due to him. Oastler, now a frail senior statesman of the movement, rejoiced at the success of his seventeen-year-old crusade.

Stephens had no part in these dramatic events. Five years later, he explained why. The earlier struggles had convinced him of the uselessness of demanding redress 'for some time to come'. Other classes must be involved, or they too would be engulfed in the coming retribution. The Act of 1847 was not passed because of public clamour out of a sense of justice; it succeeded from motives of political revenge arising from the abolition of the corn laws. Any Factory Act without restriction on the moving power of machinery would be a dead letter. Workers were too demoralized by past failures to expect any good from the new Act. Alone of the movement's leaders, Stephens did not rejoice.[29]

In any case, events in Ashton left him no reason to rejoice. He had moved nearer to his churches, first to Wilshaw and then to Fields Farm at Alt Hill, where he was within the ancient Ashton parish. A sombre survey of Ashton was made in 1844 by a local bank manager, John Ross Coulthart. It showed that while Ashton was a healthy town by contemporary standards, its slum areas were as bad as any in the country. By 1844, unprecedented distress in the north sent the cost of poor relief soaring; contrary to official policy, outdoor relief had risen. In particular, the three towns still defying the law (Rochdale, Ashton and Oldham) were badly hit. According to Assistant Commissioner Clements in November 1844, total costs in the three towns had increased by 147%, compared to a rise of 68% elsewhere in the district. This undermined the argument that the new poor law was more expensive than the old. Clements admitted to his superiors that some workhouses managed by Guardians were a disgrace to a civilized country, but claimed that those still under the old system were even worse. The commissioners seized their chance. After fierce initial resistance at Rochdale, the electoral boycott was broken by an extraordinary election held by ex-officio Guardians, and the few new Guardians so elected enforced the law.[30]

This proved to be the model for overcoming resistance at Ashton and Oldham. In August 1845 a smallpox epidemic at Ashton aggravated the distress; it was followed in successive years by outbreaks of typhus and cholera. The existing workhouse was inadequate; fears of famine were spreading. In October 1845 an election for Guardians in the Ashton Union was successfully held. Oldham Whittaker, a Hurst cotton manufacturer, became the first chairman, and Coulthart the treasurer. In March 1847 the union resolved to build a new workhouse; the curse once solemnly pronounced over Ashton had lost its potency. Nor was this all, for on 29 September 1847 Ashton was granted a municipal borough charter; the cotton manufacturer Abel Buckley, another of Stephens' Whig opponents, became the first Mayor. Whig control of the new machinery of local government was complete.[31]

There was little Stephens or anyone else could do. The old system of relief had been engulfed by the tidal wave of distress; bleak though the prospect was, only the centralized resources of the union could hope to deal with it. Stephens' gloomy reaction was seen in December 1848, when he commented on official approval of the proposed new Ashton workhouse:

> Let us not be misunderstood, we foresee no rising, no storm of remonstrance and opposition on the part of the people. That day is gone; that constitutional index of public opinion has been superseded by another and most perilous one, which is symptomatic of national degeneracy and decay – the apathy of hopelessness, the recklessness of despair. The people will see a Bastille built not even with sullen indifference, but with an undefined feeling of savage exultation – as a means of so much sooner accelerating the end of the present state of things.

However, a critical report of a Commons select committee in 1847 led to the replacement of the three Commissioners by a Poor Law Board, and some of the law's harsher provisions were dropped.[32]

In 1846, Stephens' legal restrictions ended, and he was presented with a silver cup and tea service. It was a public acknowledgment that his past services were still appreciated. In his speech, he reminded the audience of an interrupter, who shouted at a Bradford meeting shortly after his release: 'Who turned his coit?' Stephens had walked to the front of the platform and answered: 'My good man, I did. And I will tell you why I turned my coat. I turned my coat to let you, and such as you, see my coat is the same inside and out'. He assured them all he was the same Stephens he ever was, entertaining the same principles he ever did.[33]

1848 was the year of European revolution, with economic depression and a last revival of Chartism at home. Tension returned to the cotton towns; the congregations at Charlestown and King Street suddenly increased to two thousand factory operatives. In March Stephens founded the first successful Ashton newspaper, the *Ashton Chronicle*; within a year, it had a weekly circulation of two to three thousand copies. In the first issue he used the recent revolution in France to reject class alliance and attack all his old targets. Hugh Mason, now launched on the career which would culminate in his becoming the richest of all Ashton's cotton masters, complained to the Home Secretary about the 'diabolical tendency' of an article attacking his own pet scheme of Lancashire education. He warned:

> The man's talents are of a very high order – his speeches are most eloquent, and he can work up his hearers to a pitch of the highest enthusiasm. He can talk for five consecutive hours without the slightest symptom of physical weariness. At a time like this present . . . a man like Stephens possesses the power to fan the flames of social and civil disorder. We have just had two incendiary fires at cotton mills in this immediate neighbourhood . . . Stephens has asserted that in a little while, he will render Ashton too hot for the millowners. He aims at making the workpeople believe the Masters are ruthless tyrants and not fit to live.

The Home Secretary did not seem unduly worried, though police spies returned to Charlestown services, thus giving Stephens a fine opportunity to denounce the 'outrage' and to threaten legal action after a service was disturbed.[34]

Nothing revealed his new attitude more than his consent to stand for election in 1848 as a poor law Guardian. He did so 'on the express understanding that he hates the law of Malthus, and will thwart, bend or break it to the utmost of his power, whenever the parish and the poor would be gainers thereby'. He was elected, though the Board was dominated by the Malthusian Abel Buckley Wimpenny. In May, he was appointed to a committee to consider the employment of those seeking relief. It recommended settlement on the land, and came to a conditional understanding for acquiring an initial seven acres. The able-bodied unemployed would cultivate it, and eventually would become tenants. The Board adopted the report. London did not object, but wanted further details. The Board then fixed the relief at fivepence a day. Soldiers were entering Ashton during the Guardians meeting, as an indignant Stephens declared they would need them all 'to ram Mr Wimpenny's fivepence a day rate down the throats of honest, hard-working Ashton labourers'. The decision was 'monstrously cruel', and Stephens disassociated himself in writing from the Board's pro-ceedings; but though the Ashton Guardians agreed with him, others in the Union complied, and the farm was now, in Stephens' words, 'a penal settlement'.[35]

He took up individual cases of injustice by his fellow Guardians. Ann Flinders had died in the workhouse, and her daughter was refused the body until the burial club money due to her was paid to the workhouse for maintenance and funeral expenses. Although the body was ultim-ately released to the daughter, Stephens fought for an inquiry, and exposed it all in the *Ashton Chronicle* as 'robbing the living, dishonouring the dead, wrangling over the grave in the hour of sorrow and affliction'. He opposed the building of the new workhouse, with its labour test and its 'degrading jail-like regulations'. He issued vigorous letters to the ratepayers for the elections of April 1849, in which he emphasized that insufficient earnings was the cause of English pauperism. He answered accusations of extravagance against him and his friends on the Board. He was not re-elected, apparently because of spoilt voting papers; his ally Abel Swann alleged sharp practice by cotton masters. He failed again in 1851, but he kept a close, unfriendly eye on the Board's proceedings. In 1858 he attacked mismanagement and harsh conditions in the new workhouse; the central Poor Law Board intervened, and Wimpenny was forced to admit mismanagement, though he resisted Stephens' demand for an enquiry. Forced to hold one, Wimpenny excluded the Ashton press; but in December Stephens was vindicated, for 'every charge we have made has been substantiated by the Guardians'. The workhouse master resigned, but Wimpenny continued to refuse information to the press, much to the indignation of Stephens.[36]

He was convinced that the 'truly appalling' social condition of the people would encourage extremism, especially as some Lancashire cotton masters were determined to evade the law. It was this that made Stephens return to the fold of the factory reformers. Fielden's Act limited hours, but did not specify the time that work should cease; its intention was frustrated by the use of relays at staggered intervals. Thus factory machinery ran continuously, with operatives forced to accept intervening periods of idleness that kept them on factory premises up to fifteen hours a day. Factory inspector Horner concluded: 'no restriction on the hours of work could be enforced in the factories of artful men'. Trade improved and law evasion increased as more firms adopted relays to remain competitive; little attempt was made to prosecute offenders, and success encouraged the masters to petition for the Act's repeal. The factory movement revived, and by the end of 1848 it prepared for a new campaign to defend the law.

Stephens shared the traditional belief of Lancashire reformers that enforceable reform depended upon restriction of the moving power of factory machinery. The *Ashton Chronicle* exposed local breaches of the law, and as early as October 1848 its editor had memorialized the Home Secretary about them. He attacked Hindley, who made complacent speeches while his factory manager broke the law. 'Between God and Mammon, Mr Hindley must make his deliberate choice.' He drew attention to another master, John Leech, who was prosecuted for breaches of the Act, but whose case was dismissed by Abel Buckley, Ashton's Mayor and Hindley's brother-in-law. Shortly afterwards, the relay system was introduced in Leech's factory. Stephens in Stalybridge town hall moved a resolution declaring no confidence in the local bench, and asking the Lord Chancellor to take action. When women at Leech's mill left work after ten hours, millowners responded with lock-outs and dismissals.[37]

The reformers differed on the right response to relays. The lawbreaking masters had exposed a serious weakness in the Act of 1847, and their demand for a compromise over hours was persuasive. Some reformers wanted strikes, others an appeal to Parliament to uphold the Act; the plea for a new organization proved to be divisive. Hindley and Thomas Mawdsley founded the Society for the Protection of the Ten Hours' Act. Stephens, suspicious of any organization in which Hindley had a leading role, opposed strikes, and urged law enforcement and restrictions on the moving power. In April 1849, the old organization revived, and the government was memorialized to enforce the Act. On 29 May, the cause suffered a major blow with the sudden death of John Fielden, who had petitioned against relays and had counselled against violence; in mid-June it suffered another, when Home Secretary Grey promised to legalize relays, with Lord Ashley supporting a compromise of ten and a half or eleven hours, if the operatives agreed. The reformers now spoke with three voices. some wanted a compromise over hours (Ashley and Hindley), others demanded direct action (Mawdsley and the Lancashire central committee), while the majority resolved to defend Fielden's Act by constitutional means (Oastler, Stephens, and the sons of John Fielden). In September the last group formed the Fielden Society, with Stephens' new paper *The Champion* (successor to the *Ashton Chronicle*) as its organ.

Once more the ten hours cause was threatened by 'rotten friends and open foes', and Stephens minced no words. 'The battle we have to fight needs other leaders than Ashley and Hindley. They are not the men for it.' Compromise over hours meant the repeal of the Act for the benefit of lawbreakers, and merited 'the severest reprobation'. Ashley resented the criticisms of Oastler, Stephens and Sam Fielden, and thought the operatives would not listen to them; he failed to understand northern feelings for the principle of a ten hours' day. As for the real culprits, Stephens asked: 'What are we to think when masters who break the law . . . for the sake of sordid gain are looked upon as gentlemen by the world and recognized as Christians by the church?' As for the relay system: 'Down with it, or else away to jail or the hulks for those who persist in resorting to it.' He opposed passive disobedience and strike calls, and rebuffed the Lancashire central committeee's attack on Oastler. As a member of the Fielden Society's council, he took an active part in campaigning, and forming new branches. He was impressed by the growing support of Christian ministers; in November, almost all the Stalybridge clergy and ministers petitioned against relays.[38]

The crisis came in February 1850, after Baron Parke in a test case legalized relays. An angry Stephens blamed Ashley for the outcome. Fielden's Act was a dead letter, and northern reformers urged a new declaratory act banning relays and fixing working hours between six in the morning and six at night. Stephens wanted to add a curb on the moving power and a stringent punishment clause for offenders. A compromise between the Fielden Society and the Lancashire central committee to entrust a new bill to Ashley and two other Parliamentary leaders failed when the central committee denounced it as an insult to Ashley. The Fielden Society repudiated the committee, and asked the three leaders to present a new declaratory bill to be prepared by Richard Cobbett. Stephens took a leading part in this conference, and hoped to do the same in the campaign that was envisaged; but disaster was to follow.

The government accepted the case for a ten and a half hour day. Ashley refused the Fielden Society's resolutions, and accepted a government offer to abolish relays in return for agreement to the ten and a half hour day. Stephens, Oastler and even the central committee reacted strongly. On 27 May, Oastler, Stephens, the Fieldens and others denounced Ashley's 'treachery'. The government then defeated Ashley's attempt to include children in the six-to-six working day laid down in Sir George Grey's new bill, and just as easily defeated a ten hours amendment. Relays of children were still possible, and the ten hours principle was lost. Stephens lamented:

> The meanness of the Manchester school has triumphed over the honour of the English gentleman . . . Free Trade in everything, especially in flesh and blood, is henceforth to be the order of the day. As one of these millowners said lately, 'Bone is cheaper than iron!'[39]

The Lords passed the bill, Stephens noting the vote of Prince Lee, the first bishop of Manchester, against the ten hours amendment: 'There is something very shocking, very loathsome, in the sight of a bishop standing up to cover the wrong doer and crush the defenceless victim of injustice'. Grey's Act became law. It provided for a sixty-hour week within specified hours; evenings were free, and there was a half-day on Saturdays. For the Fielden Society, all this was offset by the betrayal of the ten hours principle and the cause of the factory child. Young children still worked after their elders had left the mills; thus in the judgment of Stephens, 'the name of Lord Ashley would for ever stink in the nostrils of honest men'. Understandable though it was, it was not a judgment history was to uphold.[40]

Inevitably the factory movement declined, though Stephens and Joshua Fielden continued to attack Grey's Act. He took part in the campaign for John Cobbett's bill in 1852 to restore the ten hour day for children; but Cobbett withdrew it when Palmerston, the Home Secretary promised to limit children's labour and establish a uniform working day. This he did in a bill that soon became law. A further attempt by Cobbett in 1855 to restore the Act of 1847 was defeated. Despite all their regrets, the reformers had overcome deep-rooted opposition to establish the principle of factory legislation; they knew it was too widely accepted ever to be abandoned, and that it would be extended to cover other trades. Former political opponents such as Sir James Graham and J. A. Roebuck had been converted. Stephens had long been committed to an eight-hour day, and he continued to appear on Fielden Society platforms. With Oastler and Bull in 1859, he spoke at Mossley of 'the then shameless factory system', and urged everyone to see that the law was strictly observed. The ailing Oastler was delighted by his old friend. 'He is still the same as ever . . . Make much of him; he will do you good.' At Oldham in 1860, Stephens praised John Fielden as 'the man of all men' who had brought the ten hours agitation to a first victory. Oastler, Bull and Stephens made a last united effort to oppose the renewal of the apprenticeship system. Oastler died in 1861, and although Stephens does not appear to have been present at the funeral, he preached an eloquent, long remembered memorial sermon to 'one of the best men this or any other country ever produced'.[41]

The early fifties were a watershed in Stephens' life. In the seven months after October 1851, he lost a daughter, wife and mother, all of whom died at his mother's home at Hutton in Essex. The links with his Methodist past were breaking, and in 1852 he went to live at Stalybridge with his old friend and disciple Abel Swann. On 19 May 1857 he married a farmer's daughter, Susanna Shaw, at Dalbury in Derbyshire. Between June 1858 and June 1859, they moved to The Hollins, a fine new house in the Cheetham Hill Road at Stalybridge, where he continued to live until his death. On their wedding day, the bridegroom was fifty-two, the bride not yet nineteen; his daughter Henrietta was a year older than his new wife. The two young women were acquainted, as Swann in his old age remembered that Susanna 'had come over with Miss Stephens from school on a visit'. He added that 'she was almost as clever as her husband, and could write as vigorous newspaper articles as he could'. Other than this, Susanna remains obscure. Only two of their six children survived infancy, and only one, Arthur Cornwall Stephens, was to marry and perpetuate this branch of the family. By the time of his second marriage, Stephens had private means, and the foundation of his well-stocked library and his collection of oil paintings date from this time. Years of intensive, continuous agitation began to take their toll. Though he was not quite forty-five, he wrote in February 1850 that he was 'too old to be unduly excited' by the legalization of relays. While his was never a quiet, placid ministry, the absence of nationwide agitation after 1852 enabled him to enjoy nine years of a rather less hectic existence. It was appropriate, for the morning storm clouds of threatened revolution were passing away, and the sunshine of settled Victorian prosperity was beginning to appear through the gloom.[42]

7

The Sobered Reformer

'Stephens is changed', cried the astonished radicals of August 1839. Most social historians have echoed the cry, and seem little interested in him after 1839. It is generally assumed that the change was political; the agitator became a Conservative, and in the words of Robert Lowery (who in 1856 should have known better), 'he did not mingle in public with any party again'. A *Times* editorial of 1842 actually called him a Conservative. Holyoake in 1882 agreed, and devoted a chapter in his biography to 'the two kinds of Conservatism'. Stephens's nephew Stephens Storr wrote a preface in which this was qualified: 'In politics, his leanings were Conservative.' He added that the late Lord Derby and the late John Arthur Roebuck 'were the public men with whom his heart beat most in unison'. The label 'Tory radical' is still the commonest description of his politics.[1]

As Robert Lowery confessed, 'Stephens was a riddle to many a man of shrewd judgment'. He was no more a Conservative after 1839 than he had been a radical before it. He repudiated party loyalties as unworthy of a patriot, and urged his followers to be non-party and non-sectarian. Although he said this time and again, few could bring themselves to believe it. Unlike others who repudiate party and create one of their own, he remained a solitary figure. In a sense he was a true reactionary, looking back to a remote English past before party existed. For example, in 1840, he spelt out what he meant by universal suffrage:

> ... I am for the free choice of the people in wardmote, and boroughmote, and countrymote assembled. I would go back to the days when there were no registration courts, no revising barristers, no electoral lists, no polling in booths by law-clerks with their check books and bribery oaths – and above all, no ballot box; but when the people came to hear the king's writ, and proceeded by a show of hands, and then if it were necessary, by counting the heads or 'polls', to declare on whom their choice had fallen.

No political party in the nineteenth century adopted such eccentric views. It is misleading to classify true reactionaries as extreme Conservatives; no one in Peel's Conservative party seriously contemplated a return to archaic electoral conditions. Despite his upbringing and his Oastlerite convictions, Stephens continued to repudiate the Conservative label, and it was not surprising that he was never chosen as a Conservative candidate. In July 1841 he wrote: 'Neither the Whig nor the Tory party is prepared to give to the people their ancient and constitutional rights; to place them within the pale of the law, and to protect them from the tyranny to which they are exposed'. He co-operated with parties only to further his real aims, which were, as he truthfully said at his trial, factory reform and the repeal of the Poor Law Amendment Act. After 1841, he could do it no longer through the Chartists and radicals. The Whigs were the party of his manufacturing and ideological opponents; only the Tories remained, and only a few even among them shared his social aims. In 1837, on the one occasion he stood for Parliament, he was an independent; he never ceased to be one.[2]

Nor is it true that after 1841 he repudiated his former aims. All of them reappeared in the *People's Magazine*; there was even a hint of physical force. Yet he was more cautious in what he wrote, and his style was more sober, if less exciting, than the speeches of previous years. the only change of aim was over disestablishment. As late as July 1841, he wrote: 'The connection of the church with the state is the great cause of Sectarianism, with its innumerable abominations.' By December of the same year – the year of the *Fleet Papers* – his views were 'Oastlerized':

> In the theory of the English constitution, the church is the fundamental and predominant idea. Our commonwealth is to be looked upon as a collection and consolidation of families ... It becomes, therefore, the bounden duty of the State to acknowledge the only living and true God ... and to provide the means of fitting and seemly worship on behalf and for the sake of the whole people ... The Church is more especially intended to be the divine defender, guardian, and refuge of the poor against the encroachments of the worldly spirit of Mammon ...

It was the logical culmination of Oastler's influence upon his thinking. He had been impressed by the support given by many northern clergy for the factory and anti-poor law struggles. Nevertheless, he never became an Anglican priest. Although there were many Anglicans among them, millowners were frequently identified with Dissent, and that suggested a motive for the apathy of Dissenting and Methodist churches towards the causes Stephens had at heart.[3]

By the late forties, his attitudes had hardened. Anglican renewal brought a new generation of mainly northern Irish Evangelical priests into south east Lancashire. Energetic men like William Heffill of Dunkinfield, Thomas Floyd of Stalybridge, Thomas Eager of Audenshaw and Williams of Ashton created new Anglican parishes, and were actively concerned with the plight of the poor. Stephens welcomed them as allies, and contrasted them with Dissenting ministers who 'have fawned and flattered the factory master'. In fact, 'Dissent is a growth out of the derangement of our nature'. If at times Dissent was necessary and beneficial, when the church resumed her proper office, 'she is enabled to exert her inherent virtue'. Stephens had come a long way from 1834. He had nothing in common with Edward Miall, who combined militant advocacy of disestablishment with the ideals of *laissez-faire* industrialism. By the late fifties, a younger generation of Dissenters was supporting Liberalism and social reform; there were even paternal Dissenting millowners with a genuine concern for their operatives. Hugh Mason himself became one of them, his employees at New Oxford Mills enjoying the highest wages in the district, good working conditions and many amenities; but he and Stephens remained mutually incomprehensible.[4]

There was a real change in Stephens after 1841, but it was theological rather than political. Prison reflection on the failure of Chartism in 1839 led him to conclude that God's revolution could not be equated with the ups and downs of current radical agitation; it was altogether more gradual in its outworking. His father's letter in October 1840 reinforced this; clearly it made an impression, for it appeared in his later publications. Stephens never doubted that God's revolution would come. In the words of his poem on his monument, 'this wilderness of evil must be clothed with heavenly bloom'. Nor did he doubt that it would be fierce when it came. Writing of factory labour by women and children, he wrote in the first issue of the *People's Magazine*:

Is it not right, is it not high time the wrath of a holy God was poured out upon us, for the awful sin of ever having suffered such a monstrous violation of nature to become a common household thing with us. Yea, and indeed it is; and God only knows whether the day of grace be not already gone down, and the night of his fierce anger even now darkening upon us!

His conclusion was that 'there may be a lull, but the storm is not laid':

> Our prayer is, that heaven in mercy would give us back an Alfred – one who should restore the goodly works of old, and make merry England her happy self again! But whether an Alfred or a Robespierre, the poor must be righted, or their wrongs will be fearfully avenged.[5]

However strong this sounded, it was unbacked by any commitment to radical agitation; it recognized the current lull, and that God alone knew when and how it would end. In practice, this recognition meant a great change of perspective and mood. The lull had to be taken seriously; reform of an existing order, rather than refusal to accept it or revolution to overthrow it, became all important. Slowly and painfully, and not without occasional reversion to earlier attitudes, Stephens began to come to terms with secular reality. The clearest sign of this was his acceptance of office as a poor law Guardian in 1848; opposition to the hated law of Malthus was to be within the law, and not outside it. In the renewed factory struggle, the reformers were defending the law they had carried to victory against lawless masters. Another indicator was an almost complete silence on the subject of physical force. Gone too was the feverish mood of 1838 and 1839. His new preference for the written over the spoken word resulted in a sober, even ponderous, style (though as with his sermons, he was criticized for not citing enough detailed facts to support his arguments).[6]

By the time he moved to Stalybridge, more settled times had come. Stalybridge was a growing cotton community with an excitable population. It had a high literacy rate for an industrial town, and many cultural activities; unlike its rival Ashton, it lacked parliamentary representation, and since 1828 it had been ruled by twenty-one town commissioners (one of them was that staunch Stephenite Abel Swann). Only after much party strife did it gain a charter of incorporation in 1857, when a Liberal became the first mayor.[7]

The better times had a more general origin. In spite of all he had believed, the repeal of the corn laws stabilized the price of bread, and blunted the keen edge of class politics. The dominance of Manchester school economics neither destroyed aristocratic government, nor prevented subsequent social reform. In peace and prosperity, a national consensus began to emerge. Pride in British industrial achievement as symbolized in the Great Exhibition of 1851 became widespread. Conditions were improved by administrative reform, vigorous municipal enterprise, more cultural amenities and a broadening philanthropy. The bleak rigour of economic theory remained; but the years of agitation mitigated its worst social effects. Thanks to government publications as well as factory reform and anti-poor law propaganda, public opinion had been moved by revelations of cruelty and poverty. Oastler in 1846 said that the atrocities of factory labour belonged to a bygone age; no longer were children slain, driven to suicide, or lashed. Even the Poor Law Board moderated the severity of the law of 1834. In 1852 it allowed conditional outdoor relief for the able-bodied. Squalor and injustice continued to abound, but redress was seen to be possible by reform. The language of revolution died away as it was seen that 'progress' could serve more than one end.[8]

If most of his views remained intact, the range of his activities increased. He attached particular importance to his press work. Although the *People's Magazine* soon failed, the *Ashton Chronicle* was the first successful Ashton newspaper, and its successor the *Champion* was the organ of the Fielden Society. The editor declared in its last issue that 'our pen will be immediately transferred . . . to a work of a more extensive and serious character'. He contributed stories to the short-lived *Ashton Ricker*, and the even shorter-lived *Ashton Weekly Herald*. The latter's successor as the Conservative rival to the *Ashton Reporter* was the *Ashton Standard*. The style and content of the editorials in its first year (1858–9) strongly suggest that Stephens was its first editor. It is accepted that he was the first editor of the *Oldham Standard*, which first appeared in August 1859. So highly did he rate all this that in the census of 1861, he described himself not as a minister, but as a 'yeoman and newspaper editor'.[9]

Education was another interest. In 1841, the People's School was opened by the Stephenites in Brierley Street, Stalybridge for Sunday school children of all denominations. Seven years later, Stephens took a leading part in opposing the Lancashire Public School Association, which had the support of Charles Hindley and Hugh Mason. Their plan for county boards to levy rates, build and control schools, train teachers and give undenominational Bible teaching awoke his dislike of centralization. He objected to the self-elected first board, with its powers to 'make a new Bible' and to overrule local educational bodies. At two lively meetings in Ashton town hall in early 1848, he denounced the scheme and preached against it to nearly two thousand people in a Charlestown service. He attacked 'the hasty, covert and overbearing manner in which a system, so thoroughly novel, so sectarian, so arbitrary as this, was attempted to be palmed upon the people, and passed to the legislature as having received the sanction of their deliberate judgment'. (Eventually, greater public support was given to an alternative scheme of free education which supplemented rather than replaced existing facilities, with control by municipal councils and an effective conscience clause on religion.)

His approach to primary education was determined by his desire to keep women and children out of factories to enjoy the blessings of home. He had no sympathy with 'artificial' infant schools, preferring a parental relationship that would not encourage a child to read before the age of seven. He thought that six months schooling at that age would make the child comparable to one of the same age who had been to school from the age of three. From the experience of being too tired to read or write after working alongside his own field labourers, he was doubtful about universal literacy; but since talent could be found in all classes, he decided to provide for adults whose education had been neglected in earlier life. He founded Christ College on 4 November 1856. It met at the People's School. Students paid twopence a week for an English education, and fourpence for foreign languages; there was a picture gallery, a library and a museum. Stephens himself and the Stephenite schoolmaster John Avison lectured, and among the students were the town commissioner Abel Swann, the naturalist Jethro Tinker, and the young Stephenite James France. At its inauguration in March 1857, all the speakers stressed the vital connection of education with religion.[10]

Late in 1847 he crossed swords with local teetotal societies, and the militant itinerant teetotal lecturer Dr F. R. Lees. Although virtually a teetotaller himself, Stephens disliked the hardening of the teetotal movement towards prohibition, the divorce of drinking from its economic and social context, the attempt to interpret the Bible according to teetotal principles, and the attack on the ancient institution of the public house. The ten hours battle appeared to be won, and no longer did he think that his voluntary abstinence should compel workers to conform. Within months, he was challenged to debate teetotalism on scriptural grounds. He and his friends agreed with the Stalybridge Teetotal Society on the rules of the debate and the wording of the motion – 'that the use of intoxicating drinks is absolutely sinful, being plainly forbidden by the word of God'. Dr Lees was asked to move it, and at once raised objections. Logical, pedantic and humourless, Lees was not the man to be bound by local arrangements. Stephens agreed to discuss a new motion, provided he was released from the original engagement; but the local teetotal society would not withdraw.

The subsequent negotiations rapidly degenerated into a three-sided quarrel in which published correspondence was disputed, and agreement proved impossible. Stephens played effectively on the differences between the Stalybridge teetotallers and Dr Lees. When it was claimed that the original proposition did not advance a basic teetotal principle, Stephens insisted that the local society admit this, as they stated the opposite in writing. For his part, Lees denied that he had refused the original proposition, accused Stephens of evasion, and issued a placard in Stalybridge charging the 'Ashton buffoon' with cowardice. Stephens made a last minute attempt to reach agreement for a debate, but he failed. He invited those interested to go to the town hall 'for a full view of the ass in a lion's skin'. He was lecturing too, attacking teetotallers who acted like common informers in entering widow's houses where two or three friends played innocent games of dominoes. 'If every man in Stalybridge was teetotal today, they would not have a halfpenny more wage.' A subsequent meeting of the Ashton Teetotal Society to consider the Stalybridge affair degenerated into violence. Although the Ashton teetotallers pursued the idea of a debate, Stephens would only debate on the original terms, and even then not with unprincipled persons. He intended to protect the public against 'a set of needy adventurers whose chief means of obtaining a livelihood appears to be a course of itinerant lecturing for money'. There the matter rested.[11]

Stephens was involved in local politics too. In the Crimean war, he seconded the vote of thanks at a Stalybridge patriotic fund meeting. His maverick attitude to politics was seen in 1857, when he shared a platform with Hugh Mason and Charles Hindley in support of the combative Whig Prime Minister, Lord Palmerston, whose Chinese policy had led to a temporary resignation. However, at a by-election in December 1857 after Hindley's sudden death, Stephens supported the Conservative candidate Booth Mason, Hugh Mason's brother. Hugh Mason was mayor, and the Liberal candidate Milner Gibson was a determined opponent of factory legislation; once more Ashton elected the Liberal. Stephens subsequently denounced Ashton's Whig establishment as 'a political warming-pan – a forty shilling pocket borough for a party'. Neither did Conservatives once high in his esteem escape his criticism. In 1858, Ashley (now Lord Shaftesbury) was attacked in an

Ashton Standard editorial. 'We would not trust the cause of the factory workers to his hands, and we by no means augur good from his meddling with the patronage of the Church. Lord Shaftesbury is a thorough Erastian – with him the State is everything, and the Church nothing.'[12]

Nor had Stephens forgotten his trade union interests. In 1860 he chaired two Stalybridge meetings to support the ongoing Padiham strike for the standard rate of pay, and to urge local workers to join the newly formed North Cheshire Amalgamated Factory Operatives Union. At both the Rev E. A. Verity of Clitheroe was the speaker, and after the outspoken speeches of both clerics, union membership increased. Stephens went further afield in the trade union cause. In November 1863, during a Leeds miners' dispute, he urged an eight-hour day as the most a man's body could bear for survival to old age. He was appointed chaplain of the newly formed Miner's National Association, and was one of a deputation to encourage colliers in a South Yorkshire lock-out. In 1864, he was present at the miner's conference, and he spoke at least twice in the Leeds iron workers' lock-out. The following year he spoke at Dewsbury on the need for unions.[13]

His many and varied activities did not prevent him from taking part in the wider life of Stalybridge. In 1857 he took a keen interest in the Philharmonic Society, attending concerts, speaking at celebrations, and presiding over the annual general meeting. He was an enthusiast for the Turkish baths, and in 1861 he spoke at the local baths' anniversary. He gave a history of the Turkish bath, testified to its beneficial results, and commended its use. In the same year, he began an annual visit to the Stalybridge old folks tea party; he told his elderly hearers that he had been known in the neighbourhood as 'old Stephens' for the past twenty-five years. In 1862, he returned to Woodhouse Grove School to speak briefly at its fiftieth anniversary. He was well received by a large Methodist audience.[14]

He might have been forgiven if he thought that this pleasing round of activities in easier circumstances would continue until his retirement; by 1862, after thirty years of local ministry, he was considering retirement to the Isle of Man or the Isle of Wight to write a history of the working classes. (In fact, he was never to leave Stalybridge, nor to write his history.) Four years earlier, he had urged local ministers to greater effort in the cause of the poor:

We wish all disputes about the rules and doctrines of the Church could . . . be forgotten in a holy rivalry, in a noble effort to relieve the distresses of the poor and the sick . . . Let the priesthood become a real *Ministry for the Poor*; not confined to the Church and the sickroom, but operating on the daily life of the poor. To reclaim the vicious, to counsel the improvident, to raise new hopes in the desponding, to be the friend and benefactor of all, is a noble mission. To instruct and relieve the poor is more God-like than to minister to the rich.

In 1862, his words came back to challenge him, as a civil war in north America seemed to cast its shadow over the Lancashire cotton mills, and a serious depression brought new problems and hardship to his people.[15]

8

The Cotton Famine

In the three years preceding the outbreak of the American civil war, the British cotton industry reached its zenith. By 1860, imports and exports were booming, and industrial capacity greatly increased. Raw cotton accounted for 17% of the value of British imports, and cotton manufactures for 38.3% of the value of British exports; the industry adding 7.5% to the value of the gross national income. The best and cheapest cotton came from the United States of America, which in 1860 supplied 80% of the imported cotton. 64.5% of the industry's manufactured goods were exported, mainly to India, the United States, Turkey and China. In the fifties, exports of piece goods doubled in value, and exports of yarn increased by 50%.

Inevitably there was a reaction when markets at home and abroad could no longer absorb all that could be produced. Already by 1860 there was a consequent decline of trade in England and also in India, where a succession of bad harvests destroyed the prosperity of Lancashire's most important overseas market. Orders declined, but manufacture for stock greatly increased. By February 1861 prosperity had given way to depression, as increased costs and lower prices led to the first attempts to lower wages. Thus two months before the outbreak of the American civil war, the cotton famine had begun, and it was a famine of demand, and not of supply.

This was obscured by the outbreak of the civil war in April 1861. Within a year, the supply of American cotton from the South was cut off by an increasingly effective Northern blockade, giving to many in Britain the impression that there was a famine of supply. Moreover, since the short-time working in cotton factories began only after the outbreak of hostilities, the war could be blamed very conveniently for the results of saturated markets and the contradictions of Manchester School economics. As distress in Lancashire deepened, therefore, it came to be widely accepted that the war was the cause of the depression.

The actual impact of the war was far more ambivalent. At first, it was expected to be short, and the accumulated stocks of American cotton, which kept prices low for much of 1861, indicated that there would be no immediate shortage of supply. The prospect of a short war faded with the initial Southern victories, and during the worst period of the cotton famine, large stocks of inferior Indian Surat cotton remained in Liverpool warehouses, some of it re-exported for the profit of speculators. Far from the war involving universal ruin within the cotton industry, the holders of cotton stock at least could anticipate promising rewards.[1]

Because of its supposed impact on the Lancashire cotton industry, the war was not viewed in Britain in a detached spirit. Support for the South in factory towns was far stronger than was once thought. Only a minority of unemployed workers were prepared to suffer in silence for a noble Northern cause; and that the Northern cause was noble was far from clear in 1861, since the war began over secession from the union, not over the abolition of slavery. Stephens himself has been called a Southern supporter. His editorials in the *Oldham Standard* were far more critical of the North than supportive of the South. In 1861, he affected a lofty British superiority to American quarrels – 'We flatter ourselves that a similar breach would hardly have happened anywhere else among Saxon kinsmen.' He thought that the constitution of the United States had broken down irretrievably, and he grievously under-estimated President Lincoln – as did some within his own administration. Disdain became pugnacity late in the year over the Trent affair, when a Northern warship removed two Southern agents from an unarmed British vessel. 'How upon earth are we much longer to maintain amicable relations with the ignorant, fanatical, and blood thirsty masses that constitute the town population of the Northern States of America?' It was an accurate reflection of temporarily inflamed British opinion, outraged by a high-handed Northern action on a British ship, rather than moved by any anxiety for the fate of Southern agents. Slavery was anathema to Stephens, and there is no known instance of his supporting the recognition of the Confederacy.[2]

The acid test came in 1862, when the Northern blockade denied Southern cotton to Lancashire mills, and distress began. Yet Stephens opposed joint Anglo-French mediation in the war; it was 'no business of ours anyhow'. At Stalybridge in September, Abel Swann – usually a barometer for the views of his minister – opposed recognition of the South in a formal debate, arguing that recognition meant war with the North and British acceptance of a system of slavery. There were powerful voices being raised for the recognition of the South. In October Gladstone, the Whig Chancellor of the Exchequer, spoke out in its favour. On 1 November, an *Oldham Standard* editorial urged non-interference in American troubles, and unexpectedly praised the free trader Richard Cobden's statement to that effect:

> For us to meddle in any way would be a wilder act than that which we charge upon the Americans in rushing to arms as the most direct means of composing their differences. To do this would inevitably involve us in a war with the North, and what would be the consequences of that? Would it bring us those four million bales of cotton that our wistful eyes are ever turned to, and set our mills to work again? No . . . Mr Cobden deserves all praise for this well-reasoned and impressive statement . . . Let us hope that gentlemen of position and influence, no matter to what particular class they may belong, will listen to the counsels of one who has advised them so well.

Stephens did not allow any dislike of the North to determine his attitude to British involvement in the war.[3]

Stephens understood that it was not the war, but the preceding over-production that was responsible for the cotton famine. As early as February 1861, an editorial had declared: 'We have made more stuff than we can sell.' In May, he criticized the Manchester cotton exchange for ignoring the lack of demand, and allowing large stocks of cotton to accumulate. 'Masters ought at once to limit their production, and the operatives ought, as far as they are able, to make what readiness they can against the rainy day that is coming.' The Cotton Supply Association had warned others, but had risked nothing to secure future supply. In December 1862, Stephens praised Lord Derby for his organization of relief at county level – 'Lancashire owes more to Lord Derby than to any other public man.' His son Lord Stanley had seen that over-production, not the war alone, was responsible for the famine. Stephens concluded:

> This great cotton trade, for the extension of which every other national interest has been sacrificed, rests upon a foundation of sand. We know not as yet whether it can recover (from) the blow it is now reeling under. And if it should, there is nothing to prevent a recurrence of the calamity. The whole factory system requires parliamentary revision and regulation. We produce more than the world can consume. There must be fewer mills, or as mills increase,

the hours of labour must be still further limited. Is there no other way out of the difficulty?

Three weeks later, Stephens noted the excessive hours worked in some Yorkshire woollen mills, and urged a new Factory Act with an eight-hour day and restrictions on the moving power of machinery. In all this, he showed true insight.[4]

The famine was at its worst in Ashton and Stalybridge, which had little alternative employment. Conflict began in March 1861, when employers refused arbitration by the South Lancashire Weavers Union, and insisted on wage reductions. Workers refused to accept it, and lock-outs followed. Unemployment rose, and by April south-east Lancashire and north-east Cheshire had 30,000 operatives out of work, including 4,500 at Ashton and 4,200 at Stalybridge. Against union advice, a great number of weavers visited the area to summon local weavers still at work to join them. Large and potentially ugly open-air meetings complete with banners, music and fiery oratory were held in March and April. Leaders like Jonathan Bintcliffe attacked 'capitalist oppression' and 'wage slavery' to gatherings of between 5,000 and 12,000 operatives. Starvation forced a return to work in May, and the weaver's union was destroyed. In April 1862 a letter to the *Ashton Reporter* spoke of the 'smouldering embers of dissatisfaction, which . . . will explode with a violence too terrible to be conceived'.[5]

The poor rate soared, and by the summer the poor law authorities were forced to suspend the hated labour test. By 1863, the Ashton Guardians were spending over £200,000 on indoor and outdoor relief. This was more than in Manchester; but all over the county, further relief was needed. The famine was seen as a national calamity, and voluntary relief contributions poured into Lancashire. Controlled by a central committee in Manchester, and distributed through a network of local committees, this relief created further problems. Fierce dispute arose over the fairness of its distribution; more important still, it was tied to the poor law system, which branded recipients of its own relief as paupers. Care was taken that scales of relief were not more generous than those of the Guardians. Grants were made to local committees for the creation of education and sewing classes for the unemployed, and regular attendance was made a test for receiving relief. The indignity of this scheme in practice, the unelected character of the local committees and the niggardly poor law spirit pervading their work aroused widespread discontent among the proudly independent Lancashire workers.[6]

The relief committees were a focal point of wider discontent. They tended to be composed of millowners and their allies, and thus had a Dissenting image. Unhappily the famine coincided with Dissent's bicentenary celebrations to mark their forefathers' ejectment from the Establishment; in the prevailing tension, the strident Protestantism of the Liberation Society grated on the strong Irish Catholic minorities who had suffered most from the distress. In Ashton, where the Dissenter and Liberationist Hugh Mason was the leading figure on the relief committee, a dispute in August 1862 involving Stephens' clerical allies led to all ministers of religion being excluded from the committee; the Anglican members promptly formed another. Fear that sectarian conflict could affect the distribution of relief was aired in the Ashton press. The *Reporter* contrasted disruptive Anglican attitudes with Dissenting attempts to provide relief funds from their own sources. Most churches of differing traditions offered their premises for the compulsory classes.

The crisis galvanized Stephens into activity. Gone was his desire to retire; he determined never to leave his people. In January 1862 his friend Dr John Bridges, physician to Bradford Infirmary and a *Times* correspondent, wrote to the editor of the trade union journal that 'old Stephens' had 'recovered all the energy of his youth' in allying Lancashire and Yorkshire workers in pursuit of an eight-hour day. Despite poor health, he advised Stalybridge operatives in March 1862 that 'it was a time when they should be particularly calm'. He moved a resolution against the labour test in a petition to the Mayor, Dr Robert Hopwood, and was loudly applauded. An *Oldham Standard* editorial expressed satisfaction at 'the bold, unmeasured and uncompromising manner in which the clergy denounced the New Poor-Law'. Even a few Stalybridge employers signed the petition.[7]

His attention was soon drawn to the activities of the Stalybridge relief committee. It had arisen in November 1861 among members of the Spinners and Minders Association. Its efforts were soon outstripped by growing distress, and the Mayor called two town hall meetings to enlist greater support. Soon afterwards a deputation of leading millowners – among them John Frederick Cheetham, son of John Cheetham and eventually the wealthiest Stalybridge millowner – made modest contributions, and joined the committee. At first Stephens agreed to commend it, but as he learned more, he changed his mind. It had a Dissenting image. Although the committee allowed ministers to attend, the few who did so soon fell away. Its small, unelected membership soon attracted criticism, which it resented. Although it received considerable sums from the Lord Mayor of London's fund, its proceedings were cloaked in secrecy until February 1863. Its sharp attitude to relief distribution made it unpopular. In June 1862 the committee wished it to be known that their charity was only for the deserving – 'every precaution will be taken to detect any imposition that may be practised upon them'. Recipients of relief in money were accused in the press of spending it on drink. Other deceivers were punished by witholding their tickets of entitlement for weeks on end, and persistent offenders were refused further help. Subsequent relief was given in bread and meal, and loud complaints about weight and quality led only to complacency. To this was added cant. The committee's press apologist thought it a 'truly noble sight' for men of wealth to be concerned with working-class distress. 'They are earning for themselves a corner in the hearts of the operatives which neither time nor distance can efface.'

In October, an operative deputation called for relief by ticket instead of by provisions. The committee was accused of inducing men to get drunk to stop relief, and of supplying poor bread. The Mayor had declared it unfit for human food. In Dukinfield, a petition for tickets was met by a reduction in the scale of relief. No reason was given to the public, and it was rumoured that the committee wanted to discredit the ticket system. In December 1862 the *Ashton Reporter* pointed to a division within the committee between supporters of relief in kind and relief by ticket, and noted that the prevailing system was bound to result in charges of favouritism and underhanded dealing. There were complaints over the late organization of classes, but by September, almost 400 people met in 28 classes, none of them on church premises. This was remedied by November (but by the following February, there was much resentment over the way the classes were conducted). It was all reported in the leading Ashton newspaper in 1862; despite Mayor Hopwood's later assertion to the contrary, there was much dissatisfaction at the committee's shortcomings before Stephens entered the fray.[8]

The beginning of 1863 saw distress at its height. The South was still winning victories in the war, and demand for cotton goods increased as prices rose and stocks were exhausted. Indian Surat cotton was seen as a poor substitute for American. For the first time, a real cotton famine seemed inevitable; but by the end of the year, the tide of war was turning against the South, and a decline in prices began. In Ashton during January, 1,263 worked full time, 3,111 were on short time, and 6,482 were unemployed; there was little improvement throughout the year.

Excitement in Stalybridge rose as insults met the demand for an explanation for the reduction in relief. The policy of the relief committee, the insensitivity of the Guardians and the miserly attitude of the local wealthy was too much to be borne, and a deputation waited on the Mayor for a public meeting on the subject. The Mayor refused two such requests, even though the second was supported by over 1,400 recipients of relief; it was believed this was the agreed policy of the county's Mayors. Stephens asked his congregation to pray for the committee. Numbers at his church swelled once more when he announced that he would preach on the committee's activities. He said that people had begged him to help them obtain proper relief.[9]

His eagerly awaited sermon revealed that his gift for telling illustrations drawn from life had not deserted him:

> A short time ago, a woman came to his home with a pair of stockings so thin that he had no doubt that when they were washed they would run up so that they would not fit a peastick. She had received them from the Relief committee, and there was something on the top of the leg which she could not make out. After a close examination Mr Stephens found that there were four letters on, which he had now learned should have been S.B.R.F, but by some means the tar had not run properly on the letter B, and it became an E. The letters were thus S.E.R.F . . . and a more appropriate name could not have been chosen for those who wore stockings, or anything else stamped by the Relief committee . . .

While some had bribed the committee's employees for clothes of better quality, others had fared badly:

> . . . another man received a suit of clothes, but the trousers were such that the legs came through them many a time before they got to the bottom. The man took them back, and humbly asked to change them, but he was told to take them to old Stephens, and being a dutiful subject, he did take them to old Stephens, and that gentleman would not part with them for £50.

The operatives were 'a set of cowards' for meekly accepting the insults heaped upon their wives at the committee's store. As for the committee members, they were 'shabby beggars, rogues and fools'. The dining rooms for operatives run by the millowner Leech were dubbed 'Leech's slop-kitchen'. He demanded an elected relief committee, and promised that the meeting refused by the Mayor would be held. The admiring Bridges said of Stephens:

> Now in his old age he mounted the pulpit with a pair of shoddy trousers in his hand and the 10th Psalm for his text – 'Why standest Thou so far off, O Lord, and hidest Thy face in the needful time of trouble? The ungodly for his own lust doth persecute the poor, let them be taken in the crafty wiliness that they have imagined', and thundered out denunciations against the cotton lords, the Boards of Guardians and committee men who were misusing the funds entrusted to them, and doling out rotten material instead of good.[10]

To his friend Frederic Harrison, a pro-union lawyer, Bridges wrote: 'Old Stephens of Stalybridge is the only man who speaks up and out. He has preached about it till the Oldham Guardians have openly defied the London Board, and give relief without oakum'. Bridges and his sister 'worked with all their might under Stephens' direction', despite Harrison's disapproval.[11]

On 2 February, over 1,500 adult males assembled in the Stalybridge town hall, despite the Mayor's refusal to call a meeting. Jonathan Bintcliffe was in the chair, and the Stephenites Abel Swann and James France moved resolutions. For three and a half hours, Stephens 'was listened to . . . with the most breathless attention, only interrupted by repeated responses and bursts of applause'. Stephens recounted his negotiations with Mayor Hopwood and the committee. He told the operatives:

> You are the innocent and the helpless victims of a commercial policy which it was the duty of the legislature to have restrained and checked long since. For five and twenty years I have warned you of the coming of the fearful collapse of your staple trade . . . The markets are still glutted, notwithstanding the partial stoppage of your mills for the last eighteen months. You workmen at all events, are not answerable for the idleness – the idleness! which drives you to the parish and the relief-board. Why then should they treat you with all this disrespect and cruelty?

He answered the Mayor, and clarified his own position:

> The mayor says, this committee has the confidence of the central committee at Manchester and of the Mansion House committee in London. It may have, but when those committees know what their

conduct has been, will that confidence be continued? I do not believe it. I am persuaded that the publicity given to these facts will force an investigation, and that that investigation will lead to a change. My fellow-townsmen know, as I told the mayor, that I have taken no part in your local differences and sectional squabbles. I belong to no party. I have never so much as given a vote since I became a burgess. Nor should I have stepped out now had I not been forced out by the cry of the poor.

He exhibited two pairs of worn-out trousers doled out by the committee; even the Mayor had admitted they were not fit to wear. 'The people do not get what they ought to get – good, plain strong clothing fit for their station.' Gratitude for the generosity of their fellow countrymen had been misrepresented as a desire to live on charity. The committee had wasted money on bad food for the poor, while giving £200 to relieve small shopkeepers. Lord Derby had given more for relief than the combined contributions of Stalybridge's wealthy cotton masters. As for the classes:

> He would no more undergo the school test than he would the labour test (hear hear) . . . He had seen men up to eighty-six years go hobbling and tottering along the street to those schools. He had been both to the educational and the sewing classes, and he had never seen, except in the workhouse or gaol, such sad, downcast, sleepy countenances. When he had visited them some months back, they were lively and cheerful.

The soup they got 'only swelled the belly without lining the ribs'. It was 'most insulting to the working classes' that the Mayor had stopped military drill in Stalybridge, for 'he believed that they could be trusted with arms, and that the exercise was invaluable to them on the point of health alone'. As for committee members who cursed those who came to them for relief:

> If a member of the Relief Committee used such language to his wife or daughter as this, 'Blast you, hook it', he declared that by the God in heaven, either that man or he should go down.

When Stephens finished, a memorial to the Home Secretary summarizing their grievances was agreed unanimously, and the five hour meeting ended.[12]

Stephens's own verdict on the meeting was given in an *Oldham Standard* editorial:

> The proceedings of the crowded meeting held in the Stalybridge town hall on Monday last have lifted the veil which has concealed from the public eye the real condition and temper of the working population.

His intervention reinforced strong local resolve against the cut in relief. Following Oldham, the women's classes in Stalybridge went on strike; in Ashton and Dukinfield, they marched through the streets. Inevitably tension was heightened. In mid-February, Stephens addressed two further meetings at Lees and Oldham. Hundreds were unable to enter a packed People's Hall at Lees to hear Stephens denounce the relief system. ' . . . the distinction between the Board of Guardians and the Relief Committee was a distinction without a difference'. Operatives had as little relief as would keep them alive. 'This was through twenty-nine years of tame submission to an Act of Parliament which was diametrically opposed to the law of God.' A man had a right to live by his labour, and when through no fault of their own, the people of Lees were thrown out of work 'it was the bounden duty of the state . . . to provide labour for them'. He ridiculed 'the new kind of prison houses that were called schools', which men of 73 and women between 90 and 100 were forced to attend. The indignity of mature men seeking permission from 'boy schoolmasters' to fulfil the calls of nature was given short shrift. 'I would make a polite bow to the schoolmaster, and ask him to have the goodness to lend me his hat.'

More serious in its consequences was Stephens's reference to a recent case before the Dukinfield magistrates. Three members of a class had absented themselves without leave. The schoolmaster had stopped a shilling out of their relief, and subsequently they were charged with using threatening language to him. The magistrate, one Alfred Aspland, bound them over with heavy sureties, adding some remarks about an unnamed person who stirred up discontent in the minds of the poor (this was a reference to Stephens's clerical ally, William Heffill of St Mark's Dukinfield). Unable to find the sureties, the three were sent to the Knutsford House of Correction. Stephens learned that Heffill was in trouble with his bishop after complaints had been made about his activities for the poor. He and Stephens agreed to stand bail for the three offenders, who were released. The two parsons were described at the Dukinfield relief committee by 'the great man of the village' as 'fit only for the hulks'. Stephens promised that the Home Secretary would learn how the laws were administered in Dukinfield. Like Mayor Hopwood, Aspland did not forget Stephens' disclosures.[13]

He spoke again a week later at another large meeting in the Oldham Co-operative hall. In the increase of tension throughout the area, his Lees speech had led to criticism, and he spent some time in answering it. As usual, he dismissed all personal abuse. 'Some called him an old Tory when they did not want the people to hear him, but they might call him anything so long as he was not an old Whig.' Some accused him of wearing a cross on his breast, of being a Puseyite or a Romanist, but the cross being worked on his new shirts was in memory of the one he took up in 1863:

> If he were a Roman Catholic, was there any harm in that? He did not deny it or affirm it, for he had not come there to make confession. Still he reiteraated that the members of any religious body had no right to be favoured at the expense of the socialist, the secularist, the infidel, or any other name that might be applied.

This robust and rare unsectarianism was interlaced with his stock criticism of relief committees, and his championship of the three B's for the working classes – bread, beef and beer. He assured the audience that he was better able to do a day's work than he had been thirty years earlier. 'He could talk all day and write all night, and he was ready to go to every town in England.' He sat down amid loud applause.[14]

Amid further disquieting revelations in the press about the relief committee, its three leaders wrote to Manchester to assure the central committee that until the previous Christmas, the operatives 'could not possibly have been quieter'. They had been satisfied with their relief 'until Mr Stephens appeared on the scene':

> He is an old practised demogogue, and understands well how to address masses of people, and has succeeded in gathering around him a few of the operatives of this district. His popularity is confined to (*sic*) within very narrow limits, and any impression he may make upon his audience soon dies away. With reference to any fears as to the safety or general quietness of the town, we can assure you need not be under the slightest fear ... Mr Stephens is perfectly well known here, and his followers in the event of any disturbance of the public peace would be very few ... There can be no tangible ground

for dissatisfaction, if there be any bad feeling in the town, it is entirely owing to the machinations of this ill-conditioned fellow.

This remarkable epistle, later to be passed to the Home Office, was signed R. Hopwood, James Kirk and Ralph Bates.[15] Since the letter was written almost exactly a month before the Stalybridge riot, its prophecy of future peace was no more reliable than its analysis of present unease. The three writers were anxious to retain the goodwill and grants of Manchester; thus they minimized the unrest and exaggerated Stephens's role in it. Bintcliffe's militant pressure, the steady stream of public complaint, and even Stephens' clerical allies were all ignored. By blaming Stephens, Hopwood hid the shortcomings of the relief committee behind the fearsome 'physical force' reputation of its best-known critic. It was but a short step from this to blame him for the riot itself.

The crisis came in March. On the 7th, the 'ill-conditioned fellow' and his ally Heffill spoke to nine or ten thousand people in Ashton market place, urging a monster petition for 'a fair day's wage for a fair day's work' – a phrase from Chartist times. However, the short fuse was located elsewhere. The Stalybridge relief committee abandoned its former secrecy and began to publish its proceedings in the local press. Its troubles with insubordinate scholars, low funds and discontented shopkeepers became public knowledge. At last, reasons were given for the previous month's changes in relief. The Manchester committee wanted a uniform scale, and thought that the Stalybridge Guardians paid too little, and the relief committee too much; hence the decision to deduct fourpence per week from each operative's income. Retrenchment was necessary, and the classes would be reduced and transferred to the Guardians. Finally the committee decided to prevent drunkenness by introducing relief by tickets on recognized provision shops. This last insult to the independence of the Lancashire worker was met by a petition of protest and a deputation to the Manchester committee. It promised to raise the matter at its next meeting. It was too late. The new measure was due to take effect on 20 March; the day before, the riot began.[16]

The first day was enough for Bates and Kirk, who at once promised to reconsider the ticket system. Tempers were lost, and the two men had to escape after their cab was attacked. The riot continued until the 24th, and spread to Dukinfield, Ashton and Hyde. In Stalybridge, windows were broken, shops looted, mill machinery damaged, and police attacked. On one occasion, hussars dispersed a crowd which had stoned police escorting rioters. Eventually the town's priests and clergy persuaded the operatives to accept a compromise offered by the committee; relief was to be given half in cash, and half in tickets. The riot was on a comparatively small scale, but it was regarded in the press as a national disgrace. Twenty-eight out of the twenty-nine tried for riot were Irish, and with one exception the heaviest sentence was six months hard labour; but English and Irish had shared the same grievances.[17]

Stephens took no part in the riot. An *Oldham Standard* editorial blamed 'Irish rowdies', and condemned it as 'ungrateful, deeply criminal, and positively insane'. It is likely that privately he disassociated himself from the operatives, for in April, Bridges wrote to his friend Harrison – who had accused Stephens of fear – that 'the strongest proof of courage is to have vast power over the people, and freely to abdicate it when you think them wrong. It is not by the Trade Unions Committee that he is to be judged, but by the people in governing whom they are his rivals.' Bridges added:

> Your letter moves me not a jot. I say again that Stephens is more in the right than any of you! . . . Stephens is gaining his point, in spite of the most obstinate resistance from the Mayor. The excitement in his chapel is great. The whole thing is widely fermenting. He is advocating the right to labour, and that sans phrase.[18]

Elsewhere, Stephens was blamed as the single most important cause of the riot. As early as 22 March, Aspland wrote to the Home Secretary naming Stephens, Williams and Heffill for violent language at Dukinfield open air meetings. Five days later, he wrote again to warn that until the operatives settled their differences with the committee, the riots would continue. The following day, a detailed account of the riots was sent to the Home Office; it began by saying that Stephens and others had stirred up bad feeling among the operatives. Hopwood's similar account did not name Stephens, but enclosed a copy of his town hall speech of the previous month. In April, Aspland published his accusations against Stephens, Williams and Heffill. 'But for these mischievous men, I believe that the workpeople would have continued to receive gratefully and patiently the assistance which has been so benevolently offered to them'. Any suggestion of objectivity was dispelled by a dismissive postcript against 'a silly person from Bradford named Bridges, said to be a medical man', who 'had picked up all sorts of ridiculous stories' and sent them to *The Times*.[19]

Stephens did not answer Aspland; thus it could be inferred that no answer was possible. Yet the accusers were two interested and influential parties who had been discomfitted by previous clashes with Stephens. The Stalybridge Mayor and the Dukinfield Justice of the Peace were responsible for local relief distribution; both hid the shortcomings of their respective committees by blaming the notorious old agitator. The Liberal *Ashton Reporter*, which had not been uncritical of Stephens in the past, did not blame him for the riot. It thought the relief committee 'very greatly to blame', and it defended its decision to publish Stephens' speeches despite the committee's resentment. The most that can be claimed is that Stephens' late intervention added to the general increase in tension before the riot. To claim more is to ignore the longstanding operative militancy of Bintcliffe's agitation, and the steady discontent reported in the Ashton press for almost a year. Mayor Hopwood was a Conservative. If there was a widespread belief that Stephens was responsible for the riot, it is difficult to understand why Stalybridge Conservatives only five years later could even contemplate him as a possible Parliamentary candidate.[20]

It was three more of Stephens's clerical allies, William Hoare of St Paul's, Thomas Floyd of Holy Trinity and William Bell of St John's Dukinfield, who secured £500 from the Mansion House fund for the Stalybridge operatives. In time, tempers cooled. In October Hopwood chaired a meeting of the Foresters of Stalybridge when Stephens and Floyd were among the speakers. The Mayor toasted 'the ministers of all denominations', and Stephens 'most cordially hailed him as a brother Forester'. All three were received into the society. The increasing collapse of the Confederacy from late 1864 meant a further decline in cotton prices, and more insolvent cotton manufacturers. The final Northern victory in April 1865 brought a revival of the trade, and restored full employment to the industry (though a three year depression from 1866 brought renewed gloom).[21]

If the traumatic events of the cotton famine stimulated economic thought on commercial fluctuations, it produced a sea change in the public perception of the cotton industry. No longer was it regarded as the indispensible foundation of British prosperity. The distress of Lancashire was largely confined to the county, and British commercial strength was relatively unaffected. The Manchester School lost its unique influence in national affairs, and the cotton industry became a regional rather than a national interest. Within Lancashire, political and economic liberalism was undermined. Emigration increased, and local politics were transformed. In contrast to the increasingly discredited views of their masters, cotton operatives were drawn more and more to Conservatism. Conservative Working Men's Associations, Anglican renewal, anti-Irish feeling and suspicion of free trade were all at work after the famine, contributing to Conservative victories in Lancashire in 1868, and in England six years later. In most of these developments, Stephens played a modest but prophetic part.[22]

9

The Stormy Petrel of Stalybridge

Stephens's vindication in the cotton famine did not make his last fourteen years more peaceful. On the contrary, he was involved in one town controversy after another. To some, he emerged with credit and even honour as a local elder statesman whose past services and continued activity entitled him to a respectful hearing; to others, he was a wilful and irresponsible crank who had outlived his public usefulness. Yet others were bewildered by his unpredictability, which made it difficult to trust him. His intervention in politics, especially in the School Board election of 1876, even affected men's judgment of him at the time of his death.

The cotton famine did little lasting social damage, and the return to normal times was swift. Soon Stephens was addressing meetings in his old style. Late in 1865 he preached in a full chapel for the Independent Order of Oddfellows. While upholding the need for Christian orthodoxy, he thought the church could learn from the benevolence of the 'secret orders'. Two hundred men joined the Order, and the grateful Oddfellows presented him with an inkstand and a walking stick. The following year, he was initiated into the Order with other local notables.[1]

In February 1866 he spoke on education, stressing the need for playgrounds and warning against overvaluing books – 'we read too much and think too little'. In November, he addressed 650 members of the Stalybridge Good Intent Industrial Society, and criticized the Co-operative ideal. The following month he lectured in a full town hall on trade unions, praising them but pleading for a revival of the old trade guilds to bring masters and men together. He impressed his chairman, James Sidebottom, a Stalybridge employer and the Mayor, who confessed that 'his opinions had undergone a change'.[2]

He spoke to the Spinner's Union at the Hyde Mechanics Institute in March 1867. Amid rumours of forthcoming anti-union legislation, he asserted trade union power; any government that attempted to abolish unions would go down with them. 'They wanted the hours of labour reducing from ten and a half to eight, and they intended petitioning Parliament until they got it.' The extension of the suffrage was imminent, and Stephens added: 'when they got their household suffrage . . . and sent him to St Stephens to advocate their claims, he was the man for that'. Shortly afterwards, Benjamin Disraeli introduced his reform bill. Stephens' hopes were high, for household franchise and a redistribution of seats meant a male working-class vote, and a Stalybridge parliamentary constituency.[3]

In March and April he reinforced his populist image at two lively Stalybridge meetings by opposing Sunday closing of public houses. His Liberal and Nonconformist opponents were campaigning hard in its favour. At the March meeting, Stephens arrived 'by merest chance' and made a much interrupted speech. If the meeting's promoters were against drinking in general as some of them claimed, he was 'dead against them, and the public generally were against them'. As a centre of social entertainment, the public house 'gave the poor man the opportunity of doing what the rich man did elsewhere, and which the poor man could not do anywhere else'. While he wished success to the teetotal movement in reclaiming drunkards, 'it was a serious matter for one set of men to make themselves judges over everybody else . . . to presume to impose that total abstinence on others'. After six days work, were working men to be debarred on the Sabbath from the public house? Amid accusations of claptrap and buffoonery, Stephens claimed that 'the course they were pursuing was opposed to every sound principle of political economy, public morals, and social order'. He succeeded in getting the meeting adjourned.[4]

A fortnight later, a second equally heated gathering was attended by over 900 people and the police. Stephens defended himself from criticisms of his previous speech. 'The public house is every Englishman's freehold (Shame, shame).' Earlier he had been asked if infidels would oppose Sunday closing. Aware of growing Nonconformist enthusiasm for the teetotal sentiment, he had replied: 'God bless the infidels. I know a hundred of them up and down the land, and I will back the infidels of Stalybridge against the same number of any of the people who walk out of the Iron Bridge Chapel (Shame, shame).' His speech ended in 'immense cheering', though later speakers fared worse. Amid confusion, the meeting ended at 1 a.m. without a clear result, after operatives mounted the platform to protect Stephens from possible violence. It was more than provocation on Stephens' part; to him, radical causes such as education and teetotalism were diversions from the real problem. As he once said to Dr Bridges:

> At best they are but palliatives, and if people would only call them so, I would be content; but why be so cock-a-hoop about them? Why all this ridiculous vaunting about the glories of the modern progress of this nineteenth century, *when the root is rotten*, when the breed of men and women swarming around us is growing each year feebler, and punier, and uglier?[5]

Open affront to Liberal Nonconformity could only strengthen his hold on Conservative affections. Expectations grew that either Stephens or Sidebottom would represent the party at the first Stalybridge election; in June 1867 at a Mossley party gathering, Stephens heard it publicly voiced. At once he said:

> He was no Conservative – no Tory even; he wanted to get back to the time when England was England – not split up but one body . . . He wanted the monarch to have more power . . . and it would be better if the veto of the Lords was more frequently used than it is.

He was careful to add praise for Disraeli and the Tory factory reformers, and he attacked the Liberals. He did not refuse outright the suggestion that he should stand for Parliament, and later in June the *Reporter* noted that a party intended to nominate him as a candidate.[6]

In August the new reform bill became law, and within a month a Stalybridge Constitutional Association was formed. One of its secretaries was James France, while Heffill, Swann and the Stephenite Charles Buckley moved resolutions at its inaugural meeting. Although not a member, Stephens was introduced and was received with loud applause. He was not surprised that many working people supported the banner of the altar, the throne and the cottage, for they knew that under traditional leadership, their country had become great and free. He promised that 'his influence, what little it might be, and his vote, would be given in favour of the man who would carry their principles to the House of Commons'. Once Stephens had been elected to the Chartist Convention uncommitted to the Charter; now he wanted Conservative endorsement without being tied to the party. In an age of stronger party organization, he was to be disappointed.[7]

By February 1868, he published *The Altar, the Throne and the Cottage* – 'the symbols of the English constitution, and the key to the English character'. It was to an unsectarian altar that the Constitutional Association was called:

> Let the doors of your association . . . be open wide enough for all good men to enter in at. Shut out none. The Throne of England had a breadth to cover each and every one of us. For the Protestant, for the Roman Catholic, for the Dissenter, there is an equality of freedom. Our laws confer upon us the liberty of individual conscience and the right of private judgment. But these privileges are not to be used to the disadvantage of our neighbour.

He warned against theorists, and a republicanism involving 'infidelity, communism, strife of classes, breaking-up of the holy ties of wedlock and the home'. Not party, but patriotism alone, would suffice to promote the common welfare. The battles for social reform in which he had fought had been won with few exceptions by 'the great Constitutional party', and it was the duty of working men to support it. The Government had extended the provisions of the Factory Acts to all branches of industry, and had remedied some of the flagrant abuses of the poor law. He pledged full support for 'my Lord Derby's government'.[8]

Unfortunately, Stalybridge Conservatism failed to live up to his ideals. The Irish issue resurfaced in national politics. The violence of the nationalist Fenian Brotherhood emphasized the problem of reconciling Ireland to British rule, and both British parties saw the solution in religious terms. Derby and Disraeli wanted to maintain the established Church of Ireland, but appease the non-Anglican Irish majority by endowing the Roman Catholic and Presbyterian Churches; but in March, Gladstone rallied the Liberal party and discomfitted the Government by declaring for Irish disestablishment. Both Cardinal Manning and the Nonconformists agreed with him.

Feelings ran high in Lancashire, with its strong Irish Catholic minority, and its powerful Orange Protestant backlash. Against a background of renewed ethnic tension and religious conflict, Stephens spoke at a series of stormy Constitutional Association meetings in the north to defend a faltering government. At Salford in February, he asserted that Irish emigration had nothing to do with the Church of Ireland, and he attacked its proposed disendowment. At Prestalee, he warned that Irish Church disestablishment would lead to an attack on the Church of England. In Stalybridge, he argued that the Irish Church had nothing to do with the working classes. After Gladstone's championing of disestablishment, Stephens was reminded at Dewsbury that once he had done the same. The meeting ended in uproar.[9]

There was a greater dilemma, for unsectarian conviction thwarted political ambition. Stephens' broad sympathies with the Catholic minority discredited him with the Conservative Orange interest. Orange supporters included not only his Nonconformist opponents, but his local Anglican clerical allies. Their passions were being fanned with a vengeance. In December 1867, William Murphy of the Protestant Electoral Union visited Ashton and Stalybridge to deliver violently anti-Catholic lectures. He and his friends were warmly welcomed by Booth Mason and other local Orange leaders. Murphy's agitation through most of 1868 inflamed the political tension over the Irish Church. Orange and Green gangs fought in Stalybridge streets. In April, there was a riot, and a Catholic chapel was stoned.

On 7 May Stephens spoke at a packed Irish Church meeting in Stalybridge town hall, while police armed with cutlasses patrolled the surrounding streets. Despite the boisterous atmosphere, Stephens was well received by the audience. He reminded them that Catholics were their fellow citizens, and had equal rights with themselves. The real issue was the timing of Gladstone's announcement, for he had thrown the disestablishment issue 'like an apple of discord on the floor of the House of Commons'. A year was needed to consider the question, for a three-hundred-year-old principle could not be overthrown in an hour. 'It was a Gladstone-in and Disraeli-out question.' France moved the resolution in favour of the Irish Church, and the meeting ended peacefully. A *Stalybridge News* pamphlet declared:

> The key to the complexion and character of the meeting is to be found in the loud and general cry for Mr Stephens, after the Mayor had mounted the table to put the motion. It was Mr Stephens' intention not to have spoken, but he rose to the call in order to bring the subject back to its proper issue, and give condensed expression to what he knew was the settled judgment of his fellow-townsmen.[10]

Two days later, a thousand people came to Ashton town hall for an Orange demonstration. Booth Mason presided, and Heffill spoke on 'papal aggression'. The next day, young Protestant operatives in party colours taunted Catholics on the streets. Irish assaulted English, and English retaliated by an attack on Ashton's 'Little Ireland'. Twenty houses and a Catholic chapel were wrecked; the rioters dispersed after Hugh Mason read the Riot Act, only to return later to attack another

Catholic chapel. Five hundred special constables were sworn in, and two companies of troops enlisted. Order was restored three days later. There were hundreds of injured, and thirty-four arrests. At Stalybridge, street disturbances on a smaller scale persisted from December 1867 to May 1868, and even later. This time, no one blamed Stephens for the riots.[11]

In May, Prime Minister Disraeli announced a November election on the new register. In south-east Lancashire, 'religion' was the dominant issue, and 'no popery' became a Conservative battle-cry. In Stalybridge, Sidebottom was an Orangeman, but although Stephens upheld the Irish Church, he was totally opposed to Murphyism. In late July, both Stalybridge hopefuls were interviewed by party officials; there was little doubt about their choice, especially when it emerged that Stephens could not pay for his election expenses. In vain did France protest that Sidebottom's nomination would create party discord; he was recommended overwhelmingly to a full party meeting. Stephens was called in and informed, and was allowed to speak. He told them he had done nothing to promote his own candidacy, but it had become impossible to ignore the many electors who wanted him to stand for Parliament. To become a member of Parliament was 'the legitimate object of a personal ambition'. If ever he was successful, 'he would undertake to represent the interests of the entire community, which he believed to be fundamentally the same'. (This was precisely what his pro-Orange listeners had feared.) He continued:

> Personally he had no wish to enter Parliament. There were many reasons why he should not, but until he was better acquainted with the principles of Mr Sidebottom and the preferences of the people for him, it would be a breach of public trust on his part to withdraw himself from the notice of the public, and renounce all claim to their favourable regard.

However, 'he would be the last man to divide the Conservative ranks and above all, to set one portion of the labouring people against another'. Later that week, the 'thoroughgoing Tory' Sidebottom was adopted as the candidate.[12]

The more Stephens enquired into Sidebottom's politics the unhappier he became. Two meetings between them and their mutual friends in late August ended without agreement. Their differences were gleefully reported in Hugh Mason's Liberal electioneering sheet the *Ashton News*. According to this, the Sidebottom camp thought that while

Stephens deserved to represent them, their man had a much better chance of winning in Stalybridge. As for Stephens, he thought that apart from Sidebottom's support of the Irish Church, his policy did not differ from that of the Liberal candidate, except that the latter said what he meant. He insisted that Sidebottom repudiate the Murphyites, and a promise was made to disavow the 'no popery' cry. So at least Stephens claimed a week later; but in the meantime the *Ashton News* said the two were as far apart as ever. 'Their ablest man is in the sulks. The Tories have used Mr Stephens, and then have dropped him.' Whatever may have been the truth in this routine party point-scoring, there is no doubt that Stephens was alienated from the Conservatives by their pro-Orange stance. On 31 August he wrote to the secretary of the Constitutional Association:

> Having become a mere 'No Popery' party electioneering club, you can have no claim for patronage and support from those who, believing in the Holy Catholic Church, regard their Roman Catholic fellow-countrymen as equally loyal subjects of the Crown with ourselves.

A second letter written two days later gave eight reasons why Stephens refused support for Sidebottom. He had neither been nominated openly nor informed the electorate of his specific policies. His tactics suggested corruption. Since his promise to disavow the no-Popery cry, he had consented to a blatantly anti-Papal poster. The two letters were published on 5 September and the breach was confirmed.[13]

Next Stephens turned his attention to the Liberal, his old opponent Nathaniel Buckley, whose proceedings 'were altogether at variance with ancient usage'. He urged both candidates to hold meetings without admission by ticket. He even introduced a deputation of dissatisfied Liberal electors to their own candidate, and was thanked for his gentlemanly conduct. As Sidebottom's Orange sentiments began to be voiced in earnest, Stephens made an effective gesture. The shocking truth came out at a Stalybridge Orange gathering in October – he had actually given two sovereigns for the repair of the two destroyed Ashton Catholic chapels. He had added insult to injury by telling a local Orange leader:

> If I could have my will, I would not repair them, but would build the Catholics new chapels, and allow those which have been attacked and partially demolished to remain as monuments of English bigotry.

Accurately assessing his man, he capped this by offering to defend the Council of Trent against the 39 Articles. In November, he defended Gladstone against defamation. Neither his serious nor his humorous sallies had any noticeable effect on the election result. Sidebottom won Stalybridge, the Conservatives triumphed in Lancashire, and the Liberals swept the country.[14]

Stephens' later reputation for perversity dated from this election. While he lived, the local Conservative press never forgave him for his withdrawal of support. In the Liberal press, he was 'the great puzzle of the day', a clever but untrustworthy 'old greybeard'. He delighted in mischief-making; no one would be surprised whoever he supported – 'it is this uncertainty of his next move that causes both parties to watch him so carefully'. Exasperated critics charged that 'he never was particular in sticking to the truth when it did not suit his purpose'. Others felt 'we can ill-spare so gifted a man', and hoped he might 'come out in his old colours' for the cause of freedom if only his identification with 'that crazy Dukinfield clergyman' (Heffill) did not prevent him. When Stephens withdrew from local public life after the election, the impression of thwarted ambition was deepened. In April 1870 the *Stalybridge Standard* thought his conduct over the previous two and a half years had been 'of the most unaccountable character'.[15]

Stephens withdrew partly to pursue his political ambitions elsewhere. In February 1870, he addressed the Brighton Conservatives, telling them that he came on condition that he could speak freely, and was no party man. He showed his true purpose when he was challenged to say how Ireland could be pacified: 'Send for me to stand for Brighton, and I will tell you.' His biographer Holyoake described another occasion when two members of the Carlton Club visited him in Stalybridge. (The date is uncertain, but the most likely time is after the election of 1868.) 'They wished Mr Stephens to stand for a certain borough, and that his election to parliament should cost him nothing. They added that they wanted to keep the seat until a certain person was ready to take it. Mr Stephens opened his door, and desired these gentlemen to leave his house at once'.[16]

He also needed to withdraw to reconsider his position. He had done this as far back as December 1838. In recent years, his hold on the operatives had been shaken twice, first by trade union militancy in the cotton famine, and then by the popularity of Murphyism and the success of Orange Protestantism at the polls. Even Abel Swann had been a member of the Orange Order. In March 1870 he returned to

Stalybridge public life, and in an eloquent address entitled 'What is it you want?' he diagnosed the basic problem as one of party. 'In ranging yourselves under the banner of party . . . you ceased to be what you had been, and I therefore could not be of you'. Sound judgments could be made by returning to the pre-party constitution and by constant self-questioning. He left no doubt about what he wanted. He opposed Liberal social legislation. He wanted mothers to be at home to bring up their children, a fair day's wage for a fair day's work, and renewed understanding on the causes of increasing national disorder. He asked if national unity was not distracted by religious differences. In a moving peroration, he urged trust in God rather than in numbers. His two and a half hour speech was cheered, but there were sour comments in the Conservative press.[17]

In May, Stephens went to Copenhagan for the wedding of his daughter Henrietta to Alfred Earle, who had been warmly recommended by his brother Professor George Stephens. Both then visited the Swedish branch of the family. In March 1871 at a Stalybridge by-election after Sidebottom's death, the Liberal Nathaniel Buckley won the seat. Stephens was roused by the licensing bill, which had Evangelical support. With Swann and France, he denounced its injustice to the poor, and its principle of centralization. At the annual dinner of the South Lancashire Licensed Retailers Association in 1872, he said that the root of drunkenness was the factory system. The bill to limit licensing hours pandered to 'fanatics and sectarians'. After it was passed, he reminded a town hall protest meeting: 'In no age has the Church of the living God ever condemned the drinking of fermented liquor.' Neither Bible, reason nor experience condemned it. The Act was impracticable, and he defied it. He was away when another Stalybridge meeting called for its repeal. Feelings ran high, for on 3 November over ten thousand people demonstrated outside temperance leader Hugh Mason's house in Ashton; they were only dispersed by soldiers.[18]

His libertarian instincts made him highly critical of the Education Act of 1870, with its compulsory school attendance and education rate. He still believed that mothers should be freed from the factory to bring up their children. 'Education simply means growth.' His spokesman Abel Swann opposed any attempt to exclude the Bible from day schools. In the census of 1871, Stephens' two sons were returned as 'scholars at home', and in September the School Board learned that he was educating his children. In August 1872, he prepared the defence of a

Stephenite mill operative prosecuted by the Stalybridge School Board for not sending his eight-year-old daughter to school. At first Jonathan Schofield claimed that he taught her at home, and asked defiantly if School Boards superseded parental authority; but later he argued that he had a 'reasonable excuse' for his conduct under the Act. The girl satisfied the court, and the case was dismissed. The *Reporter* thought Schofield an exceptional man, and commented that 'the defence put into his mouth was prepared by a very shrewd and clever member of society who "knows on which side his bread is buttered"'. Later it was revealed that the girl had attended school until three or four months before the case, and this scarcely vindicated her father's ability to teach.[19]

He continued his trade union involvement, and his campaign for shorter hours. At Darwen he argued for a fifty-four hour week, and at Padiham for an eight hour day. He spoke on the high price of meat at Stalybridge. In December 1872 he welcomed to Stalybridge two Government commissioners enquiring into the conditions of factory labour. One of them was his old ally Dr Bridges. They attended a Sunday afternoon service and an evening conference. The Liberal *Ashton Reporter* proudly declared:

> They had wended their way to the unpretentious chapel in King Street to hear the voice of the man who came forward more than thirty years ago to fight the battle of the working men and women, and to 'invoke the power of God against the oppressor'. The Rev J. R. Stephens was at his post, and with his usual tact and foresight he fixed upon a passage of Scripture . . . to bring home to them some of the most telling arguments in favour of factory reform. Many of his assertions will be ratified by scores of our readers.

He attended the Leeds Trade Union Congress of 1873, and was impressed by Joseph Arch, the Primitive Methodist local preacher whose Agricultural Labourers Union was having such a dramatic impact in the south. The Congress urged its members to prepare for the forthcoming election by supporting candidates of any party who wanted the repeal of unjust labour laws. In late February, Stalybridge was the first to respond by forming a Trades Council for this purpose. At a meeting chaired by Stalybridge's sympathetic leading industrialist, John Frederick Cheetham, Stephens spoke of the Congress and carried the proposal for a Trades Council. He became its corresponding secretary.[20]

By August 1873, rumours in the Manchester press that Stephens would be Conservative candidate for Stalybridge at the next election were denied by the local party chairman, Napoleon Ives. With a suitable Conservative still lacking, Stephens was announced as an independent candidate. On 2 September, he read a Trades Council declaration for direct labour representation in Parliament, with priority given to labour questions. The *Reporter* thought it represented the principles of Stephens, and that his object was mischief; he would stand and be defeated. At the end of September, he resigned his secretaryship because of a conflict of interests. In a covering letter to the Council, he revealed that many had asked him to stand for Parliament. 'The old parties are wearing out, and the people are weary of them . . .'[21]

Without warning, Gladstone called an election for February 1874. Stephens was ill in bed, and the only nominations were Buckley for the Liberals, and T. H. Sidebottom for the Conservatives. The Liberal *Stalybridge News* jeered: 'Happily for newspaper men and the public, Mr Stephens was not able to gratify his speechmaking propensity, and this is a public blessing for which electors cannot be sufficiently thankful.' His six friends who claimed to be a national party were 'the Ishmaels of political society, their hand being against every man, and every man's hand against them. They are Tories, but Tories of a malignant and peevish caste . . . They are political nobodies.' Unhappily for the Liberals, Sidebottom recaptured the seat, the Conservatives won a decisive victory in the country, and Disraeli became Prime Minister. For the first time, trade unionist Liberals entered Parliament; later they came to be known as 'Lib-Labs'. Although 1874 ended Stephens's Parliamentary ambitions, some of his wider aims were realized through the Conservative victory.[22]

Stephens and Arch met again at the 1874 Trade Union Congress, and Arch was invited to Stalybridge. Stephens was among the speakers who called on the town to aid the agricultural labourers in the lock out by every means in their power. 'These men have set the ball rolling, and there was now one more chance for England to be free.' He proposed a local relief committee, with himself as a member, to co-operate with the Manchester relief committee on their behalf.[23]

His declining health forced him to accept that his days and those of the Stephenites were numbered. At the age of seventy, he was admitted to the Stalybridge old folks tea party. He had spoken there many times before, and now he told them:

He came to Stalybridge nearly forty years ago, and he loved it so much, and the people had hugged him so tightly that he had never been able to get away, and he did not want to get away. He had worked hard in his time, and the harder a man worked, minding at the same time how he lived, the better he would be for it, and the longer he would live. When he got up on Sunday morning, he had the gout in both feet, and his throat was made up so that he could scarcely speak, but he got up, and went to his work, and preached three times, and if the three sermons could be put together, the length of them would be nearer five hours than four in the time taken for their delivery, and yet he was there that night, all the merrier and all the jollier for having done that hard day's work.

A member of the committee replied that they owed him a debt of gratitude they would never be able to repay. 'They owed it to Mr Stephens that there was a certain independency about the working classes of Stalybridge which was not to be found in other places.' In November 1875 King Street closed, and he retired from the ministry to be known henceforth as 'plain Mr Stephens'.[24]

A last, damaging outburst of political passion followed. He was still willing to stand for public office, and in December 1875 a Conservative split on the Stalybridge School Board forced an election for three vacant seats. Two dissident aldermen saw Stephens, who agreed to stand as an independent. Both the Liberal *Reporter* and the Conservative *Standard* attacked him; neither thought he would be elected. He refused to withdraw, and the Conservative chairman Napoleon Ives suggested a reason:

It was simply to air his crotchets at the School Board. Joseph Rayner Stephens would use all the three hours of School Board meetings himself. Since he was opposed to a School Board, why should he seek election to it? . . . Everybody that they met said 'What an inconsistent member, what is he, a Churchman, or what is he?' Nobody could understand him.

The following evening, Stephens replied at his adoption meeting. Just as he opposed the Act of 1834 and accepted office as a Guardian, now he hoped to make the best of a bad law by using it to reform the School Board. He dealt with hecklers, and asked the electors to return him at the head of the poll.[25]

On 10 January 1876, they confounded his critics by doing so. Stephens had 2,627 votes to the next successful candidate's 1,494. Both newspapers blamed Irish Catholic voters for his triumph, and the Conservative *Standard* was bitter towards him. Stephens attributed his victory to a rejection of party; he had won without any organization. As for the compulsory education of 'gutter children', Stephens said:

> The poor hungry children now asked for bread, and they were given a book, and for clothing they were given a slate – (applause). This was called religious education, but it would not do – (applause). They must begin at the right end, and shift the slums, and restore the village green again. He would have large public playgrounds . . .

When the Board met in March, Stephens plunged it into discord by objecting to the presence of the attendance officer, whose information to the Guardians on school absentees resulted in the stoppage of relief. After a second stormy meeting in April, his attendance fell off. Amid talk of the abolition of School Boards, he was re-elected in 1877, but he had the least votes of the nine successful candidates. His days of public service were over.[26]

By 1877 his gout was severe, but he remained cheerful. Shortly before the end, his friend Holyoake was a guest, and listened to the many conversations Stephens had with his visitors. Holyoake thought that 'his talk was the most remarkable to which I had ever listened. Newness of idea, aptness of quaint illustration, singular richness of language, a picturesque eloquence devoid of all effort, gave the impression of a new quality of speech.' His nephew Stephens Storr wrote of his uncle's daily round:

> Sometimes he would rise early and take very long walks: at other times he would sit up and read far into the night; take his breakfast in bed in the morning, and perhaps not get up until the afternoon. In company too, he would oft-times keep the whole table in a roar of laughter, or when on a serious subject, in rapt attention; whilst at another time – with different surroundings – he would be still, and seem to be dull and listless. He smoked too much and Turkish-bathed too much . . . No man I ever knew had so keen a sense of humour in himself . . . [27]

As far as health permitted, he could now enjoy his leisure interests. Though few details remain, he had maintained them throughout. His newspapers included his poems and children's stories, though neither were of great merit. He was a connoisseur and collector of rare and valuable oil paintings. His library included books in English, French, Latin, German, Greek, Spanish, Italian, Swedish and Danish. He had ten volumes of the works of Martin Luther, Samuel Wesley's *Life of Christ*, Greek and Latin lexicons, and Hebrew manuscripts. He owned a day and night telescope.[28]

On the morning of 18 February 1879, he repeated the Lord's Prayer in a loud voice, and died shortly afterwards. The cause of death was congestion of the kidneys, persistent vomiting and exhaustion. On 1 March, his coffin was carried shoulder high to St John's Church Dukinfield. There was a private service, but the streets and churchyard were crowded. In the Ashton district, 'there were thousands of mourners because this man was going to his long home'. For a hundred years, the King Street baptismal font marked the grave. The inscription reads:

In loving memory of

JOSEPH RAYNER STEPHENS

Born March 8th 1805,
Died February 18th 1879,

He hath done what He could.

The press obituaries varied. *The Times* called him the leader of the northern Chartists and recalled his imprisonment. The *Manchester Guardian* in an editorial stressed his literary gifts, but concluded that he gave up for party what was meant for mankind. The local press was far too close to recent contentious politics to be generous. The *Standard* belittled him, and the *Reporter* exaggerated his faults, and thought that 'the age most congenial for a man like Mr Stephens has passed away'.[29]

His collections were sold, and his widow moved to London. Soon a memorial fund was established to honour him with a monument, as with Sadler, Oastler and Fielden, with the ever loyal pair France and Swann working hard on the committee. The decision to erect a monument led to the writing of Holyoake's biography. He had few illusions about the difficulties, for he devoted a preliminary chapter to elusive source material and poor press reporting. He added to the problem by his over-tactful choice of what was available, especially in the later period. His anti-Anglican bias distorted his account of both Wesleyan Methodism and the leading factory reformers. The result was a book favourably reviewed at the time, but recognized as defective since.[30]

On 19 May 1888 the granite obelisk was unveiled in Stamford Park Stalybridge. The face of the old man and a verse of his best known poem 'Scatter the seed' appeared on it. Hundreds of people came for the last rally of the Stephenites. Old Abel Swann presided over a battery of speakers, including Members of Parliament, trade unionists, local dignitaries, family and old friends. All paid tributes to the one- time Champion of the Factory Child, and agreed that he played a part in the great improvement in the lot of the working classes over the years; a veil was drawn over recent, contentious matters. The *Stalybridge Herald* atoned for earlier Conservative antipathy:

> Mr Stephens was the man for the time. He laid bare to the country the great evils under which the factory operatives groaned. He exposed in unmeasured terms all tyrannical acts which reached his ears, and woe be to that local employer who came under his sweeping condemnation. He was merciless, but the times required plain speaking; yet he was merciless only to those who had no mercy for others. He held a wonderful fascination over the people. They felt they could trust him, they placed themselves entirely in his hands, and he never betrayed them.[31]

One by one the surviving faithful departed. Swann died in 1892, and France in 1906. On the centenary of the Champion's birth in 1905, Susanna, Arthur and Henrietta laid wreaths in Stamford Park; the following year, old friends gathered there on the anniverary of his death. The three surviving children went their various ways. Henrietta's son was born in 1876, but her husband died at Shebbear in Devon. She married a son of one of the founders of the Bible Christians, a predominantly west country Methodist denomination. At her death in 1906, leading Bible Christian ministers attended the funeral; she was remembered in the area for her goodness to the poor. In 1885 George died in an accident in Texas. The piano tuner Arthur Cornwall married in 1887, had eight children and died in London in 1907.[32]

Susanna outlived her husband, both sons, and two grandchildren. She survived the First World War, which destroyed the Victorian world that she and her husband had known. She had returned to her native Derbyshire, where she died in broken health at the age of 82 on 28 December 1920; an official of the Shardlow workhouse signed her death certificate. On it, she was described as 'widow of Joseph Rayner Stephens, a worker's advocate'. Her funeral was conducted by a Wesleyan Methodist minister.[33]

10

The Stephenites

Until his retirement in 1875, Stephens remained a minister of the gospel in pastoral work. His churches were the base from which he emerged to fight for Christian justice, and to which he returned to minister to his devoted flock. He never deserted the Stephenites, and they supported him in prison as well as in the pulpit. He shared their trials, and they found that his were reflected in their chequered church life. In the words of the *Ashton Reporter* after his death, 'he was from first to last a curious compound of minister and agitator'. The ministerial part of the compound was basic, for Stephens saw his agitation as an expression of his ministry; he was not a secular agitator, but one who served a Christian body set within the wider community. Some account of the Stephenites is necessary if Stephens is to be understood.[1]

The full story of the Stephenites is unlikely ever to be known. No church records seem to have survived, except for three plans of worship and the Charlestown chapel deed. Stephens' prison writings throw some light on his churches, as do his speeches, some scattered press reports, a few miscellaneous documents, and reminiscences written long afterwards. Of his church buildings, only the People's School remains. The font on the Dukinfield grave has vanished, though his communion vessels have survived. For the earlier years, even the *Christian Advocate* is less informative than might have been expected. In the disruption of 1836, its editor was caught between a desire to support his brother's churches, and a prudent concern not to alienate his Wesleyan reform readers. The result was a minimum of information and some subtly ambiguous editorials. Holyoake had little patience with earlier Methodist complexities or later Anglican sympathies, and misunderstood the material he used.

The resulting obscurity created its own myths. One was that whatever church troubles Stephens had when he became a factory agitator were with the Wesleyan Methodists. As has been shown, there is no foundaton for this. Another myth was that the Stephenites were more of a political than a religious movement. This was a judgment of hindsight. It was never the intention of Stephens, and despite an inevitable influx of sympathetic unbelievers in recurring times of social crisis, the surviving Stephenite data from 1839–40 dispel it. When these myths are discounted, we are left with a genuinely Christian movement fully involved in the turbulent social and political life of the neighbourhood. Its history falls into three unequal phases. Up until September 1836, the Stephenites struggled to establish an identity as a reformed Methodist circuit. In 1836 they exchanged Wesleyan reform for factory reform, maintaining and broadening this new identity in the midst of radical ferment; their image was still that of a Methodist body. After 1841, they became increasingly pro-Anglican, while remaining independent and continuing on the Christian social path with growing difficulty, until their demise in 1875.[2]

The Ashton separatists of 1834 wanted an independent 'apostolic church' governed by the rules laid down by Christ in the gospels. 'No rule or law shall be framed in the church but what is formed on them, either in the spirit or the letter.' As Wesleyan reformers, they were opposed in theory to ministerial supremacy; but in practice, they were devoted to their increasingly forceful minister. Old habits died hard, and Stephens was the son of a ministerial father who was to be called 'next to Mr Bunting himself, the most unbending champion of authority that the Methodist connexion could produce'.[3]

After November 1834, it was not a separate Ashton apostolic church that arose, but a group of churches that followed Methodist precedent by calling itself 'the Ashton circuit'. In its formation, Stephens battled with Wesleyan superintendents and Warrenite dissidents. At Ashton, his followers had occupied Mill Lane Sunday school with the approval of the school's own trustees. At Stalybridge there had been a struggle for the Sunday school premises; it was won only by the casting vote of John Cheetham, the millowning Congregationalist chairman of the trustees. 'He could not bring himself to stop Stephens' ministry there, depriving a large body of industrious and intelligent men – many of whom were his own servants – of the means of obtaining religious instruction at those hours which were alone suited to their worldly occupations.' (Soon Cheetham would have cause to regret his action.) A visitor to Stalybridge in November 1834 reported that Stephens' followers numbered over 200, with many more friends. Others were to be found at Hyde, Hooley Hill and Dukinfield.[4]

In the tug of war between the Wesleyan Association and the

Stephenites for separatist Methodist societies, there was confusion and overlap. The usually well-informed diarist Edwin Butterworth twice referred to Stephens in 1836 as a Wesleyan Association minister. There was a close understanding between the separatists of Ashton and Oldham, although the latter went their own way. The Oldham circuit plan included Shaw, where a new chapel was opened in June 1835 'for the followers of Mr Stephens and other seceders from the Wesleyan Methodists'. At Royton, where the Stephens agitation deprived the Wesleyans of a congregation, the chapel was re-opened by Wesleyan reformers in September 1834. When the Sunday school anniversary services at the newly acquired King Street chapel at Stalybridge were taken in November by Stephens, it was reported that the membership was over 250. They 'have a neat chapel, two Sunday schools, and are about to build a very large school. The whole circuit is in a very happy and flourishing condition.'[5]

The situation was transformed by the conversion of Stephens to factory reform. Before it, the fading of disestablishment seemed to make the Ashton circuit nothing more than a separate Warrenite body. After January 1836, the new cause deflected the circuit from the church-based objectives of Wesleyan reform. In addition, the factory issue aroused resentment among certain pro-Wesleyan reform leaders and trustees, who knew that the livelihood of most of the members depended upon the goodwill of their millowning employers. They disapproved as strongly of their minister's addressing factory meetings as the Wesleyan Conference had of his addressing disestablishment meetings. (All Methodist bodies had a 'no politics' rule, even if only the Wesleyans enforced it strictly.) Despite their constant cry of 'civil and religious liberty', few Associationists were active in working-class movements before 1850; the *Christian Advocate* was unique in uniting the two reform causes. Thus there was growing tension in the circuit between those who put Stephens before Wesleyan reform, and those who put Wesleyan reform before Stephens.

Stephens knew that a crisis had come as early as February 1836, when he was asked to go to London for the parliamentary lobbying. He required twenty-four hours to consider it because 'he felt it would prove the most paralysing and destructive step to himself that he could possibly take. He knew full well that if he did that work in the spirit of his Master, to him only would he have to look for his reward.' At once opposition began. The 'overlookers' in his chapel tried to stop him going to London, and posted a placard; 'but he told them that he would not preach to them again unless the placard with withdrawn, and in less than six hours they granted him freedom of speech'. He remembered 'much painful expostulation with some of the people who attended my chapel to no purpose'.[6]

As his reputation for extremism increased, the objections of his critics hardened. By August and September, disaffection became disruption. Stephens said at Blackburn:

> I now preach nothing but factory sermons, and am determined to preach only such, until the question be settled; and I have given notice to my congregation that if they desire to hear other sermons, they must go to places other than mine.

From the pulpit, he called millowners 'murderers and swindlers' even when one was present; he himself had been called a 'madman'. In early August, he was deprived of two places of worship which could seat about a thousand people. By mid-September, he wrote to his father that he had lost five out of seven preaching houses by his part in the factory question. His father commented in his diary: 'Had he served the God of Israel instead of the calves of Jeroboam, he would not have been so easily forsaken'.[7]

The key battle was fought at King Street, Stalybridge. Stephens in a speech told part of the story:

> . . . there was a large placard stuck up against my chapel at Stalybridge, by some of the factory masters' tools (whom I call lickspittles), and this placard was as follows: 'Stephens' Evangelical Cotton Manufactory and Lunatic Asylum for Turned-off Parsons, Admittance gratis.' I got hold of that placard through some of the lads who are always about, and I took it for my text the next time I preached there (Laughter and cheers). I showed the cotton masters that mine was an Evangelical cotton manufactory, and the only one in that neighbourhood conducted on such principles; and I told them besides that every one ought to be, and that every one shall be so, or no cotton should be manufactured.

Stephens taunted his enemies, because they 'could not give him "the bag"'. It was not through want of trying. Abel Swann in his old age remembered their attempt:

> One Sunday night the leaders locked us out. Mr Stephens came as usual to the chapel at night, and finding King Street full of people,

enquired the cause, and was told that the door of the chapel had been locked against him by Robert Kershaw and William Clegg, the trustees and local preachers. Mr Stephens said it was his chapel, sent for a blacksmith and had the doors broken open, and the service took place as usual. The congregation was very excited, and many who were unable to get inside the building got ladders and listened at the open windows. Not one half of the people who were there could gain admission. In his sermon, he made reference to the conduct of the trustees. He could not, he said, see what they had to make any bother about; at any rate, he did not sacrifice his rights as a man and a citizen when he became their preacher.

Stephens retained the loyalty of most of the congregation at King Street. The dissidents left, and on 24 October Kershaw, Clegg and others in the name of the Wesleyan Methodist Association licensed a building in King Street, where 'upwards of twenty persons' met for worship. Not for another fourteen years was the Booth Street Association chapel opened, and its origin was traced only to a town mission in 1839. At its opening, many cotton masters contributed liberally; Kershaw was regarded as its spiritual father, and was remembered by his co-religionists as a just employer and a true philanthropist.[8]

The issue had been resolved, but very few wanted to draw attention to what had happened; thus except at King Street, the process of separation is shrouded in deep obscurity. The pro-Stephens forces were strong at Ashton, but there seems to have been no split there. They were in possession at Newton, Hyde, but some joined the Association. In July 1837 the *Advocate* reported that the chapel at Shaw had been reopened by the Association, 'but the circumstances we need not here detail'. Stephens still preached for the Oldham Associationists, but in August 1836 he spoke there of 'the impropriety of Sunday school education, advocating the observance of the Sabbath either for strictly religious worship, or harmless recreation'. Since Sunday schools were a great source of Association strength, doubtless this was another salvo in the battle. In March 1837, Stephens relieved his feelings at Middleton by attacking all his foes:

> The Wesleyan Conference he censured in strong terms; but said the Association or Warrenites were even greater tyrants than the Wesleyan Conference. He denounced them all, namely new poor-law makers, commissioners,, mill-owners, Wesleyan Methodists, Associationists or Warrenites, by reading the curses in the twenty

seventh and twenty eighth chapters of Deuteronomy . . . He spoke for about three hours.[9]

Brother John in the chair of the *Advocate* had to be more careful. He reported his brother's speeches, but not details of the disruption. He wrote two-edged editorials. In October he criticized Evangelical Christians who had lost sight of the ten commandments, and went on smoothly to speak of the 'English slave-proprietors' of mills who had threatened his brother's life, and called him a 'cast-off parson':

> As to his being a 'cast-off parson', that conveys reproach not to him, but to those who, boasting of Wesley as 'their venerable founder', thrust out of their communion a man more nearly resembling that illustrious Reformer . . . than any of his successors.

No reader unaware of recent events in Stalybridge would assume that the reference was to Stephens' pro-Association opponents; but it was not the Wesleyan Conference that had just thrust him out from its communion, or labelled him a 'cast-off parson'.[10]

The result of the disruption was drastic. Two years later Stephens said that 'his rich friends forsook him, and instead of being a minister extensively respected, and receiving a support equal to his wishes, he became a shepherd to a few scattered sheep in the wilderness'. He preached in the open air. 'He went to the highways and hedges – he stood upon his own doorstep . . . and there instead of preaching to congregations of 200 or 300 only, he had preached to 3,000 persons, and on one occasion to as many as 12,000.' Soon there were two new Stephenite buildings. At Charlestown, one of the poorest parts of Ashton, a large, plain chapel arose in Wellington Road. Built by subscription for the Stephenites, it could hold 1,100 people, and could be used as a meeting room on weeknights. On 8 June 1837 thirteen Stephenite trustees took the lease of the new premises, and the old Wesleyan building was abandoned. In September 1838, the Hyde Working Men's Institute was opened. It had two large rooms which could hold 1,600 to 2,000 people. The lower room was used as both school and chapel, and Stephens preached twice at the opening. Locally it was known as 'Stephens' Chapel'.[11]

The character of his churches changed. Numerically, the exodus of Association liberals was more than made up by an influx of working class radicals. Instinctively they rallied to the minister who had imperilled his livelihood in their cause. The occupations of the Charlestown trustees were: carter, warper, painter, clockmaker, machine-maker, dresser, weaver, bookseller, butcher, joiner, currier, draper and coalminer. Just as the departing Associationists tended to be uncritical of their liberalism, so many of the new recruits accepted without question the politics of working-class radicalism. Although they had long since been exposed to the influence of the writings of Thomas Paine and Richard Carlile, such unbelief as they had did not prevent them from joining Stephens; doubtless with many, unbelief was only skin deep, while others had never turned against Christianity. They were united in their support for their increasingly bold minister,, and through him were open to the direct challenge of the Evangelical gospel.[12]

Their employers reacted strongly. In June 1838, Stalybridge mill-owners determined to drive Stephens out of the neighbourhood by depriving him of his financial support. They began to discharge Stephenites from their employment; hundreds were turned out into the streets. A relief committee was formed, with the Stephenite John Durham as secretary. Stephens waived his stipend, and an appeal on his behalf was made by the *Northern Star*. Radical meetings took collections. In Halifax it was said:

> An open religious persecution is begun, and the Rev Mr Stephens is made the scapegoat of the concern, provided they can only manage to drive him forth into the wilderness, so that the people may lose the benefit of his ministrations. He who was the pride and glory of a certain class of influential individuals in those parts a few years ago when he advocated the question of a separation of Church and State, is now forsaken and alone, treading the wine press by himself . . . while the mammon of unrighteousness is engaged in slaying the poor of his flock, that they also may be removed out of his vineyard.

By mid-September the discharged Stephenites were allowed to resume work under new masters, and the short but dangerous persecution subsided.[13]

Once more Stephens had survived, and was left basking in the love and admiration of his flock. Durham gave four reasons why – their minister preached the truth, he never inculcated sectarian dogma, he befriended the needy and he opposed their oppressors. (Durham included among the oppressors the Christian minister 'who knows the truth, but who for the sake of the loaves and fishes dare not speak the truth'.) Stephens entered local folklore. Verses were set to music in his honour – 'Our Champion Stephens leads us on to glorious victory.' His portrait appeared on working-class crockery. He was beloved for his pastoral understanding of his people, and his striking 'political' preaching made the common people hear him gladly. *The Observer* reported in 1838 that he had one of the largest provincial congregations in England; it could not be less than 2,500 people:

> He is represented to be a preacher of great talent. All who have heard him speak in public concur in saying that his acquirements as a public speaker are of a very superior order. His delivery is fluent, his voice pleasant, and his elocution is in every respect in good taste.

The Trollopes were more critical, both of the 'miserable little chapel' they attended and of the preacher:

> Presently Stephens arrived, and the man who had been ranting in the pulpit, merely it seemed to occupy the people till he should come, immediately yielded his place to him. Stephens spoke well in that place of the cruel and relentless march of the great juggernaut, Gold. But I did not hear anything which seemed to me to justify his great reputation.[14]

Despite the 'proletarianizing' of the Stephenites, they continued to produce quarterly plans in time-honoured Methodist style. The earliest that has survived is for May to July 1839, and on it are Sunday and weeknight appointments for ten churches. Thirty-one preachers headed by Stephens are listed. Love feasts, a sacrament and quarterly collections appear; the solitary sacrament was to be taken by Stephens, as were the services involving quarterly collections. Quarter-days and preachers' meetings are shown; in form, the plan is indistinguishable from current Methodist plans. No name other than the Ashton circuit appears on it. When the members wrote to the *Northern Star* after their minister's imprisonment, they called themselves by the cumbersome title 'The Members of the Society lately worshipping under the pastoral care of the Revd J. R. Stephens'. Lacking a name for themselves, inevitably they were called Stephenites.[15]

The theatrical Stephens and the uninhibited operatives made public worship unpredictable. In few Methodist services would the minister suddenly observe:

> I perceive there are spies among this assembly, but as there is to be a collection made tonight, I need not tell you that you will soon be able to know who those spies are, because they will not contribute

anything. But woe to that man who attempts to capture me, for I am
armed with my brace of loaded pistols and polished steel dagger with
its silver handle.

A discomforted Goddard was forced to contribute with the others: 'My
readers can imagine my position, altho' I was incognito, to be in
company with ruffians of the lowest type.' Nor was this all. Stephens told
Londoners, 'Where I preach, every man has not only the power but the
right to stand up in his pew, or to ascend the pulpit if he pleases, and
there in the face of the congregation propound his views of the truths I
endeavour to teach.' One such occasion was in August 1839, when the
farewell sermon provoked spirited dissent:

> (Two or three voices: 'That will not do'.) Yes, it will do. (Nay it won't
> do.' Yes, it shall do. (It will not do.) Stephens: It will do; it shall do. (A
> voice: I will fight blood up to the eyes before that shall do.) Stephens:
> So will I fight blood up to the eyes; but I will not shed a drop of blood,
> nor will I see a single drop of blood shed, unless I know that in
> shedding my own blood, and in the shedding of my neighbour's
> blood, I am likely to get what I want either for myself or for my
> children that are to come after me. Let not that good friend behind
> me be angry. They are none the worse men that are all pluck . . .

If the congregation were 'ruffians of the lowest type', they were the very
people whose general absence from Christian worship in the nineteenth
century has been noticed repeatedly by social and church historians.[16]

Stephens accepted the right to unbelief, befriended the unorthodox
and the secularist, and even on occasion invited them to his churches.
Richard Carlile came to Charlestown in 1838 to debate with Stephens
on the best way to improve the lot of the people, with all proceeds going
to the Charlestown building fund. Although he opposed the principles
of Paine and Carlile, Stephens worked with unbelievers who were social
reformers. Though he was firm in his own faith, many of his flock in the
late thirties were far less secure in theirs. It is very difficult (if not
impossible) from the surviving evidence to determine how Christian
they were. One pointer is to trace what little is known of the careers of
five Stephenite leaders.

John Broadbent the clockmaker was a trustee of Charlestown chapel.
He came from a staunchly Wesleyan family, and was a local preacher in
1834; he served the Stephenites in the same capacity, and on the 1839
plan, he was appointed to conduct a Stalybridge love feast. In 1838 he

moved the resolution to boycott those who had given evidence against Stephens. A physical force Chartist, he served a year's imprisonment for conspiracy to incite the people to arms. He imbibed his political principles in the United States, and Major Williams in 1840 thought that he might be induced to emigrate. Williams considered him 'a man of some mind'. He 'had his own ideas about religion, but is more inclined to Mr Stephens than anyone else'. He appears on the plan of 1852, but not on that of 1853–4.[17]

George Johnson the hatter was another local preacher on the plan of 1839. An ex-Wesleyan, Johnson chaired the Charlestown Christmas tea party in 1838, and later suffered imprisonment as a Chartist in the Kirkdale House of Correction. There his interviewer thought him 'a religious enthusiast who makes the scriptures his text book for worldly conduct. He stated to me, I only consider myself bound to obey the laws of man, when in consonance with that of God, as laid down in the scriptures. He is wholly engrossed with this subject, and an intimate friend of the Rev Mr Stephens at Chester Castle.' He seems to have dropped out of the Stephenites by the forties, although he spoke warmly of Stephens at the presentation of 1846. He took part in the Chartist agitations of 1842 and 1848, and in the factory campaign in 1849. By the sixties, he had emigrated to America.[18]

John Avison was a Stalybridge cotton operative who was discharged for his part in the ten hours agitation. Laboriously he prepared himself to become a schoolmaster. His name appears in the list of Stephenite preachers on the 1839 and 1852 plans, and he taught at the People's School. He became the general secretary of the Fielden Association, and contributed to the *Ashton Chronicle*. He was arrested in 1842, and was bound over to keep the peace. After he moved to Saddleworth in 1843, he was the principal of a Wesleyan day school for over thirty years, and president of the Saddleworth Literary and Philosophical Society for over twelve years. An admirer of Stephens, Avison spoke at the presentation in 1846, and was a member of the Stephens memorial committee in 1881.[19]

Charles Dain was a Stalybridge confectioner and later an auctioneer; at one time, he had invested money in a cotton mill. In 1832, he was the first person in Stalybridge visited by Stephens, and he followed his minister and friend out of Wesleyan Methodism. He remained a consistent Stephenite until his death in 1871; his name appears as a preacher on all three of the surviving Stephenite plans, and he was a trustee of the People's School. He was in no doubt about the beneficial effects of Stephens's ministry. At the Christmas tea party in 1838, Dain said:

> For nearly seven years he had sat under Mr Stephens's ministry, and he would challenge the whole world to point to any clergyman whose pulpit labours had affected so great a change in the morals, the habits and the general conduct of society at large. This was the real reason why Mr Stephens was so much hated by the rich. He was raising the poor – lifting them up out of that degraded and demoralised state in which he first found them. They were coming over from practical infidelity to practical Christianity – were becoming an intelligent, thoughtful, religious, neighbourly, and patriotic people; and this change did not suit the rich . . . Mr Stephens has been charged with setting master and servant at variance. He had done the very opposite. He had found them at variance. He had striven to reconcile them. To the workmen he had taught obedience, diligence, respect and good conduct in all the relations of life. To the employer he had taught justice and mercy towards those in his service – the royal law of Christ – and he was sure if Mr Stephens's advice were taken and acted upon by all, we should have very different times.[20]

Abel Swann the tailor was the quintessential Stephenite. A Yorkshireman who came to Dukinfield in 1829, Swann was a Wesleyan local preacher who became one of Stephens's greatest friends and disciples. His name appears in the list of preachers on all three Stephenite plans. He was involved in all Stephens's campaigns, as has been apparent in earlier chapters; for three years, he even gave Stephens a home after the death of his first wife. Swann completed his education as an adult pupil of the People's School. He gave many years of selfless public service, first as a Conservative Stalybridge town commissioner and later as a councillor. He served for thirteen years on the Stalybridge School Board. He was constantly in the columns of the local press, defending his own or his minister's policies, describing himself as a Cobbett-type radical. He belonged to the Druids, the Oddfellows, the Orange Order, and the Conservative party, as well as to the Stephenites. After 1875 he rejoined the Wesleyans, but still loyal to previous teaching, he was expelled in 1881 for opposing the Sunday closure of public houses. In 1888, he presided at the opening ceremony of the monument in Stamford Park, emphasizing the great debt that the people of the district owed to Stephens for what he had done for them.[21]

Two out of these five leaders seem to have lost their Christian vision (Broadbent and Johnson), while the other three retained it. Two of the three (Dain and Swann) had been Wesleyan preachers before 1834, but so had Broadbent, so this was no guarantee of future fidelity; Johnson too had been a Wesleyan. All five were united by their personal attachment to Stephens. If they were at all representative of the swollen rank and file in the late thirties, mighty dilemmas of faith must have flourished within the Stephenite churches.

The dilemma was not lessened when in the summer of 1839 M'Douall accused Stephens of indecent assault. It is noteworthy that during the crisis, the Stephenites tried to function as a court of church discipline. Stephens was suspended from his ministry, and the next senior preacher Joseph Hilton chaired the boisterous open-air meeting that enquired into the charge. The period of suspension was short, for in early July it was announced that Stephens was to return to his pulpit to explain the causes of his differences with M'Douall. He satisfied the Stephenites, since no more was heard of the charge.[22]

When Stephens was imprisoned, he realized clearly that the survival of his churches was at stake. Inevitably his removal meant a decrease in church attendance and in pulpit supply, as well as a prospect of attempted proselytism by other interested political or religious movements. Though the details are obscure, the dangers were real enough. As early as September 1839, the circuit local preachers wrote to him of an abortive attempt to close their chapel doors; they reassured him that 'we are yours in Christ, and with you . . .' An anxious Stephens began to write a stream of pastoral letters from Chester Castle to encourage the faithful:

Let your first and most strenuous exertions be directed to maintain your own independence and comfort as a society. Your chapels and schools must be supported first of all . . . Impress this upon the minds of your congregations. Tell them it is my most earnest wish – my entreaty – my command that they should preserve inviolate and unimpaired those institutions which I have laboured to set up amongst them.

In October he thanked the people of Hyde for 'the stand they have made against the men who are plotting both against me and them'. He warned the circuit against those who 'would seek to snare you by the formation of secret societies for political purposes' – possibly a reference to O'Connor's attempt to win over the Hyde and Stalybridge Stephenites in November 1839. At Stalybridge, 'wicked men' (the persecuting local cotton masters) had long 'been in league to break you up'.[23]

The dissension may not have been entirely political. In March 1840 he wrote to circuit leaders in rarely used christological and trinitarian language. Stephens reminded them that despite doctrinal diversity, there should be no differences about the need for Christian deeds to others. By such deeds 'we show the likeness we bear to our Father in heaven, and the kinship we claim to our Healer, Leader and Holy brother Jesus, the one Saviour of the world'. In all that he said and did, Christ had shown that his followers must display the same kind of love to others as he had borne towards all. '. . . we cannot, when we have all this before our eyes, be under any mistake as to the way by which we are bound to prove our fellowship and oneness with the Son; as the Son is fellow and one with the Father, who with the Holy Ghost is God over all, blessed for evermore'. Certainly Stephens warned against sectarianism with monotonous regularity. 'In religion bear in mind you are not a sect – in politics, never belong to a party.'[24]

Nor did he neglect other matters. 'Keep up your religious services steadily and zealously. Whatever else you do, fill your chapels and keep them out of debt'. True religion was 'the yielding up of the whole man, body, soul and spirit to the guidance of the truth as it is in Jesus'. He thought that 'plain, simple earnest and energetic appeals made to the understandings and hearts of men will never fail to produce corresponding fruits'. 'The great work of snatching our fellow men out of the burning will always be the first and last business of true, zealous and devoted ministers of the gospel'. He wanted preaching to be free from jargon, winning, and authoritative. He was pleased that many had come forward to supply preaching for the plan. He advised preaching from house to house, since in March 1840 he noted there were between thirty to forty preachers on the plan, but only seven preaching places (three less than the previous July). While he was grateful for his flock's financial support, he constantly reminded them of the needs of the poor. He urged plain Bible teaching in the Sunday schools, with plenty of Whitsuntide merry making for the children, 'not forgetting the currant cakes and the treacle beer'.[25]

By April 1840, the immediate danger had passed. Charlestown was enjoying 'a still and pious calm', and six months later Stephens wrote to King Street Stalybridge: 'You have outstood it all, and you still stand.' He asked for a 'unanimous and affectionate' call to return to them after his release.[26]

Despite the survival of his three main causes at Ashton, Stalybridge and Hyde, Stephens had no easy task when he returned in 1841. The 'hungry forties' were not conducive to the prosperity of small Christian bodies, and emigration ('self banishment' to Stephens) began to sap Stephenite strength. Their minister's break with Chartism meant smaller congregations, though they tended to increase dramatically at times of social crisis. One positive achievement was the opening in 1841 of the People's School at Brierley Street, Stalybridge, for Sunday school children of all denominations. Eleven trustees headed by Charles Dain took possession of the site in May, costs being met by voluntary contributions and a mortgage. Two years later it was reported that the Stephenites had 127 Sunday school teachers and 790 scholars, as well as 520 'readers in scriptures'.[27]

In February 1844 large placards in Ashton proclaimed THE PEOPLE'S CHURCH IN DANGER. Charlestown's mortgagee had demanded his money, and the trustees were unable to pay. Stephens was to be empowered to prepare a new deed transferring the mortgage to him, and conveying the chapel as security; but as he would not guarantee further debts of £80, the trustees refused to act. By March agreement was reached, and the chapel conveyed to Stephens and his trustee James Henwood of Hull, one of his wife's relations. The mortgagee was paid £351, and all ended well.[28]

Although in 1848, 1,500 factory operatives returned to Charlestown, they had gone again by the time of the religious census of 1851. Although Stephens refused to co-operate, about a hundred adults and eighty scholars were counted at Charlestown on census Sunday by the registrar, who was told that when Stephens preached, the congregation doubled.[29]

Stephens' growing pro-Anglican sentiment was reflected in two later plans for April to July 1852 and October 1853 to January 1854. They are no longer headed 'Ashton circuit', though on one of them appears the words 'the quarterly vestry of the whole circuit'. Services at the three remaining churches of Ashton, Stalybridge and Hyde are given under the Prayer Book Sunday lessons for matins and evensong. 'Methodist' survivals included love feasts, Sunday school anniversaries, and a much reduced list of local preachers – fourteen on the first, and nine on the second, with one probationer. Despite his Anglican sympathies, Stephens refused ordination into the priesthood, as earlier he had refused dissenting overtures for a chapel of his own.[30]

Stephens' move to Stalybridge was followed in 1856 by the sale of Charlestown chapel for £420 to the Roman Catholics. Hyde is heard of no more, so presumably the circuit and his ministry outside Stalybridge came to an end. At the remaining Stephenite church at King Street, the service in 1857 was 'that of the Church of England, with very effective intonation and chaunts'. Stephens lectured at the newly-founded Christ College in the People's School. In these years, King Street enjoyed a more normal church life. Thus in 1859, the choir, the minister and some of the congregation dined at the Commercial Inn, where £30 was raised for a larger organ. Forgetting old controversies, Stephens presided at a Booth Street Wesleyan Association meeting, at which another spoke on the comforts of home.[31]

He attacked the spread of American-style revivalism in 1858. An editorial in the *Ashton Standard* did not mince words:

> The men who get up these religious extravangancies have no credentials to show in proof of the reality of their mission. They are not more learned, nor more devout, nor more virtuous, and certainly not more humble than the great body of Christian teachers whom they pretend to excel in zealous concern for the souls of the people. On the other hand, they are for the most part distinguished for their ignorance, their vulgarity, and coarse-minded familiarity with sacred things . . . All Christians are agreed in believing Holy Scripture to contain all things necessary for salvation . . . But does it follow from this that unauthorized individuals are at liberty to use its language, attach a meaning to its phrases, and put a construction upon its statements to suit their own peculiar objects? Yet that is what is done, not only without any scruple, but with the boldest effrontery by the disciples of the revivalist school. No heresy was more impudently maintained by an appeal to the Bible in proof of its divine sanction than the wild delusion now under review . . .

Shrewdly he seized on one specific point:

> It is both curious and instructive to note that in the American awakenings, now exciting so much attention, that *negroes* are not admitted to their meetings. For the white to associate with the black in the presence of HIM with whom there is no respect of persons would be too great a condescension; it would be a social degradation to which they could not bring themselves to stoop.

In 1868, it was reported that Stephens opposed the Protestant Evangelical Mission, but nevertheless he had been invited to lecture at one of its meetings.[32]

For the last time, the cotton famine of the sixties brought back the crowds to King Street; but again they fell away when the crisis passed. Although their minister remained a controversial figure in town life, the King Street congregation was dwindling due to continued emigration and marriage into other churches. By the early seventies, the events of 1834 were a remote memory; some of the stalwarts such as Charles Dain had died. Stephens was an old man with an intimidating reputation from a stormier past; in more settled times, less exotic churches than his were more to churchgoing taste.

There were new recruits. The most promising was James France, who worked from the age of nine in a cotton mill, and eventually rose to become an overlooker. He was fully involved in the later factory movement, contributed to the *Ashton Standard* when Stephens was editor, was active in the cotton famine, and took a leading part in the Stalybridge Conservative party. An ardent Stephenite, France was a local preacher on the 1853–4 plan. After the closure of King Street in 1875, he became an Anglican. He was secretary of the Stephens memorial committee, and always remained an admirer of Stephens; but there were not enough men of his calibre to offset Stephenite losses.[33]

The moment of truth came in 1875. On 20 June, Stephens conducted the usual King Street anniversary services. His theme was change, in church, state and in life and manners. It was an apt choice, for change quickly came to King Street. On 17 July an advertisement in the *Ashton Reporter* declared that the church was to let; it continued to appear until the issue of 6 November. Without prior notice, an irate Stephens preached his last sermon on the 7th. Few details have survived, but basically it was a history of his ministry, enlivened by pungent comment. He began.

> If you think I am going to preach a farewell sermon or a funeral sermon, you are mistaken. If ever my funeral sermon is preached, I should like to preach it myself, for the very good reason that nobody else can do it.

He had found in his agitation for the ten hours' bill that all churches and chapels worked for their own advantage. 'With the close of his ministry he would give up the title "Rev" and be plain Mr Stephens.' He ended by dividing the church furniture among what remained of his congregation (about thirty in all), and he advised them to go to whatever church they chose. He seemed to be upset by his failure to let the chapel, which was later acquired by an aereated water company.[34]

It had been fifty years since a young Wesleyan probationer had gone to Beverley, and forty-one years since his retirement from Wesleyan Methodism. Oddly enough, the Wesleyan Conference of 1875 relaxed its rules for ministers by allowing them greater freedom as Christian citizens. Though the new rule was drawn up to safeguard connexional peace and unity, which in his day the young Stephens had violated, it was ironic that its real purpose was to allow ministers freedom to advocate disestablishment. There is no known reaction from the miscreant of 1834 to this remarkable change of heart. He had long since found freedom as a Christian citizen to proclaim a coherent social Christian message that his former church had yet to find.[35]

He outlived the Stephenites by a little over three years. They had loyally supported him, enabling him to exercise a rare and remarkable ministry; with his retirement, their work came to an end. His genuinely non-sectarian convictions prevented the sect from ever becoming a permanent and fully developed denomination. As he had written in prison:

> I know how easy it was to make followers, and build up a sect, but thank God, my heart always shuddered at the wickedness, as my mind rose above the littleness and empty outside show of the being the head of one of the thousand and one so-called religious bodies with which the land is overrun. Instead, therefore, of doing anything to induce men to join themselves to me, and pin their faith upon my sleeve, I ever stood aloof from this kind of leadership, and strove rather to bring all, to whichsoever of the jarring creeds and warring churches they might belong, to hear, read, think, mark and learn for themselves, asking wisdom of God, who has promised to guide all aright that walk in the way he sets before them.

In his reaction from Wesleyanism, he was opposed also 'to the establishment of societies having a directive centre over which individual localities have no control'. This too inhibited Stephenite development. A larger price had to be paid for these attitudes. With the demise of the Stephenites, there vanished the last, faint possibility that their minister's received teaching would affect the coming recovery by the churches of the social dimensions of faith.[36]

11

Conclusion

In south-east Lancashire, Stephens was never quite forgotten. His memory was quietly treasured in Ashton and Stalybridge. Some still living in 1976 could remember a gale on Hartshead Pike being called a 'Stephens wind'. The Stamford Park monument, the People's School, the Hollins and the sadly impoverished grave survive. Blue commemorative plaques appear on the remains of the old Stalybridge town hall. However, Rayner Stephens Way has vanished in an Ashton redevelopment scheme; and unlike that other celebrated nineteenth-century Ashton divine, John Wroe the licentious prophet, Stephens has never had a series of television programmes devoted to his exploits. On the wider scene, he was being forgotten while he still lived, for he was a disturbing figure from a previous age; and after his death, Holyoake's biography remained his sole popular memorial. Nevertheless, in Britain today the Revd Ian Paisley demonstrates that the 'political parson' is not extinct. The notion of a revolutionary traditionalist may seem a contradiction in British terms, but not in black Africa, where potent appeals to tradition were made in successful struggles against an alien colonialism.[1]

One major reason why Stephens' memory faded was the belief that his perceived inconsistencies rob him of true greatness. Even his admirers, in choosing for his epitaph the words 'he hath done what he could', were admitting that he was not a figure of the first rank. For many outside the charmed circle, he championed and abandoned causes with equal alacrity. As a Christian patriot, he claimed the right to participate in politics in order to press for social reform. At different times, he was a liberal disestablisher and a traditional upholder of the constitution, a Wesleyan reformer and a pro-Anglican, a supporter of radicals and Tories, of teetotallers and publicans. A sectarian leader who opposed sectarianism, he split his own followers by taking up factory reform. His unrestrained fervour for his chosen causes did not stop at the public advocacy of violence, resulting in the alienation of much potential support. Although he mistrusted political reform, he became the magnetic orator of Chartism, only to repudiate it at his trial. Such a record did not inspire confidence in his judgment. To Chartists he was a turncoat, and to later critics an unpredictable, pretentious and untrustworthy 'old greybeard'. Others since tend to agree, seeing in such a mass of contradictions the cause of his comparative failure. They echo the words of Napoleon Ives in 1876, who applied to Stephens the ancient adage of Horace that he 'had been like a mountain in labour, and had brought forth a mouse'.[2]

Stephens was not an original thinker, but (like John Arthur Roebuck, a politician he admired), a man of fiercely independent judgment, which he had won at some cost by his resignation from the Wesleyan ministry. Like Wesley, he was a man of one book, by which all things were to be judged. His Wesleyan roots gave him a foundation of biblical humanitarianism that undergirded all his agitations. Factory and poor law reform were not the outworking of political theory, but the inescapable, minimum demands of Christian social justice in a newly industralized society, and thus imperatives for a professedly Christian nation. Despite all its religious activism, the nineteenth century was not an age of faith; yet Stephens was remarkably true to his vision. His troubles arose because in order to realize it, he was prepared to be opportunistic in everything else. Throughout his public life, he had warned against the evils of absolute party and sectarian loyalties, and in practice he refused to be bound by them, despite the impression so often created. In his own way, he embodied the late Professor Butterfield's celebrated advice to hold to Christ, and for the rest be totally uncommitted.[3]

His worst mistakes were in politics. Chartism was a fortuitous extension of his social aims, and despite the fleeting fame it brought, it involved him in insoluble dilemmas over physical force. There is little doubt that for decades after his death, his violent language discredited him. The Congregationalist minister Joseph Parker, writing in 1899, recalled in his youth a portrait of Stephens hanging in the house of his radical father:

> There I often gazed on it with wonder and awe. The man looked innocent enough in his black coat and white neckerchief... Here was a man who threatened to preach 'Edinburgh into flames' and 'Glasgow into ashes' if the Government withheld such and such from the working classes, and yet this wolf in sheep's clothing looked all

over, from top to toe, like a Wesleyan minister accustomed to class meetings and hymn books!

However, the language of Christian physical force is less shocking to a later Christian generation in newly developing countries, familiar with liberation theology and confronted by the problem of Christian participation in armed struggle against oppression.[4]

Another damaging factor was his backward-looking political vision. A bold social agitator who caught the attention of Marx and Engels, Stephens drew inspiration from King Alfred and the ages of faith, via Richard Oastler. He could evoke a powerful myth of bygone Christian social concern:

> The house of God was not then a den of thieves, who plundered the altar to starve the poor and enrich themselves. The poor were the children of the church, because they were the cherished brethren of Jesus . . . Oh England, how deeply hast thou fallen! . . . In the time of which I now speak, the religion of the country was the law of the country, and its law was its religion; substantially they were one . . .

He painted a vivid picture of the thirteenth-century church sanctioning an idealized Magna Carta:

> Cathedrals like those of York, Lincoln and Westminster, crowded with the bold and stalwart yeomanry of England trooping in their thousands from hut and homestead and hall, leaving their weapons piled up outside the gates of the sanctuary, standing uncovered in the house of God and thundering forth, as with one heart and voice the terrible 'Amen' after the bishops dashed the candles to the ground, exclaiming with the congregated multitude: 'thus let him be extinguished and stink in hell who dares to violate this charter of our liberties'. And then, by way of contrast, think of the maudlin meetings that have been held in our large towns, to ascertain the reasons why the people no longer go to church as their fathers did. Never, never more will that sight be seen again until justice – equal and impartial justice – is again restored and effectually administered. Priests and people must alike invoke, maintain and practice it.

However potent was the magic of the speaker on his Stalybridge audience, any resemblance to the realities of contemporary politics was purely coincidental. Peel's Conservative party declined 'Tory radicalism' and came to terms with industrial capitalism; thereafter there was no future for Oastler's ideology. As for the churches, even if all denominations had agreed with him, they lacked the power to restore a British Christendom. Stephens was opposed to the spirit of the age, and complete success was bound to elude him.[5]

Within his limitations, Stephens accomplished a good deal. No one could deny his substantial contribution to the success of the factory movement. He lived long enough to rejoice in Disraeli's three Factory Acts of 1874, 1875 and 1878, which finally established the ten hours principle, gave protection from exploitation to factory women and children, and consolidated factory and workshop legislation under a single Act. The Factory Acts were to provide a model for future social legislation. He had helped in all this, but had long since gone on to campaign for an eight hour day. Contrary to his hopes, he never lived to see the repeal of the 1834 poor law; but anti-poor law agitation had forced government to weaken the law's Benthamite rigour in practice, and by 1863 Stephens pointed out that no one then argued that poverty ought to be punished. In that sense, Stephens found confirmation for his social judgments from his fellow countrymen. He understood correctly the cause of the cotton famine, and did his utmost to make the nation aware of the real condition of the operatives. His less spectacular but solid work for trade unionism over many years earned him respect and support from a new generation of workers, who had been in their cradles when he had been at the height of his fame. His last known letter on public affairs was written to encourage George Howell, secretary to the Parliamentary committee of the Trades Union Congress, and one of the 'junta' of trade union leaders.[6]

In Ashton and Stalybridge, Stephens in the desperate years gave the cotton workers a badly needed self-confidence to stand up to their masters. Even the possession of weapons was a sign of human dignity. 'I found that the badge of a bondsman was the print of the lash on his naked back – the mark of a freeman the trusty sword hung over the door-post of his castle-cottage.' He kept hope alive, and inspired self-respect and principled resistance. As late as the cotton famine, Dr Bridges called him 'the only man who speaks up and out'. Even when they disagreed with him, the operatives who knew him respected and loved him, because he instinctively responded to distress and injustice. He listened to hundreds of them in their own miserable homes, knew their plight and tried to relieve it as best he could. He believed that no one living had visited so many alleys and back portions of towns as he had. He spoke to the people in their own dialect, and could voice their social aspirations in speeches of unrivalled if fleeting power. He retained his hold on them in later life, despite his often eccentric interventions in local affairs. He never confined his ministry to fellow Christians. It was the rare Victorian parson who could conduct a funeral service for an unbeliever like his friend Harry Hindle, conveying human warmth and Christian conviction in the same address; but as he said, he was concerned not only with those who knew the gospel, but also with those who did not.[7]

In the last analysis Stephens must be seen as a minister, not as an agitator. Here his scattered seed seemed to fall on stony ground, for despite his unusual gifts and pioneering ministry in the pulpit and the press, he had little impact on the recovery of a Christian social gospel within the churches. This came through the Christian socialist fathers Maurice, Ludlow and Kingsley, who raised the banner in 1848. More cerebral than the factory reformers, they did not use the language of romantic Christian violence, nor were they unduly influenced by an Anglo-Saxon Christian golden age; but they were far less effective in terms of working-class support and legislative achievement. Maurice's movement was short-lived, but it shaped the future. In the seventies and eighties, the teaching of Maurice on the kingdom of God influenced a younger generation of both Anglo-Catholics and Nonconformists, and shortly after Stephens' death, a new Christian collectivism arose within the Protestant churches.

Stephens' Christian influence was more generalized in character. He was among the first to fight for Christian social values in an increasingly secularized society. 'I have asked especially whether the principles of our modern political economy can be made to quadrate with the statements of divine revelation . . .' He struggled against fatalistic economic theories that were accepted without question by most Christians of all persuasions, and politically he challenged Christian support for the prevailing Liberal–Conservative consensus. His isolation was such that it was not entirely pretentious for him to exclaim in his last sermon that he was 'the only minister who faithfully preached the truth'. In this, he illustrated another saying of Professor Herbert Butterfield – that a religion does not need to be successful, for its function in human history is to be in opposition. In the long run, his prophetic passion, undaunted courage and unchanging testimony within Christian circles that thought him incurably wrong were more significant than tangible results. It was fitting that when a modest recognition came at last, it was from a Wesleyan Methodist source.

S. E. Keeble was the leading Wesleyan social activist of his time. In 1922, he wrote his most important book, *Christian Responsibility for the Social Order*, and included Stephens in an historical survey of social Christians:

> What use might not have been made of this powerful speaker, with his intense hatred of the un-Christian conditions under which the people groaned, had he but been retained within the Church by patient, tolerant and far-seeing statesmanship, and given scope and a mission!

It never happened, but at last this latter-day Wesleyan lament recognized that Stephens had 'done what he could'.[8]

What he and the other factory reformers had done was to make many English factory workers aware that despite the complacency of the churches, the realm could still be purged of bitter things. Christian redress was still a possible alternative to secularist social reform, whether of a Liberal or a Marxist kind. It was an awareness that was conveyed in the crucial twenty years before 1850, when working-class consciousness was being forged. In Britain for decades it was to be a major factor in preventing a total divorce between the worlds of faith and work. It questions the argument that no Christians of any stature broke through the class barriers in sacrificial concern for the new industrial proletariat, so that Christian shoulders bore 'the burden of proletarian unbelief'.[9]

Stephens died confident in the ultimate triumph of God's cause. He had set it forth in the last verse of his best-known poem:

> Scatter the seed! the teeming seed,
> Wide as the world abroad;
> Soon it will show itself indeed
> The garden of our God;
> We work and wait – we toil and trust,
> Sure that the end will come;
> This wilderness of evil must
> Be clothed with heavenly bloom!

He had scattered the seed, and the end was sure.[10]

Key to Abbreviations Used in the Notes

Further details of books referred to may be found in the Bibliography

AC	*Ashton Chronicle*
AH	*Ashton Herald*
AN	*Ashton News*
AR	*Ashton Reporter*
AS	*Ashton Standard*
ASR	*Ashton and Stalybridge Reporter*
AWH	*Ashton Weekly Herald*
AWR	*Ashton and Weekly Reporter*
CA	*Christian Advocate*
DNB	*Dictionary of National Biography*
FM	J. T. Ward, *The Factory Movement 1830–1855*
HO	*Home Office Papers*
HO MH	*Home Office: Ministry of Health*
HO TS	*Home Office: Treasury Solicitors*
MSA	*Manchester and Salford Advertiser*
MC	*Manchester Courier*
MCh	*Manchester Chronicle*
MG	*Manchester Guardian*
Mins W.C.	*Minutes of the Wesleyan Conference*
MT	*Manchester Times*
NS	*Northern Star*
NTA	*National Temperance Advocate*
OS	*Oldham Standard*
PLC	*Poor Law Comission*
PM	*People's Magazine*
PP	*Political Pulpit*
RT	J. T. Ward, *Revolutionary Tory*
SH	*Stalybridge Herald*
SN	*Stalybridge News*
SR	*Stalybridge Reporter*
SS	*Stalybridge Standard*

SMM	*Stephens's Methodist Magazine*
SM Mag	*Stephens's Monthly Magazine*
WHS Proceedings	*Proceedings of the Wesley Historical Society*
WM Mag	*Wesleyan Methodist Magazine*
WMA Mag	*Wesleyan Methodist Association Magazine*

Notes

1 The Methodist Minister

1. The twelve children were: Barnabas (b. 1797), Sharon (b. 1799), Rebecca Eliza (b. 1800), John (b. 1802), Jabez (b. 1803), Joseph Rayner (b. 1805), John (b. 1806), Mary (b. 1808), Samuel (b. 1810), Edward (b. 1811), George (b. 1813), and Mary Ann (b. 1819). Barnabas, the first John, Jabez and Mary died in infancy. (Sampler in the possession of Mr and Mrs R. S. Unwin.) The family motto was Deo Non Fortuna (Through God, not by chance), but it is uncertain how old it is. See also G. J. Holyoake, *Life of Joseph Rayner Stephens*, Williams & Norgate 1881, pp. 19–26; M. Taylor, *Joseph Rayner Stephens, Political Preacher*, Ph.D. thesis. University of California 1966, pp. 27–30; J. Stephens, *The Advantages which Man derives from Woman*, 3rd edn 1828; J. R. Stephens, *The Political Pulpit*, Sermon 9, 9/6/1839, p. 78.
2. *Wakefield Free Press* 24/10/1863. *Minutes of Wesleyan Methodist Conference* 1841, pp. 155–6. Methodist Archives Centre *MAM PLP 100 10 4*. *Wesleyan Methodist Magazine* 1811, pp. 895–906. Anon., *Wesleyan Takings* 1840, 1.351. J. N. Clark, *English Society 1688–1832*, CUP 1985, pp. 235–247, and L. Colley, *Britons: Forging the Nation 1707–1837*, Yale University Press and London 1992, pp. 18f. stress the crucial role of Protestantism in cementing British patriotism.
3. *Stanford Rivers Baptismal Register* 1774–5; Holyoake, p. 22.
4. *Champion* 20/1/1839, p. 2. F. C. Pritchard, *Woodhouse Grove School*, 1978, pp. 38–9. J. F. Smith (ed.), *Manchester School Register* 3.1, pp. 136–7 (Cheetham Society, Vol. 93). Holyoake, pp. 27–8. *Nottingham and Newark Mercury* 29/3/1839, p. 98. *Manchester Guardian* 5/6/1876. W. E. A. Axon, *Cheshire Gleanings*, 1884, pp. 109–110. *Manchester and Salford Advertiser* 20/8/1836. *Christian Advocate* 22/8/1836, pp. 271–2. *Rebecca Stephens –James Helsby*, 20/11/1821. Holyoake, pp. 28–9.
5. *J. Stephens-McNicholl*, Jan 1824. His father noted Joseph's 'considerable gifts' but thought he wanted 'more time for the study of Divinity, and especially of our standard works.' *Galland-Bunting* 30/6/1825, in W. R. Ward (ed.), *The Early Correspondence of Jabez Bunting 1820–1829*, Royal Historical Society, Camden Fourth Series Vol. 11, pp. 112–3.

Wesleyan Candidates Book, 1825. J. T. Ward, 'Revolutionary Tory', *Transactions of the Lancashire and Cheshire Antiquarian Society*, 1958, Vol. 68, p. 94.

6. *Wesleyan Missionary Society minutes*, 1826. *Wesleyan Methodist Magazine* 1837, p. 532. *Owen–Watson* 7/10/1825. *Ordination certificate*, 29/5/1826, in the possession of Mrs D. Stephens-Krook. Ordination did not affect probation, which continued until Stephens' reception into full Connexion at the Conference of 1829; see *W. M. Minutes*, 1829, p. 47. See also J. C. Bowmer, 'Ordination in Methodism', *Proceedings of the Wesley Historical Society*, 1974, Vol. 39, pp. 121–7.

7. See R. Murray, *A Brief History of the Church in Sweden*, Stockholm 1961, and O. Hagen, *Preludes to Methodism in Northern Europe*, Norsk Forlagsselskap, Oslo 1961. Stephens said that Owen had no English workers (*Stephens–Morley* 27/7/1826); by 1830 his successor noted five (*Scott–Morley* 3/9/1830). Later writers (Hagen, p. 37) refer to workers brought from England. Owen in 1830 wanted 'a good Large Society among the Swedes and English' (*Owen–Morley* 4/7/1830), and Scott saw 'the principal sphere of usefulness . . . among the Natives' (*Scott–Morley* 3/9/1830). However, by 1837 he was saying that no Swedish Society could be formed (*W. M. Mag.* 1837, pp. 535–6). It it hard not to conclude that the Missionary Society in 1826 aimed at Swedish converts rather than ministering to English residents; much later, an article in the *London Quarterly Review* (1869, p. 305) explicitly stated that this was the object from the start.

8. *Stephens–Morley* 27/7/1826, 22/8/1826, *W. M. Mag* 1828, pp. 132–3. *W. M. Mag* 1837, p. 535 minimized Stephens' connection with the approach to Count de Geer; after 1834 there is a marked tendency in Wesleyan sources to belittle Stephens' Swedish ministry because of his subsequent English notoriety.

9. Holyoake, pp. 34–5. *Stephens–Morley* 20/4/1827. *Owen–Morley* 30/12/1826.

10. *Stephens–Morley* 20/4/1827. Holyoake, pp. 31–2, quoting from Bloomfield's letters of 5/6/1829 and 13/11/1829 to Stephens. All favourable references to Stephens are omitted from Georgiana Lady Bloomfield's *Memoir of Lord Bloomfield*, 2 vols, 1884. See also G. Scott, *A Coronet laid at the feet of Jesus*, 1856, and *W. M. Mag.* 1846, pp. 1091–5, 1886, pp. 426–9. For Stephens' duties at the embassy, see Holyoake, p. 30, Axon, p. 110. A. Gordon, *DNB*, 54, pp. 178–9. Oastler in 1839 said that Bloomfield wanted to get Stephens an appointment in the Church of England, but Stephens declined (*Northern Star* 6/4/1839).

11. *Stephens–Morley* 20/4/1827, 11/5/1827, 17/12/1827, 11/8/1828. *A. Gordon*, *DNB*, pp. 178–9. According to *Observer* 30/12/1838, Stephens visited France, Germany, Norway and Finland, and he told a prison inspector in 1840 that 'he had been in Germany some time on business

connected with the Wesleyans' (*HO 20/10*). Neither source mentioned Sweden! He offered to visit Germany three times while in Sweden (*Stephens–Morley* 9/12/1826, 11/5/1827, 3/4/1829). It is possible he went at some time between November 1829 and July 1830, when he had left Sweden and was without a British circuit; Bloomfield wrote to him on 13/11/1829 desiring either his return to Sweden, 'or that any project may be realized'. See Holyoake, p. 32.

12. *Stephens–Morley* 9/12/1826, 11/6/1827, 11/8/1828.

13. Holyoake, pp. 35–41. C. de Montalembert, *Lettres a un Ami du College*, L. Cornudet, 1827–30, 1873, p. 183. I am indebted to Mr B. Aspinwall for this reference. *Ashton Standard* 4/12/1858, p. 4.

14. *Stephens–Morley* 29/1/1829, 3/4/1829. *Missionary Society minutes* 27/5/1829, 1/7/1829. *Scott–Morley* 9, 11/8/1830. *Northern Star* 6/4/1839, p. 1. Holyoake, pp. 31–2. For later contrasts between Stephens and Scott, see Georgiana Lady Bloomfield, *Memoir of Lord Bloomfield*, 1884, 1.310, *W. M. Mag.* 1886, pp. 427–8. Scott was careful to distance himself from Stephens and occasionally was sharply critical (*Scott–Morley* 4/7/1834, 10/10/1834). For the end of the mission, see *W. M. Mag* 1840, pp. 164–9, 1847, pp. 820–3. Scott's connections with Swedish pietists and American Methodists form a bridge with the later, successful Methodist work in Sweden.

15. See D. Hempton, *Methodism and Politics in British Society*, Hutchinson 1987, pp. 116–148.

16. Holyoake, pp. 41–4; Holyoake omitted the year at Newcastle, thus misleading later writers. See *W. M. Mag* 1831, p. 628, *Christian Advocate* 16/6/1834, p. 190. B. Gregory, *Sidelights on the Conflicts of Methodism*, Cassell 1899, pp. 93, 128–132.

17. J. T. Ward, *RT*, p. 94. E. A. Rose, 'Ashton Churches and Chapels', *Victorian Ashton* ed. S. A. Harrop and E. A. Rose, 1974, pp. 62, 64. W. M. Bowman, *England in Ashton-under-Lyne*, Ashton 1960, p. 140, 186.

18. Rose, p. 67. Bowman, pp. 235f.

19. Rose, p. 65. E. A. Rose, *Methodism in Ashton-under-Lyne 1797–1914*, Ashton 1969, pp. 11, 20, 14, 4.

20. Rose, *Victorian Ashton*, p. 60. His two booklets on Methodism in Ashton-under-Lyne give a detailed account. See 2.11 for Hutchinson.

21. Quotations from the *Circular to Wesleyan Methodists* supplied by courtesy of Dr D. Gowland. See also E. A. Rose, *Methodism in Ashton-under-Lyne 1797–1914*, pp. 33–4. *Stephens–Holgate* n.d. but postmark apparently 5/8/1833; supplied by courtesy of Dr W. R. Ward. *CA* 16/2/1835, p. 53.

22. *W. M. Mag* 1832 had given a cautious approval of the Reform Act. *MSA* 5/1/1833, p. 4; *Circular to Wesleyan Methodists*.

23. M. Tylecote, *The Mechanics Institutes of Lancashire and Yorkshire before 1851*, Manchester 1957, p. 251. E. A. Rose, *Methodism in Ashton-under-Lyne 1797–1914*, p. 34. *Champion* 20/1/1839, p. 2. Hindley is dealt with

favourably by J. W. Follows, *Antecedents of the International Labour Organisation*, Oxford 1951, pp. 10–21, and more critically by Tylecote, pp. 247f, and J. T. Ward, *The Factory Movement 1830–1855*, Macmillan 1962. Ward reflects the complaints of factory reformers. *Mason–Grey* 6/3/1848, in *HO 45/2410*.

24. For the church and state crisis of 1834, see O. Chadwick, *The Victorian Church*, 1966, Vol. 1, pp. 60–100; W. H. Mackintosh, *Disestablishment and Liberation*, Epworth 1972, pp. 15f; W. R. Ward, *Religion and Society in England 1790–1850*, Batsford 1972, pp. 126–134, 156–9, 167, and chapter 7. For Ashton, see E. A. Rose, *Victorian Ashton*, p. 65, *Methodism in Ashton-under-Lyne 1797–1914*, pp. 34–5, and *Manchester Times* 1/2/1834, p. 3.

25. D. Hempton, *Methodism and Politics in British Society 1750–1850*, Hutchinson 1984, pp. 180–1, 185–6. W. R. Ward, *Religion and Society in England 1790–1850*, chapter 6. B. Gregory, *Sidelights on the Conflicts of Methodism*, Cassell 1899, p. 162. *W. M. Mag.* 1833, pp. 727–8.

26. *CA* 12/5/1834, p. 150.

27. *MT* 1/2/1834, pp. 2, 3; *CA* 10/2/1834, p. 43.

28. *MT* 1/2/1834, pp. 2, 3; *CA* 10/2/1834, p. 43; *MT* 8, 15/3/1834; *The Case of the Rev. Joseph Rayner Stephens, Wesleyan Methodist Minister, collected from the Christian Advocate Newspaper*, 1834, p. 5.

29. *Bunting–Grindrod* 11/3/1834 in W. E. Ward, *Early Victorian Methodism*, Oxford 1976, p. 51. E. Butterworth, *Diary*, March 1834. R. Rees, *Diary*. B. Gregory, p. 154. *Bowers–Bunting*, 29/4/1834 in W. R. Ward, *Early Victorian Methodism*, pp. 60–2. *MT* 5/4/1834, p. 4. *CA* 12/5/1834, p. 150. G. Smith, *History of Wesleyan Methodism*, London 1870, Vol. 3, pp. 205f.

30. *Hare and J. Stephens–J. R. Stephens* 16/4/1834, in Holyoake, pp. 48–9. *Grindrod–Bunting* 17/4/1834 in W. R. Ward, *Early Victorian Methodism*, Oxford 1976, p. 59. *CA* 12/5/1834. Holyoake, pp. 48–9.

31. B. Gregory, p. 152. *Bowers–Bunting* 29/4/1834, *Grindrod–Bunting* in W. R. Ward, *Early Victorian Methodism*, pp. 60–2, 63.

32. *Bowers–Bunting* 29/4/1834. *Case and Resolutions of the Manchester District Meeting* 12/5/1834; *Grindrod–Bunting* 1/5/1834.

33. *Bowers–Bunting* 29/4/1834. *CA* 12/5/1834, p. 150. *MT* 24/5/1834. *Case and Resolutions*, 12/5/1834. B. Gregory, pp. 152, 153.

34. *CA* 5, 12/5/1834. *MT* 24/5/1834. *Case and Resolutions*, 12/5/1834.

35. *MT* 3, 10/5/1834, *CA* 5, 12, 19, 26/5/1834, 2, 9, 16/6/1834. *Case and Resolutions*, 12/5/1834. *Stephens's Methodist Magazine*, June, July 1834.

36. *CA* 2, 16, 20/6/1834. *Beecham–Bunting* n.d. postmarked 5/7/1834 in W. R. Ward, *Early Victorian Methodism*, p. 79. *Minutes W. M. Conference* 1834. Rose, *Methodism in Ashton-under-Lyne 1797–1914*, p. 37.

37. *CA* 9/6/1834, 3/11/1834, p. 348. *Hargreaves–Bunting* 4/7/1834 in W. R. Ward, *Early Victorian Methodism*, p. 79; O. Rattenbury, *Flame of Freedom*, Epworth 1931, pp. 80–2. I am indebted to Dr O. A. Beckerlegge

for drawing my attention to this source.

38. The main primary sources for the Stephens case at Conference are: (i) *Turner–T. P. Bunting* 5/8/1834, in W. R. Ward, *Early Victorian Methodism*, p. 82; (ii) *Stephens's Methodist Magazine*, Sept. 1834, pp. 146–156, and corresponding issues of the *Christian Advocate*; (iii) Gregory's *Sidelights*, pp. 150–164. Unlike much of Gregory's treatment of Fowler's contemporary notes on Conference debates, he reproduced Fowler in some detail on the Stephens case, refuting the charge of the Chartist historian Gammage that Conference was politically prejudiced; see J. Kent, *The Age of Disunity*, Epworth 1966, pp. 118–120. However, Gregory omitted most of Stephens' speech, given in *SMM*. John Stephens' accounts, which must have been 'leaked' by a Conference minister, produced a garbled version of Bunting's speech. *SMM* August 1834, pp. 81–8. *Diary* of Richard Reece. *SMM* Sept 1834, pp. 148, 153. See also *SMM* Oct 1834, p. 195, *CA* 3/11/1834, p. 348.

39. *SMM* Sept 1834, pp. 149–150. *Turner–T. P. Bunting* 5/8/1834.

40. *Turner–T. P. Bunting* 5/8/1834. Gregory, pp. 154–7.

41. *Turner–T. P. Bunting* 5/8/1834. Gregory, pp. 157–165. *SMM* pp. 151–3, 155–6. *SMM* included an account of John Stephens the younger's attempt to enter Wesley's Chapel during the Conference debate; he sent a message to the President seeking admittance where 'under your presidency, a meeting is now being held'. There was no reply.

42. Many recent historians follow Holyoake (pp. 47–7) and R. C. Gammage (History of the Chartist Movement, Newcastle 1894 pp. 55–6) in linking the factory issue with the Conference proceedings of 1834. See J. T. Ward, *RT*, pp. 94–5, though he avoided it in *FM*, p. 130; G. Parsons, *Religion in Victorian Britain*, Manchester 1988, Vol. 2, p. 42; R. Davies, *Methodism*, 1963, p. 152; see also *Proceedings of the Wesley Historical Society*, Feb. 1967, Vol. 36, pp. 16–21, and J. Kent, 'The Wesleyan Methodists to 1849', *A History of the Methodist Church in Great Britain*, Epworth 1978, Vol. 2, pp. 221, fn. 17. I shall return in Chapter 2 to the undated Stephens letter quoted by Holyoake.

43. See W. R. Ward, *Religion and Society in England 1790–1850*, p. 158 for this criticism of Bunting. In the *Journal* of the Northern Branch of the Wesley Historical Society for August 1968, Dr Ward thought Bunting's political shrewdness may have been greater than his moral straightforwardness in opposing disestablishment in 1834. Dr J. Kent in *The Age of Disunity*, Epworth 1966, p. 89 quoted Joseph Entwisle's approval of Connexional neutrality in 1829, even though this senior Wesleyan minister was an opponent of Catholic emancipation; he supported the District Meeting's suspension of Stephens (Gregory, p. 157). No one has thought Entwisle odd or lacking moral straightforwardness in any of this; it was the representative ministerial view that Wesleyan Methodism as such should be neutral on public issues that did not directly affect its interests.

44. Gregory, p. 164, 162. Bunting had admitted that 'Mr Stephens was not called upon to approve the resolutions, that would have been tyranny', but only to abstain from agitation (Gregory, p. 157). The pledge did not cover 'any peculiarities of private opinion', but required 'his readiness to meet as a Wesleyan Methodist minister the wishes of his brethren and to consult the peace and order of the Connexion' (*Minutes of Conference*, 1834). As will be seen, by 1875 even the Wesleyan Conference conceded that ministers were citizens, and should be allowed more freedom of expression.

45. *Champion* 20/1/1839, p. 2. *CA* 25/8/1834, 22, 29/9/1834, 13, 20, 27/10/1834, 10/11/1834. *SMM* Oct 1834 pp. 193, 199. *An Apology for Wesleyan Methodism in a letter to the Rev. Thomas Robinson, Minister of the Methodist New Connexion*, by a Wesleyan Methodist, 1834, p. 24.

46. *CA* 27/10/1834, *SMM* Oct 1834, pp. 199, 193–4. *MT* 27/9/1834. *Stockport Advertiser* 3/10/1834.

47. A. Marcroft, *Historical Account of the Unitarian Chapel, Oldham*, 1913, pp. 59f.

48. *CA* 27/10/1834, 3/11/1834. In the *Leeds Mercury* there was an intriguing description of 'the Stephenites, alias Union Methodists' who 'are called radicals' (*CA* 17/11/1834, p. 362). It could refer to a momentary Stephenite desire to negotiate with the Warrenites. Certainly there was an overlap between the two reform movements; but the stronger Association went its own way, and was prepared only to absorb Stephenite causes (See Chapter 10).

49. *SMM* Nov. 1834, p. 238. Silver box inscribed 17/12/1834 in the possession of Mrs D. Stephens-Krook. For Grey's attitude to disestablishment, see W. H. Mackintosh, *Disestablishment and Liberation*, Epworth 1972, pp. 15f.

2 Transformation

1. *Champion* 20/1/1839, p. 2. Holyoake, p. 166. For the misplaced letter, see Holyoake, pp. 44–6. It referred in passing to 'Elizabeth', and Hindley's privilege of free postage as an MP; since Stephens' marriage and Hindley's election occurred only in January 1835, it could not have been written by Stephens as a Wesleyan minister. Further references to severe weather and a Newcastle visit suggests it was written shortly after his Newcastle speaking tour of 12–16 January 1836. A footnote in Holyoake, p. 45, showed that he knew the year of Stephens' marriage to Elizabeth Henwood. Either Holyoake was confused by the undated letter, or he misled his readers by suggesting a link between the charges of the Wesleyan Conference and the factory issue. If the latter, he succeeded only too well. See *W. H. S. Proceedings* Vol. 36, 1967, pp. 16–21.

2. See D. Hempton, *Methodism and Politics in British Society 1750–1850*, Hutchinson 1984.

3. *MSA* 20/8/1836, p. 3. *CA* 22/8/1836, pp. 271–2. J. Stephens, *The Mutual Relations, Claims and Duties of the Rich and Poor*, 1819, especially pp. 35–6. *Stephens–Bunting* 1/2/1821, as in W. R. Ward, *The Early Correspondence of Jabez Bunting, 1820–1829*, Camden, London 1972, pp. 61–2. *MAM PLP 100.10.4.*

4. *Stephens–Morley* 20/4/1827, 11/5/1827. *MSA* 27/9/1834. J. C. D. Clark, *English Society 1688–1832*, Cambridge 1985, p. 241. Hempton, p. 208, quoting *W. M. Mag 1830*, p. 434. *MSA* 23/1/1836, p. 4.

5. Richard Reece's *Diary*, 1834.

6. *Ashton Reporter* 18/4/1867, p. 7.

7. Gregory, p. 150. Butterworth Diary, March 1834. See Chapter 1 ref. 13 for Montalembert. Holyoake, p. 39. *Ashton Standard* 4/12/1858, p. 4.

8. Butterworth *Diary*, March 1834.

9. Butterworth *Diary*, March 1834. *CA* 9/4/1832, p. 117.

10. *CA* 5/9/1831, 10, 17, 31/10/1831, 7/11/1831, 6, 20/2/1832, 9/7/1832, 17/12/1832, 3/2/1834. *Champion* 30/9/1838, *Northern Star* 6/10/1838. See also *NS* 11/5/1839, when Stephens said that he had been trained to think that poverty was the result of profligacy and crime, and *Ashton Chronicle* 10/3/1849, when he claimed to have devoted twenty years to the study and structure of civil society.

11. *NS* 6/10/1838.

12. J. T. Ward, *RT*, p. 94. D. Gowland, *Political Religion and Religious Politics in South-East Lancashire 1834–5*, pp. 7–8 (unpublished thesis). W. M. Bowman, *England in Ashton-under-Lyne*, Ashton 1960, p. 439.

13. J. T. Ward, *RT*, p. 94. *Ashton Herald* 5/8/1893, p. 7.

14. S. A. Harrop, '19th Century Housing in Ashton', p. 34, 36, and O. Ashmore, 'The Industrial Archeology of Ashton-under-Lyne', pp. 86–106, both articles in *Victorian Ashton*, ed. S. A. Harrop and E. A. Rose, Ashton 1974.

15. Ibid, p. 37. *AH* 5/8/1893, p. 7.

16. *NS* 11/5/1839. *Ashton Reporter* 8/10/1859, *Oldham Standard* 25/8/1860. E. A. Rose, *Methodism in Ashton-under-Lyne 1797–1914*, Ashton, p. 21. *CA* 12/5/1834, p. 149. *SMM*, pp. 194–5.

17. Living standards before 1850 remains a highly controversial issue. See E. J. Hobsbawm and R. M. Hartwell, 'The Standard of Living during the Industrial Revolution: A Discussion', *Economic History Review* 16 1963, pp. 119–134. The pessimistic view of decline (Hobsbawm) fits Stephens' perspective more naturally than its alternative. E. J. Hobsbawm, *Labouring Men*, Weidenfeld and Nicolson 1965, p. 124, E. P. Thompson, *The Making of the English Working Class*, Pelican 1968, p. 209. See J. Kent, 'The Wesleyan Methodists to 1849', pp. 268–9, *A History of the Methodist Church in Great Britain*, Vol. 2, Epworth 1978, for the Toryism of Bunting and Oastler.

18. *Champion* 20/1/1839, p. 2. *CA* 20/10/1834, pp. 332–3.

19. MSA 31/1/1835. *CA* 2/2/1835. *Champion* 3/2/1839.
20. *CA* 2/2/1835. *AH* 5/11/1892. *Watchman's Lantern* 1835, p. 384. *Oldham Circuit Plan* April–July 1835. *CA* 14/8/1835. *MSA* 2/1/1836. Stephens was not mentioned as being present on 9 March 1835 at Ashton when Oastler denounced Hindley; see *MSA* 14/3/1835. Oastler and Stephens did not meet until later that year. When the Advocate published Stephens' first factory speeches in March 1836, the editor had to state that they were 'an answer to the numerous enquiries that had been made *as to what he was doing*'; see *CA* 21/3/1836, p. 84.
21. J. T. Ward, *FM*, p. 134. *Champion* 3/2/1839, p. 1. C. Driver, *Tory Radical*, Oxford 1946, p.325. For Stephens on Oastler, see *Sketch of the Life and Opinions of Richard Oastler*, Anon, 1838, reprinted from the *Northern Star*, 31/3/1838–21/4/1838.
22. For Oastler, see Driver's biography. See also F. Driver, 'Tory Radicalism?' in *Northern History* XXVII, 1991, pp. 120–138, which shows that even in Huddersfield, the alliance between Oastler and local Radicals was strategic rather than ideological.
23. Driver, pp. 428, 425.
24. J. Knott, *Popular Opposition to the 1834 Poor Law*, Croom Helm 1986, pp. 40–4.
25. Driver, p. 295. J. T. Ward, *FM*, p. 127, quoting from the *Agricultural and Industrial Magazine*, 1835.
26. Ibid. Driver, p. 306.
27. K. Marx and F. Engels, *The Communist Manifesto*, int. A. J. P. Taylor, Penguin 1967, p. 106.
28. O. Chadwick's *The Victorian Church* ignored Oastler altogether.
29. *Nottingham Mercury* 29/3/1839, *NS* 6/4/1839. See also *NS* 20/4/1839: 'Stephens differs from me in politics, but that is no reason why I should not love him.' *Sketch of the Life and Opinions of Richard Oastler*, Anon., 1838, p. 12.
30. The argument follows J. T. Ward, *FM*. It is impossible to ascertain which of the three Manchester conferences was the one where Stephens and Oastler met.

3 *The Political Preacher*

1. *CA* 14/12/1835, 11/1/1836. According to *CA* 1/2/1836, the Newcastle reformers failed to get an account of the visit into the northern liberal press.
2. Holyoake, p. 10.
3. *MSA* 23/1/1836, p. 4. *CA* 8/2/1836, p. 45. *MSA* 13/2/1836, 5/3/1836. *NS* 6/10/1838. J. T. Ward, *RT*, p. 96, *FM*, pp. 146–7.
4. *MSA* 5/3/1836, *CA* 14/3/1836, p. 82. J. T. Ward, *RT*, pp. 96–7, *FM*, p. 147.
5. *CA* 14, 28/3/1836, pp. 99. *MSA* 9, 16/4/1836. *Blackburn Gazette* 20,

27/4/1836. J. T. Ward, *RT*, pp. 96–7, *FM*, pp. 151–3.

6. J. T. Ward, *RT*, p. 97. *FM*, pp. 155–7. *MSA* 18/6/1836.

7. *Blackburn Gazette* 20/4/1836, p. 3. *MSA* 18/6/1836. M. Tylecote, *The Mechanics Institutes of Lancashire and Yorkshire before 1851*, Manchester 1957, pp. 250–1. *MSA* 20/8/1836, *CA* 22/8/1836. Oastler and Stephens' meeting at Stockport on 15 August was five days before the better known one at Ashton, which is usually stated to be their first. (See J. T. Ward, *RT*, p. 97, *FM*, p. 160, C. Driver, *Tory Radical*, Oxford 1946, p. 325). Butterworth *Diary* 18/8/1836, *Leeds Times* 20/8/1836. For O'Connor, see J. Epstein, *The Lion of Freedom*, Croom Helm 1982, p. 36. *MSA* 27/8/1836.

8. *Blackburn Gazette* 27/4/1836, *Preston Chronicle* 13/8/1836, 5/9/1836. *CA* 22/8/1836. For the Stephenite division, see Chapter 10.

9. J. T. Ward, *RT*, p. 98, *FM*, pp. 161–2. Driver, pp. 326–9. *CA* 26/9/1836.

10. *CA* 10, 17/10/1836. J. T. Ward, *RT*, p. 98, *FM*, p. 162. Driver, p. 329.

11. *CA* 17, 31/10/1836, 7/11/1836.

12. Butterworth *Diary* 11/11/1836. *MSA* 7/1/1837. *CA* 9/1/1837. J. T. Ward, *RT*, p. 98, *FM*, pp. 165–7. Driver, pp, 329–330.

13. *CA* 10, 17, 31/10/1836. S. A. Weaver, *John Fielden and the Politics of Popular Radicalism 1832–1847*, Oxford 1987, pp. 26–27.

14. *CA* 9/1/1837.

15. See J. Knott, *Popular Opposition to the 1834 Poor Law*, Croom Helm 1986, Chapters 1–2. Stephens was familiar with the arguments of William Cobbett, whose obituary had appeared in *CA* 22/6/1835; see *CA* 22/8/1836. See also *MSA* 25/2/1837, for a repetition of Cobbett's case that the poor had a right to relief from the soil, a right acknowledged before the reign of Elizabeth. Stephens knew Cobbett's sons, James Paul and John Morgan Cobbett. J. T. Ward, *FM*, p. 173. For Stephens on the Act of 1834, see especially *Bradford Observer* 18/5/1837, *NS* 2/12/1837, 6/1/1838, all quoted by M. Taylor, *Joseph Rayner Stephens, Political Preacher*, 1966, pp. 265–6. *Political Preacher* 6/1/1839, pp. 18–20. *NS* 23/6/1838.

16. The Ashton Union was composed of Ashton, Droylesden, Denton, Haughton, Dukinfield, Newton, Godley, Stalybridge, Matley, Hattersley, Mottram and Tintwistle. Ashton was allowed five Guardians, Dukinfield two, and the others one each. *MSA* 4, 25/2/1837, 11, 29/4/1837, 10/5/1837. *Ministry of Health Papers MH12 5413 140243*. Butterworth, *Diary* 22/4/1837. See also N. Edsall, *The Anti-Poor Law Movement 1834–44*, Manchester 1971, pp. 83–4, 90. Knott, pp. 147–8.

17. *MSA* 28/1/1837. *MSA, Leeds Intelligencer* 20/5/1837. Knott pp. 112–122. Driver, pp. 351–2. Lord Brougham had read that in the Peep Green Speech Stephens was supposed to have said: 'Sooner than sit down under this Bill they would light the tocsin of anarchy.' He commented that Stephens misunderstood the word 'tocsin'. See J. T. Ward, *RT*, p. 99, *FM*,

p. 179.

18. *New Moral World* 29/4/1837, 27/5/1837, quoted in M. Beer, *A History of British Socialism*, 1940 edn, Vol. 2, pp. 15–17. *MSA* 20/5/1837. For Bernard, see Epstein, pp. 43–7.

19. Butterworth, *Diary* 21/6/1837, Holyoake, p. 57. *MSA* 1, 15, 28/7/1837. *To the Electors of the Borough of Ashton-under-Lyne*, 7/7/1837. *CA* 7/8/1837. *Times* 9/1/1839. J. T. Ward, *RT*, pp. 99–100, *FM*, p. 181.

20. S. Robinson, *A Letter to Charles Hindley Esq. MP*, Ashton 1837, p. 15. The previous year, Robinson as Vice-President of the Ashton Mechanics Institute, had made a veiled attack on Stephens when he referred to 'the half information and shallow reasonings of every ignorant and interested demogogue, who chooses to constitute himself their (the operatives) advizer and leader'. See M. Tylecote, *The Mechanics Institutes of Lancashire and Yorkshire before 1851*, Manchester 1957, p. 252. *MH 12 5413 140243. Power–PLC* 22/10/1837. *Muggeridge–PLC* 26/10/1837.

21. J. Easby, *J. R. Stephens Unveiled*, 1837. Another attack by an Ashton surgeon was answered by an operative, William Clarke. See J. T. Ward, *RT*, p. 100. *Times* 9/1/1839. *NS* 19/1/1839. *Leeds Times, Leeds Intelligencer* 11/11/1837. *NS, MSA* 2/12/1837. J. T. Ward, *RT*, p. 100, *FM*, p. 183.

22. Knott, pp. 174–6. Epstein Chapter 2. J. T. Ward, *FM*, p. 182. Holyoake, p. 181.

23. J. Epstein and D. Thompson (eds.), *The Chartist Experience*, Macmillan 1982, pp. 156–8, D. Thompson, *The Chartists*, Wildwood House 1984, pp. 21–3. *NS* 30/12/1837, quoted by Holyoake, pp. 117–122. *MSA* 7/10/1837.

24. *MSA* 7/10/1837. Holyoake, pp. 117–122.

25. *Northern Liberator, Newcastle Chronicle, NS* 6/1/1838. His motive for this violent language is considered in Chapter 4.

26. *Northern Liberator* 13/1/1838. *Blackwood's Magazine* 1838, p. 234. Although J. T. Ward puts the Glasgow speech before the Newcastle speech of 1 January, it was made on 4 January. See J. T. Ward, *RT*, pp. 100–1, *FM*, pp. 183–5.

27. For Brougham, see *NS* editorial, 31/3/1838. J. T. Ward, *RT*, p. 101, *FM*, pp. 188–9. For Place, see Ward, *RT*, p. 101, *FM*, p. 186, quoting *Place MSS. 27820 f. 219, 27821 f. 226*, J. Jephson, *The Platform*, 1892, Vol. 2, p. 255, R. F. Wearmouth, *Methodism and the Working Class Movements of England 1800–50*, Epworth 1937, p.131, J. C. Gill, *The Ten Hours Parson*, SPCK 1959, p. 186. If O'Connor's speeches 'rarely matched the reckless abandon of Stephens' (J. Epstein, *Lion of Freedom* 1982, p. 95), the difference between them is one of degree rather than of kind. Although Kemnitz and Jacques (T. M. Kemnitz and F. Jacques, 'J. R. Stephens and the Chartist Movement', *International Review of Social History* 19, 1974, pp. 2, 221) stated that unlike Stephens and Oastler, O'Connor did not advocate arming, during the anti-poor law struggle O'Connor at Newcastle

had upheld the right to arm, and added, 'war to the knife' with the poor law bill. Also he had said that those who passed the poor law bill were guilty of murder and were worthy of death (See *Northern Liberator, Newcastle Chronicle* 6/1/1838).

28. *MSA* 6, 27/1/1838, *Northern Liberator* 13/1/1838, *NS* 3/2/1838. Driver, p. 369. J. T. Ward, *RT*, p. 102, *FM*, p. 187.

29. *NS, MSA* 10/2/1838. Knott, pp. 126–7. For the consequences, see Chapter 4, pp. 148–9.

30. *NS* 17/3/1838.

31. *MH 12 5413 140243. Worthington–PLC* 7/4/1838, *Power–Lewis* 25/4/1838. Edsall, pp. 140–1. *NS* 26/5/1838, Knott, pp. 4–5.

32. For the Oastler articles, see *NS* 31/3/1838–21/4/1838; later they were republished as an anonymous pamphlet, *Sketch of the Life and Opinions of Richard Oastler*, 1838. Holyoake, pp. 84–5. Driver, pp. 376–8. J. T. Ward, *RT*, p. 102, *FM*, p. 189. *NS* 24/11/1838.

33. *NS, Leeds Times* 9/6/1838, *Birmingham Journal* 16/6/1838. Weaver, p. 191. For Saddleworth, see *NS* 16/6/1838. According to *Place Papers 27820 f. 141*, Stephens also said at Saddleworth: 'There was no hope of anything being done for them unless they resorted to physical force, and the only question was, when they should commence burning and destroying mills' (See J. T. Ward, *FM*, p. 189). Place added that John Collins of Birmingham reported the speech to the council of the Birmingham Political Union. (See A. Briggs (ed.), *Chartist Studies*, Macmillan 1959, p. 27). For Keighly, see *NS* 4/8/1938.

34. F. C. Mather, 'The Government and the Chartists', *Chartist Studies*, ed. A. Briggs, Macmillan 1959, pp. 374–5. Edsall, p. 162. The Commissioners did not take advantage of Stephenite difficulties in the summer of 1838 to introduce the Act into Ashton. *MH 12 1413 140243. Once an Opponent– PLC* 20/7/1838.

35. *NS* 10/2/1838, *MSA* 22/9/1838.

36. *MSA* 22/9/1836; Kemnitz and Jacques, especially p. 214.

37. There are several varying accounts of the Kersal Moor speech. The one quoted is from *MSA* 29/9/1836. See also *NS* 29/9/1838, J. T. Ward, *RT*, p. 103, *FM, pp. 191–2, and A. Briggs, Chartist Studies*, Macmillan 1959, p. 34.

38. *Champion* 30/9/1838, *NS* 6/10/1838, *CA* 15/10/1838. B. Harrison and F. Hollis, *Robert Lowery, Radical and Chartist*, Europa Publications 1979, pp. 109–112. The three contemporary accounts have much in common, but Lowery, though an eye-witness, wrote in 1856–7, and reflected on what he had heard. He alone mentions Stephens' denial of Chartism, but the pro-Chartist press at the time was unlikely to include it. Since it is known that Stephens never claimed to be a Chartist, the Queen's Theatre denial is inherently probable. However, Lowery's memory may not always be accurate. He said he first met Stephens at Kersal Moor (p. 109), but at least

he had been present at Newcastle on 1 January 1838 (*Northern Liberator*, *Newcastle Chronicle* 6/1/1838). The Queen's Theatre speech is useful for Stephens' earlier career.

39. *MSA* 6/10/1838. Epstein, p. 119f. M. Taylor, *Joseph Rayner Stephens*, unpublished Ph.D thesis, California 1966, p. 211f. For Carlisle, see *NS* 27/10/1838, *Champion* 4/11/1838. For Norwich, see *Norfolk Chronicle*, *Norfolk Gazette* 3/11/1838, *NS* 10/11/1838. I am indebted to the late Mr E. Youngs for the full text from the two Norfolk papers. See also J. T. Ward, *RT*, pp. 102, 104, *FM*, pp. 192–3.

40. *NS* 10, 17/11/1838. J. T. Ward, *RT*, p. 105, *FM*, pp. 192–3.

41. For Stephens and O'Connor on arming and physical force, see Epstein, pp. 116–131, Kemnitz and Jacques, pp. 219–224. See also *NS* 17/11/1838.

42. Briggs, pp. 376–7. *NS* 17/11/1838, 15/12/1838. *Home Office papers TS 11/814.* J. T. Ward, *FM*, p. 193. H. Goddard, with int. by P. Pringle, *Memoirs of a Bow Street Runner*, Museum Press 1956, pp. 154–5.

43. *NS* 15, 22/12/1838, 4/5/1839. *H. O. TS 11/814, H. O. 40/38. MG* 12/12/1836. *MSA*, 15/12/1838. Goddard, pp. 155–6. *Trial of the Rev. J. R. Stephens*, p. 15.

44. For Chartist criticism of Stephens, see *NS* 24/11/1838 (Muntz), 1/12/1838 (Edmonds), *True Scotsman* 1/12/1838 (Duncan). See also Epstein, pp. 122–3, Kemnitz and Jacques, p. 222. *TS 11/814. Stephens's Vindication*, 13/12/1838. *CA* 22/12/1838.

45. *H. O. 40/38*. Goddard, pp. 156–7. Letters of Lord Francis Egerton, *Egerton–Lock* 22/12/1838. *TS 11/814. Champion* 6/1/1839, *MSA* 29/12/1838, *Times* 1/1/1839, *NS* 5/1/1839. Goddard, p. 157.

46. Goddard, pp. 157–60. J. T. Ward, *RT*, p. 105, *FM*, pp. 193–4, Holyoake, pp. 143–4.

47. *MG* 30/12/1838, *Observer* 31/12/1838, *Standard, Sun* 3/1/1839, *Times* 3, 5/1/1839, *NS* 5/1/1839. J. T. Ward, *RT*, p. 105, *FM*, p. 194. Holyoake, pp. 144–5.

48. *Trial*, p. 15. *Sun, Standard* 3/1/1839, *NS* 5/1/1839, R. F. Wearmouth, *Methodism and the Working Class Movements of England 1800–1850*, Epworth 1937, pp. 131–2.

49. *NS* 29/12/1838, 5/1/1839, which quoted a wide range of press opinion on the case. On O'Connor's alleged desertion of Stephens, see Epstein, pp. 123, 136, fn. 117. J. T. Ward, *RT*, p. 105, *FM*, p. 195. *Sun, Standard* 3/1/1839 *NS* 12/1/1839.

50. *Copies of the True Bills Found Against the Rev. J. R. Stephens*, 1839, pp. 21–2. *Charter* 7/4/1839, *TS 11/814. Trial*, pp. 12, 26. *NS* 13/4/1839, p. 4. *Copies*, p. 3.

51. *Copies*, pp. 22–3. *Times* 3/1/1839, 4/5/1839.

52. *Champion* 3/2/1839, 6, 20, 27/1/1839, 11/4/1839. *The Charter* 24/3/1839, 21/4/1839. The history of the defence fund is full of

obscurities. For example, *NS* 9/2/1839 mentioned two funds, a Stephens fund and a Stephens defence fund.

53. *The Political Preacher . . . An address delivered at Ashton-under-Lyne*, 6 January 1839 by Joseph Rayner Stephens, Manchester 1839, and *A Sermon preached by the Rev. Mr Stephens*, London 1839; *The Political Pulpit*, 1–13, (February–August 1839). The sermons also appeared in *NS*. In two of them (preached on 26/5/1839 and 3/8/1839) his real attitude to Chartism is revealed. Harrison and Hollis, *Robert Lowery*, 1979, pp. 234–7. Kemnitz and Jacques, p. 225, quoting *NS* 13/4/1839. R. F. Wearmouth, *Some Working Class Movements of the 19th Century*, London 1948, pp. 177–8, 181.

54. The Marcus pamphlets are discussed in J. Knott, *Popular Opposition to the 1834 Poor Law*, Croom Helm 1986, pp. 237–243. Knott said that Stephens suggested one of the Poor Law Commissioners was the real author (p. 238) but omitted his denial (see *Champion* 20/1/1839, from the *Times* letter of 11/1/1839). In the full text of the Ashton sermon of 6/1/1839, which antedated the Commissioners' rebuttal of the 9th, Stephens attacked the pamphlets, but did not attribute them to any of the three Commissioners. Knott used the anti-Stephens *Leeds Mercury* of 5/1/1839 as his source. Stephens himself saw the statement in 'a Manchester paper notorious for its uniform misrepresentations of everything I have ever advanced', i.e. the *Manchester Guardian*. In his *Times* letter he added: 'I am always exceedingly careful of what I say on these as well as on other matters.' Knott concluded that J. P. Cobbett is probably nearest to the truth in thinking that Marcus was a Tory who intended to injure the Whigs (Knott, p. 240).

55. *NS*, *MSA* 27/4/1839. His friends the Gordons lived at Dudley, and Stephens probably stayed with them. John Gordon had resigned from the Wesleyan ministry over disestablishment in September 1834. He met Stephens at Birmingham in November 1834. His son Alexander became a noted Unitarian minister; he wrote the article on Stephens in the *Dictionary of National Biography*. D. Thompson, *The Chartists*, Wildwood House 1984, pp. 74–5. J. T. Ward, *RT*, p. 106, *FM*, p. 195. *Times* 4/5/1839, *Champion* 5/5/1839. R. F. Wearmouth, *Some Working Class Movements of the 19th Century*, London 1948, pp. 102, 104. *Annual Register* 1839, p. 67. *PP 6* (Shepherd and Shepherdess Fields), *PP 7* (Primrose Hill), *PP 8* (Kenington Common), all on 12/5/1839.

56. *PP 9* (Ashton 26/5/1839). *PP 10* (Stalybridge 9/6/1839), *PP 11, 12* (Ashton 9/6/1839).

57. *PP 13* (Ashton 3/8/1839) p. 102. *Stephens's Monthly Magazine*, Jan 1840. For the Convention, see D. Thompson, pp. 63–76, Epstein Chapter 4.

58. The main press sources for the M'Douall charge are *MSA* 22, 29/6/1839, *MG* 26, 27, 29/6/1839, *MT*, *MC* 29/6/1839, *Times*, *Sun* 1/7/1839, *Champion* 7/7/1839, *Charter* 11/8/1839. *NS* is silent, though earlier it reported his previous friendship with Stephens (27/4/1839). See also Kemnitz and Jacques, p. 224. In *MSA*, a paper usually friendly to

Stephens, the editor Condy (*MSA* 6/7/1839) claimed to have seen Stephens' written confession, and promised to publish full details; but he did not do so. Two papers hostile to Stephens claimed that his signature had been obtained through a threat to his life (*MG, MT* 29/6/1839). The growing Chartist distrust of Stephens made them ready to believe M'Douall. The animosity between M'Douall and Stephens over the defence fund continued in prison; see Chapter 6. For more general criticism of M'Douall, see C. Godfrey, 'The Chartist Prisoners 1839–1841', *International Review of Social History* 24, 1979, Pt. 2, pp. 208–9, and D. Thompson, *The Chartists*, p. 105. See also article on M'Douall in *Biographical Dictionary of British Radicals*, ed. F. J. O. Baylen and N. J. Gossman, 1984, Vol. 2, pp. 323–6. For Stephens' renunciation of the defence fund, see *Times* 1/7/1839; Stephens specified 'reasons of a private nature' in his letter to Richard Moscrop, stressing that the trustees decided to use the whole fund for its original purpose (*NS* 9/11/1839, p. 2). Holyoake is silent on the charge, but published two letters with a bearing on it. In the first, the solicitor Richard Cobbett informed Stephens of his troubles with the 'little Doctor' (M'Douall) over the non-payment of his bill (Cobbett–Stephens 28/8/1840, Holyoake, pp. 176–9); in the other, O'Brien wrote a friendly letter to Stephens in prison mentioning 'the malicious efforts of certain parties to destroy your usefulness by undermining your popularity and influence' (O'Brien–Stephens 4/9/1840, Holyoake, pp. 179–180). Holyoake was inferring that M'Douall caused trouble, and O'Brien was still friendly with Stephens after July 1839.

59. *PP 13* (Ashton 3-8-1839). Earlier versions of the farewell sermon are reported in *MSA* 20/7/1839, *MT* 27/7/1839; see also *NS* 17/8/1839.
60. *PP 13* (Ashton 3 8 1839). T. M. Kemnitz and F. Jacques, 'J. R. Stephens and the Chartist Movement', *International Review of Social History*, 19, 1974, pp. 213–4, 220–4. J. Epstein, *The Lion of Freedom*, Croom Helm 1982, pp. 95–6, 117–121.

4 *The Question of Physical Force*

1. The drawing is reproduced in N. A. Spence, 'Joseph Rayner Stephens', *Looking Back at Stalybridge*, ed. A. Lock, Stalybridge 1989, p. 44.
2. *True Scotsman* 1/12/1838.
3. Goddard, p. 155. See *CA* 26/9/1836 for another example of his boasting; he has 'put out a candle with a bullet' and 'split a bullet on the edge of a penknife. This is the way I meet the threats of our adversaries'. For *Stephens's Vindication* see *NS* 22/12/1838, p. 5.
4. Holyoake, p. 28. *MG* 5/6/1876. Axon, p. 109–110. *Ashton Standard* 4/12/1858, p. 4.
5. Driver, p.179.
6. *CA* 12/5/1834.

7. *MSA* 5/3/1836, *CA* 14/3/1836. *Clegg–Fielden* 9/7/1836 (*Fielden Papers*).
8. *Political Preacher*, 6/1/1839, pp. 18–20.
9. *Newcastle Chronicle* 6/1/1838.
10. *Newcastle Chronicle* 6/1/1838. Robert Lowery (See Chapter 3, note 38) in 1856 wrote of Stephens' language: 'I believe he so spoke with the hope and expectation that the Government would indict him for seditious opposition to that law . . .' i.e. the Poor Law Amendment Act. (Quoted in B. Harrison and F. Hollis, *Robert Lowery, Radical and Chartist*, Europa Publications 1979, p. 112.) Epstein (p. 123) thought Lowery was probably correct in this. Subsequent challenges to Russell in Stephens' speeches (as in *NS* 16/10/ 1838) appear to confirm it; also his confusion when indicted for something other than opposition to the new poor law tends to the same conclusion. Since the end of 1837, the proprietor of the *Manchester Guardian* had urged government to send an agent to take notes of Stephens' speeches (J. T. Ward, *FM*, p. 185). Stephens quickly learned of this, and it enabled him to challenge Russell more directly.
11. See Chapter 3, notes 32, 33 and text.
12. See Chapter 3, notes 40, 41 and text. Some idea of the dilemma Stephens faced and the feelings it aroused can be seen in Colin Morris' ministerial advice to an enquirer that a Christian was justified in using violence to win freedom in what was then Rhodesia. See C. Morris, *Unyoung, Uncoloured, Unpoor*, Epworth 1969.
13. *NS* 27/10/1838, 17/11/1838. Kemnitz and Jacques, p. 218. Chapter 3, note 40 and text.
14. *NS* 16/10/1838, *Leeds Times* 20/10/1838. *NS* 10, 17/11/1838. *PP 11*, Ashton 3/8/1839, p. 103.
15. *HO 20/10. PP 8*, Ashton 26/5/1839, p. 70. *PP 10*, Ashton 9/6/1839, p. 93. *PP 11*, Ashton 3/8/1839, pp. 102, 103, 103*.
16. *PP 11, Ashton 3/8/1839, p. 101. NS* 5/1/1839, p. 8.
17. *Stephens's Monthly Magazine*, Feb. 1840.
18. *WW Mag* 1837, p. 552. *Watchman* 9/1/1839. J. Kent, *The Age of Disunity*, Epworth 1966, pp. 135, 144–5.
19. *PP 3*, Stalybridge 24/2/1839, p. 23. *NS* 9/3/1839, p. 6.

5 *The Man and his Message*

1. *Times* 1/1/1839, *Observer* 30/12/1838. *WM Magazine 1882*, p. 77. *NS* 6/ 10/1838. The four children were Henrietta (b. 1837), one, name unknown, d. 1838 (*NS* 14/4/1838, p. 8), Lucy (b.and d. 1839), Mary Holroyde (b. 1841 d. 1851).
2. *Observer* 30/12/1838, *Times* 1/1/1839. H. O. *20/10 XL 142525.* Holyoake, p. 227. *Stephens–Morley* 9/12/1826. J. T. Ward, *RT*, p. 115, fn. 131. Holyoake, pp. 218–9. See *CA* 19/10/1835 for the South Australia Company, of which Samuel Stephens was the colonial manager. The only

source for Stephens' shares in the 'Australia Company' is J. Easby's vituperative *Joseph Rayner Stephens Unveiled*, 1837, p. 11; but there seems no reason to doubt the truth of this particular statement, and given the known family interest, it is inherently likely. For a late letter of his father's, see Holyoake, pp. 182–3.

3. *Stephens–Morley* 9/12/1826. *Nottingham and Newark Mercury* 29/3/1839, 5/4/1839, PP 6 Primrose Hill, p. 56. *Sun* 3/1/1839, *Times* 4/1/1839, *Champion* 3/2/1839, *CA* 31/10/1836, 7/11/1836, *NS* 9/3/1839, *NS* 30/3/1839, p. 6.

4. *CA* 10/10/1836, p. 324. *Our Champion Stephens* (leaflet). *NS* 18/5/1839, 6/3/1839. Goddard, p. 157. *MG* 26/6/1839, *Times* 27/6/1839.

5. *Champion* 6/1/1839.

6. *NS* 26/1/1839. For Stephens and others on women's liberation, see E. Yeo, 'Chartist religious belief and the theology of liberation', *Disciplines of Faith* ed. J. Obelkevitch, L. Roper and R. Samuel, Routledge and Kegan Paul 1987, pp. 417–421. Stephens was still heavily influenced by his father's sermon *The Advantages that Man derives from Woman*, which he reprinted in his magazines of the forties.

7. *Times* 1/1/1839. *NS* 6/1/1838. *CA* 15/10/1838.

8. B. Harrison and F. Hollis, *Robert Lowery, Radical and Chartist*, Europa Publications 1979, pp. 110–2. J. T. Ward, *RT*, p. 106, fn. 76, *FM*, p, 206. E. A. Rose, *Methodism in Ashton-under-Lyne, 1797–1914*, pp. 50, 53. B. Gregory, *Autobiographical Recollections*, London 1903, p. 211. A more detailed analysis of Stephens' oratory is given in M. Taylor's unpublished 1966 Ph.D. thesis *Joseph Rayner Stephens, Political Preacher*.

9. F. H. Amphlett Micklewright, (*Notes and Queries* 1/1/1944 pp. 8–12) thought that Stephens's creed was basically political, and suggested possible influence from Coleridge and Swedenborg. As far as the latter is concerned, as far back as 1827 he was concerned that the standard Swedish Lutheran textbook was written by a Swedenborgian; it abounded 'in many and dangerous errors', and he urged the gift of Watson's *Institutes* and other Methodist theological works to Swedish libraries (*Stephens–Morley* 11/5/1827). Swedenborgian lectures at Charlestown in 1846 (W. M. Bowman, *England in Ashton-under-Lyne*, Ashton 1960, pp. 140–1) are no more significant for Stephens' beliefs than Chartist meetings held there in the same period. Stephens' basic tolerance was spelt out in 1834: 'Diversity of sentiment, either in religion or politics, ought never to unsettle or break up private friendship. With him it never had, or never would' (*SMM* Oct 1834, p. 196).

10. *CA* 7/1/1839. *Champion* 6/1/1839. *NS* 6/10/1838.

11. *Stephens–Morley* 29/1/1829. *CA* 26/9/1836, p. 307.

12. *CA* 22/8/1836, 17/10/1836, p. 332. *NS* 11/5/1839. *PP* 4 Ashton market place, pp. 21, 24–5.

13. There are two versions of the sermon of 6/1/1839 – A London version (*A*

Sermon preached by the Reverend Mr Stephens, 1839) and a longer Manchester version (*The Political Preacher*, 1839). The quotations used here are from the London version, pp. 2, 4.

14. *The Political Preacher*, pp. 16–17. I am indebted to Professor J. Kent for the stress on providence.
15. *A Sermon*, p. 4, 6–7.
16. *PP* 6 (Shepherd and Shepherdess Fields), 7 (Primrose Hill), and 8 (Kenington Common), all preached on 12/5/1839.
17. *Political Preacher*, p. 29. Dale A. Johnson, 'Between Evangelicalism and a Social Gospel: The Case of Joseph Rayner Stephens', *Church History*, 42. 2 June 1973, American Society of Church History.

6 Crisis and Recovery

1. There are at least two accounts of the trial from Chartist sources – (i) the *Champion* 18/8/1839 is an eye-witness account, and was later published as a pamphlet, (ii) *NS* 24/8/1839, published as the *Trial of the Rev. J. R. Stephens* by Joshua Hobson of Leeds. This is the one usually quoted; extracts appear in Holyoake, pp. 147–164, Holyoake stated (p. 164) that its source was F. B. Templeton's verbatim shorthand report of the trial. Both agree broadly on Stephens' speech, though occasionally the *Champion* is more detailed. I have followed the second, with occasional amplification from the first. Stephens himself neither prepared nor corrected any account of his speech, and complained that one pamphlet was 'so full of errors that I had not patience to read it through' (*Stephens's Monthly Magazine* Jan. 1840, p. 12). Specifically he objected that at Leigh he did not say that under universal suffrage he would be the first to go to the block; it would be the Radicals on gaining power who would see to that. Templeton's account agrees; interestingly, the *Champion* omits the statement.
2. *Champion* 18/8/1839, p. 6. *Chester Chronicle* 23/8/1839.
3. *TS* 1/815, p. 5. *PP* 13, Ashton-under-Lyne, 3/8/1839, p. 104. Trial of the Rev. J. R. Stephens, p. 9. Holyoake, p. 152.
4. *Trial*, pp. 3–5. *Champion* 18/8/1839, p. 5. Holyoake, pp. 147–50.
5. *Trial*, pp. 5–8. Holyoake omitted the cross-examinations. W. H. Chaloner, 'Reminiscences of Thomas Dunning', *Transactions of the Lancashire and Cheshire Antiquarian Society*, LIX, 1947, p. 118. Dunning thought Stephens a fool for defending himself.
6. *Trial*, pp. 8–28. *Champion* 18/8/1839, pp. 5–6. Holyoake, pp. 150–167. Stephens wanted Russell to testify about the Ashton factory fire.
7. *Trial*, pp. 8–17.
8. *Trial*, p. 18. Chaloner, p. 119.
9. *Trial*, pp. 20–28.
10. *Trial*, pp. 28–31.
11. *Trial*, pp. 31–2.

12. *Trial*, p. 32. Holyoake, p. 174.
13. C. Godfrey and J. Epstein, 'H. O. 20/10: Interviews of Chartist Prisoners 1840–41', *Bulletin of the Society for the Study of Labour History*, 1977, 34, pp. 27–34. C. Godfrey, 'The Chartist Prisoners 1839–1841', *International Review of Social History* 1979, 24, pt. 2, pp. 189f. *DNB*. Stephens's ordinary prison diet was a pound of bread a day, a quart of gruel at breakfast, 1½ pounds of potatoes at dinner, and a quart of gruel at supper. For his reaction to harsh visiting magistrates, see *SM Mag.* Feb. 1840, p. 46, Jan. 1840, p. 7. *The Charter* 12/1/1840, p. 803. In the *Ashton Reporter* 22/21879, a visiting magistrate ordered Stephens to remove his hat; when the order was ignored, the magistrate knocked it off. Stephens wrote to the Home Office, and allegedly the magistrate had to replace it on the prisoner's head.
14. *H. O.* 20/10, W. J. Williams interview with J. R. Stephens, 30/10/1840. *SM Mag.* Aug 1840, pp. 187–192, Feb. 1840, p. 46, Jan. 1840, p. 3. Holyoake, p. 175.
15. *SM Mag.* Jan. 1840, pp. 7–8, March 1840, p. 61, June 1840.
16. *H. O. 20/10 XL 142525. SM Mag.* Jan, Feb. 1840. There is a good example of the attitudes of prison chaplains to Chartist prisoners in A. Briggs, *Chartist Studies*, Macmillan 1959. The Monmouth chaplain enquired into the religious affiliation of the Newport prisoners 'to discover in what congregations sedition throve best'. He found that at least 41 out of 49 were sectarians, 'their lapse into dissent, and their progress in Chartism keeping pace one with the other' (D. Williams, 'Chartism in Wales', pp. 241–2). Such attitudes were hardly likely to stimulate prison chapel attendance by non-Anglicans.
17. *SM Mag.* Feb. 1840. *H. O. 20/10 XL 142525.*
18. *H. O. 20/10 XL 142525.* It should be remembered that M'Douall had been released by the time of Williams's visit in October 1840.
19. *H. O. 20/10 XL 142525. SM Mag.* Jan. 1840, p. 6, April 1840, p. 91. NS 6/6/1840, p. 7, 13/6/1840, p. 6, 25/7/1840, p. 7, 9/11/1839, p. 2. The Charter 1/12/1839. Holyoake, p. 177, quoting from a letter of Cobbett to Stephens of 29/8/1840, in which M'Douall is called 'the little Doctor'. *SM Mag.* Aug. 1840, p. 190. *H. O.* 20/10. See also interview with Abel Swann in *Ashton Herald* 5/11/1892, in which Swann stated that Stephens had spent every halfpenny in getting better dinners for the other prisoners.
20. *SM Mag.* March 1840, p. 68f. *NS* 2/11/1839, p. 4. Epstein, pp. 160–1, 199–204. See also Chapter 3, note 52. In June 1839 the Chartist National Defence Fund was founded by O'Connor when many more Chartists were being arrested.
21. Epstein, pp. 201f; *NS* 16/11/18439, p. 8, 9/11/1839, p. 2, 30/11/1839, p. 5. *The Charter* 1/12/1839. *NS* 7/12/1839, p. 4, 4/1/1840, 27/6/1840, 11/7/1840, 1/8/1840, 19/9/1840. See also Godfrey, pp. 208–9. S. A. Weaver, *John Fielden and the Politics of Popular Radicalism 1832–1847*, Oxford 1987, p. 223. Epstein, pp. 160–1, 199–204. The defence fund issue

remains confusing. M'Douall himself confounded two Chartist defence funds, stating that he had no previous knowledge of one of them (*NS* 19/9/1840, p. 5).

22. Stephens said the fund was 'only a few hundreds', and apart from £150, he had not touched any of it, leaving it in the hands of his committee. See *SM Mag.* Jan. 1840, p. 12. Also *SM Mag.* Mar. 1840, pp. 69–70, Aug. 1840, pp. 187–192, Oct. 1840, pp. 228–9, Jan. 1840, p. 14.

23. Holyoake, pp. 182–3. *Wesleyan Methodist Minutes of Conference 1841*, pp. 155–6. Holyoake, p. 21. *Times* 23/2/1841. *H. O. 20/10*.

24. *NS* 6/3/1841, 17/4/1841. Census, 1841 gives an address at 49 Copeland Street, Chorlton. *Stalybridge Standard* 22/2/1879 states that he lived at Greenheys for three or four years after his release.

25. *True Scotsman* 6/2/1841, *NS* 15/5/1841. For the Stephens–Buchanan debate on Socialism, see *NS* 28/8/1841, 4/9/1841; see also *New Moral World* 1841, p. 110, *People's Magazine* Nov. 1841, pp. 346–352. Abel Swann in his old age seems to be recalling the same debate in *Ashton Herald* 5/11/1892, but he calls Stephens' opponent McDonald. He adds that Stephens was reluctant at first to debate, because the speakers had known one another in their college days. Unlike the impression from the *NS* account, Swann thought Stephens won the debate – 'after that discussion no Socialist ever volunteered to meet him again'.

26. *PM* November 1841, p. 325, April 1842, p. 99, July 1841, pp. 218–9, August 1841, pp. 226–7, September 1841, p. 286, February 1842, pp. 42–7. On home colonization, see *PM* August 1841, pp. 229f, November 1841, pp. 324–5, 327. *Bradford Herald* 10, 17/3/1842, *Bradford Observer* 10/3/1842. Butterworth Diary 26/2/1843, 26/3/1843.

27. *Times* 4, 6/8/1842, *Nottingham Review* 5/8/1842, *NS* 6, 13/8/1842. D. Thompson, *The Chartists*, Wildwood House 1984, pp. 265–6. Stephens took no part in later Chartist activity, but in 1848 he raised funds for the defence of Chartist prisoners accused of the murder of an Ashton policeman. See H. Davies, 'A Shot in the Dark', *Victorian Ashton* ed. S. A. Harrop and E. A. Rose, Ashton 1974.

28. J. T. Ward, *RT*, pp. 111–2, *FM*, *p.260*. *Times*, *Manchester Courier* 16/12/1843. S. A. Weaver, *John Fielden and the Politics of Popular Radicalism 1832–47*, Oxford 1987, p. 247.

29. *Ashton Chronicle* 13/1/1849, pp. 4–5. See also *MT* 21/2/1846. Oastler held a meeting for the bill at Charlestown chapel in 1844, but this does not imply Stephens' support, as Chartist meetings were also held there throughout the forties.

30. Details from Coulthart's report are given in Chapter 2. *HO MH* 12/5413–5415, especially Clements–Commissioners 26/11/1844. See also N. Edsall, *The Anti-Poor Law Movement 1834–44*, Manchester 1971, pp. 253–4.

31. *HO MH* 12/5413. *MSA* 24/10/1846, p. 8. W. M. Bowman, *England in*

Ashton-under-Lyne, Ashton 1960, pp. 334–8.

32. *Ashton Chronicle* 2/12/1848, p. 4. J. Knott, *Popular Opposition to the 1834 Poor Law*, Croom Helm 1986, pp. 217–8.

33. *MT, MSA* 21/2/1846. The cup is now in the Grosvenor Museum, Chester.

34. *AC* March 1848 p. 6, 7/10/1848, p. 1. *HO* 45/2410, Mason–Grey 6/3/1848.

35. *AC* April 1848 pp. 6–7, 24/6/1848, p. 5, 8/7/1848, pp. 1, 5, 22/7/1848, pp. 13–14. *HO MH* 12/5415 *XC* 142566.

36. L. Swallow, *Shameful Treatment. Important Enquiry before the Poor Law Guardians, from the Manchester Courier*, 7/6/1848. *HO MH* 12/5415 *XC* 142566. *AC* 23, 30/12/1848, 13/1/1849, *MC* 16/1/1849. *AC* 10/6/1848, p. 4, 10, 17, 24, 31/3/1849, 7, 14, 21/4/1849. *Ashton Times*, April 1851. *Ashton Standard* 10, 16/10/1858, 20, 27/11/1858, 4, 18/12/1858. Ashton Poor Law records 1857–8. *Ashton Reporter* 27, 30/10/1858, 6/11/1858.

37. *AC* 29/4/1848. J. T. Ward, *FM*, p. 346, *Popular Movements c. 1830–1850*, Macmillan 1970, p. 72. S. A. Weaver, *John Fielden and the Politics of Popular Radicalism 1832–1847*, Oxford 1987, p. 275. *AC* 7/10/1848, 16, 23/12/1848, 13, 20/1/1849, 3, 24/2/1849, 21, 28/4/1849.

38. J. T. Ward, *RT*, pp. 112–13, *FM*, pp. 356, 360–2, 368. *AC* 13/1/1849, 17/2/1849, 30/6/1849, 28/7/1849. On Ashley, see G. Battiscombe, *Shaftesbury*, 1974, pp. 210–11, and S. A. Weaver, p. 286. *AC* 15/9–3/11/1849, *Champion* 10/11/1849.

39. *Champion* 16, 23/2/1850, 9/3/1850, II, 2, 7. J. T. Ward, *RT*, pp. 113–4, *FM*, pp. 371–390, Weaver, pp. 282–6.

40. *Champion* II 12. J. T. Ward, *RT*, pp. 113–4, *FM*, p. 390, Weaver, p. 286.

41. *Champion* II 19. J. T. Ward, *RT*, p. 114, *FM*, pp. 394–7, 400–3. *Oldham Standard* 8/10/1859, 25/10/1860, *Ashton and Stalybridge Reporter* 21/9/1861.

42. Death certificates of Mary Holroyde Stephens (13/10/1851), Elizabeth Stephens (6/1/1852), Rebecca Eliza Stephens (25/1/1852). *Ashton Reporter, Stalybridge Standard* 22/2/1879. Application for marriage licence and certificate, 1857. Stalybridge Poor Rate books, 1858–9. The six children of the second marriage were: Henry Rayner Beresford (b. 15/5/1858, d. 10/1/1862), Lucy Elizabeth (b. 18/2/1861, d. 20/1/1862), Arthur Cornwall (b. 18/2/1861, d. 15/6/1907), George Alfred (b. 23/4/1863), Mary Rayner (b. 14/5/1865, d. 29/3/1868), Amy (b & d. 18/1/1867). *Ashton Reporter* 9, 16/8/1879 lists in an auctioneer's notice the collection 'made during the last thirty years by the late well-known connoisseur' Stephens. The sources of his private income were probably his numerous newspaper editorships, shares in the South Australia Company, and his late mother's estate.

7 The Sobered Reformer

1. Robert Lowery, 'Passages in the Life of a Temperance Lecturer', *Robert Lowery, Radical and Chartist* ed. B. Harrison and P. Hollis, Europa Publications 1979, p. 112. *Times* 6/8/1842, p. 4. Holyoake, Chapter 9, pp. 184–198, p. 11.

2. Lowery, p. 112. J. R. Stephens, *Sketch of the Life and Opinions of Richard Oastler*, Leeds 1838, p. 12. *SM Mag.* January 1840, pp. 14–15. *PM* July 1841, p. 219.

3. *PM* July 1841, pp. 222–4. December 1841, p. 362. For alleged Anglican offers of ordination, see *Ashton Herald* 24/5/1888, 5/11/1892, *Ashton Reporter* 26/5/1888. Karl Marx in 1843 mistook Stephens for an Anglican priest; see J. T. Ward, *RT*, p. 116 fn. 119.

4. *Champion* II. 12–14. For Miall, see W. H. Mackintosh, *Disestablishment and Liberation*, Epworth 1972, pp. 12–17. J. Holland, 'Hugh Mason', *Victorian Ashton* ed. S. A. Harrop and E. A. Rose, Ashton 1974, pp. 7, 9. N. Kirk, *The Growth of Working Class Reformism in Victorian England*, Croom Helm 1985, p. 294, quoting *Ashton Reporter* 18/4/1868.

5. *PM* January 1840, pp. 3, 6.

6. *New Moral World* 13/2/1841, p. 94.

7. *Ashton Weekly Reporter* 11/8/1855. H. and D. King, 'Stalybridge – A New Town', *Looking Back at Stalybridge* ed. A. Lock, Tameside 1989, pp. 27–33. See also S. Hill, *Bygone Stalbridge*, 1987 edn, *Manchester Times* 5/7/1854, p. 7, *Ashton Ricker* 5/7/1856, *Ashton Reporter* 14/3/1868, *Ashton Herald* 12/3/1892, 5/11/1892.

8. *NS* 28/11/1846, p. 6; J. Knott, *Popular Opposition to the 1834 Poor Law*, Croom Helm 1986, pp. 217–8.

9. The last known issue of the *People's Magazine* was in June 1842. *Champion* II 26, p. 413. *Ashton Ricker* 5/7/1856. *Ashton Weekly Herald* 9/5/1857. Although it is difficult to identify the frequently changing editors of 19th-century provincial newspapers, the internal evidence for a Stephens editorship of the *Ashton Standard* before February 1859 is strong. The editor upheld the Oastlerite slogan of the Altar, the Throne and the Cottage (2/1/1858), was anti-sectarian (10/4/1858), advocated an eight hour day, and asked 'ARE THE MASTERS READY FOR ANOTHER FIGHT?' (22/5/1858). He thought that 'the radicalism of the sturdy English labourer is the toryism of the English gentleman' (7/8/1858). He constantly attacked the Ashton Board of Guardians (2/10/1848 et al). When the editorship changed 'within the last month', there were charges that the paper had changed its principles (19/3/1859). There are two scraps of supporting external evidence. In Stephens's obituary in the *Stalybridge Standard* 22/2/1879, p. 4, it was stated that he contributed leading articles to the *Standard*. In James France's reminiscences, a sentence begins: 'When Joseph Rayner Stephens sat in the editorial chair of the *Ashton Standard* . . .' (*Ashton Herald*

5/8/1893). The view taken here is that he was editor from January 1858 to February/March 1859. For the *Oldham Standard*, see *Warwick's Guide to British Labour Periodicals, 1790–1860*. *Oldham Standard* editorials to 1862 are among the surviving Stephens family papers. Census return, 1861. For the 19th-century Ashton press, see P. M. and D. L. Williams, *Extra, Extra, Read all about It'*, Ashton, n.d.

10. Deeds of the People's School, 1838–81. At the time of writing, the People's School is the last surviving Stephenite building. *MG* 2, 8, 9, 16/2/1848, *MC* 16/2/1848. W. R. Ward, *Religion and Society in England 1790–1850*, Batsford 1972, pp. 283–4. *Ashton Weekly Reporter* 7, 15/3/1857. Stalybridge Annual 1927, pp. 45–7. *Ashton Herald* 2/8/1895, 5/8/1893.

11. *MC* 15/12/1847, 12, 19, 22, 25, 29/1/1848, *National Temperance Advocate* IV 1848, pp. 29–30, 38–40, J. R. Stephens – Samuel Ashton 22/3/1848 (owned by Mr Anthony Ashton, who kindly supplied a photocopy), the Swann–Grundy correspondence in *Ashton Reporter* 22/2/1879, 18, 22, 29/3/1879, and Holyoake, pp. 209–210. See also B. Harrison, *Drink and the Victorians*, Faber 1971, and 'Teetotal Chartism', *History* 58, 1973, pp. 193f. In the text, the contemporary *Manchester Courier* account is followed, with Abel Swann's two letters in the *Reporter* of 18, 29/3/1879. *MC* 29/1/1848 reproduced a letter to Lees in which Stephens showed every intention of pursuing the debate. Although Swann wrote much later as a Stephens partisan, his letters are in broad agreement with *MC* and the Stephens–Ashton letter of 22/3/1848. Swann's offer in 1879 to his opponent Grundy to produce Lees' letter refusing to discuss the Stalybridge proposition, or to recommend anyone else to do so, was not taken up – a fact that must be given due weight in this confusing dispute. The very existence of such a letter would directly contradict the *National Temperance Advocate*'s statement that 'Dr Lees never declined, but often accepted this proposition' (NTA p. 39), and that the Lees propositions as the ground of the proposed debate 'were the ORIGINAL ones' (NTA p. 29). The *NTA* accounts seems designed only to ridicule Stephens.

12. *MT* 6/12/1854, *AWR* 14/3/1857, *AS* 10/4/1858. J. Holland, 'Hugh Mason', *Victorian Ashton* ed. S. A. Harrop and E. A. Rose, Ashton 1974, p. 11. *AS* 27/11/1858.

13. N. Kirk, *The Growth of the Working Class Reformism in Victorian England*, Croom Helm 1985, pp. 255–6. *ASR* 15/9/1860, *AS* 1/12/1860. *Wakefield Express* 7/11/1863. *Wakefield Free Press* 24/10/1863. *The Beehive* 21/11/1863, 14, 21/5/1864, 2, 23/7/1864, 17/9/1864. *Leeds Intelligencer* 14/5/1864, 16/7/1864. Holyoake, pp. 132–4.

14. *AWR* 27/6/1857, 10/10/1857. *AS* 16/2/1861. *AR* June 1861. J. T. Slugg, *Woodhouse Grove Reminiscences*, 1885, pp. 209, 222.

15. *AR* 14/2/1863. *AS* 18/12/1858.

8 *The Cotton Famine*

1. For the background to the cotton famine, I am indebted to Dr D. A. Farnie's article 'The Cotton Famine in Great Britain', *Essays in honour of W. O. Henderson, Great Britain and her world, 1750–1914*, ed. Barrie M. Radcliffe, Manchester University Press 1975, pp. 153–178. However, opinions will differ among those competent to judge about the 'luxurious standard of living' said to have been enjoyed by the Lancashire cotton operatives since 1830 (p. 167).

2. Farnie, p. 177 fn. 36. For Stephens as a Southern supporter, see the passing reference in W.R. Ward, *Religion and Society in England 1790–1850*, Batsford 1972, p. 283. *OS* 20/7/1861, 14/12/1861.

3. *OS* 9/8/1862, *AR* 27/9/1862, *OS* 1/11/1862. The *Ashton Standard* was pro-South (see *AS* 3/1/1862), but by then Stephens was no longer its editor (see Chapter 7 reference 9).

4. *OS* 23/2/1861, 11/5/1861, 6, 27/12/1862.

5. N. Kirk, *The Growth of Working Class Reformism in Mid-Victorian England*, Croom Helm 1985, pp. 256–260.

6. Farnie, p. 168. A. Lock, 'The Role of Local Clergy and Ministers in the Stalybridge Riots of 1863', *Looking Back at Stalybridge* ed. A. Lock, Stalybridge 1989, pp. 69, 72.

7. *AR* 6, 13, 20/9/1862, 14/2/1863. Bridges–Beesley 20/1/1862, in S. Liveing, *A 19th Century Teacher*, London 1926, pp. 100–1. For Bridges on Stephens, see Holyoake, pp. 204–5. *AR*, *OS* 8/3/1862.

8. *AR* 14/2/1863, 21/6/1862, 5, 26/7/1862, 16/8/1862, 4, 25/10/1862, 8/11/1862, 6, 20/12/1862. Kirk, pp. 258–262. On the classes, see *AR* 27/9/1862, 27/11/1862. *The Unemployed Operatives of Lancashire and the Lancashire Relief Committees*, Oldham 1863, pp. 16–20. Lock, pp. 72f.

9. Farnie, p. 171. Kirk, p. 258. *AR* 31/1/1863.

10. *AR* 31/1/1863. Liveing, p. 101–2. Holyoake, pp. 211–2, included a reminiscence of Stephens' daughter Henrietta about her father's preaching during the cotton famine, after he had sustained a head injury from a heavy fall. She remembered it as an example of her father's 'wonderful strength of will'.

11. Liveing, p. 102.

12. *AR*, *AS*, *OS* 7/2/1863. *AR* has the fullest account of the town hall speech; that in the *Unemployed Operatives* is a condensed and carefully edited account. The four resolutions passed at the meeting called for an elected relief committee, a change in its constitution, fair wages, and the existsing workers' committee to watch over their interests.

13. *OS* 7, 14/2/1863, *AR* 14/2/1863. Kirk, p. 262.

14. *AR*, *OS* 21/2/1863.

15. *AR* 21/2/1863. *HO* 45/7523.

16. *HO* 45/7523. *AR*, *AS* 14/3/1863. Kirk, p. 262. Lock, pp. 82–3.

17. Kirk, pp. 262–4. P. Joyce, *Work, Society and Politics*, Methuen 1980, pp. 150–2. Lock, pp. 82–4.
18. *OS* 28/3/1853. Liveing, pp. 102–3.
19. *HO* 45/7523. *AR* 18/4/1863. In *AR* 9/5/1863, an anonymous letter writer pointed out that Aspland's quotations from Stephens' speeches did not tend to a breach of the peace.
20. *AR* 4/4/1863.
21. Lock, pp. 88–9. *AR* 17, 24/10/1863. Farnie, pp. 171–2.
22. Farnie, pp. 173–6.

9 The Stormy Petrel of Stalybridge

1. *AR* 30/12/1865. Holyoake, p. 212. *AR* 29/12/1866.
2. *AR* 8/2/1866, 24/11/1866.
3. *AR* 23/2/1867.
4. *AR* 30/3/1867. B. Harrison, 'Teetotal Chartism', *History* 58.113, June 1973, pp. 193–217.
5. *AR* 13/4/1867. Harrison, pp. 193–217. Stephens' words to Bridges come from an undated proof slip in the Stephens family papers called *Home Affairs. The Coming Struggle* ed. J. S. Storr. This material was intended for Holyoake's biography, but 'for certain reasons was not inserted in the book'.
6. *AR* 1/6/1867, 21/11/1868 quoting 15/6/1867.
7. *AR* 14/9/1867.
8. *The Altar, the Throne and the Cottage, A Speech by Joseph Rayner Stephens*, Stalybridge 1868. This was a condensed version of a speech delivered at several branches of the Manchester Constitutional Association, and was published by special request. Since Derby was still Prime Minister (pp. 6, 10), the pamphlet must have been published at the latest by February 1868. A later speech with the same title is found in *Preston Herald* 2/5/1868.
9. *MC* 20/2/1868, *AR* 7, 21/3/1868, *Yorkshire Post* 21/4/1868.
10. For the Murphy riots, see Kirk, pp. 321–4, 338–341, Joyce, pp. 257–261, G. J. Stevenson, *Popular Disturbances in England 1700–1870*, Longman 1979, pp. 283–4, W. Glover, *History of Ashton under Lyne and District, 1884*, pp. 317–327. For Stephens' Stalybridge meeting, see *AR* 9/5/1868, *Ashton News* 9/5/1868, 11/5/1868, *Report of a Public Meeting of the Ratepayers of Stalybridge convened by the Mayor and held in the Town Hall, Thursday May 7th 1868*, especially p. 19. In Stephens' defence of the Irish Church, there is an echo of Bunting's argument against him in 1834. Wesleyan Methodism was in his mind that night, for he attacked the current Wesleyan President for committing Wesleyans to disestablishment.
11. Kirk, p. 322. Joyce, pp. 260–1. *AR* 16/5/1868.
12. Kirk, pp. 340–1, *AR* 1/8/1868, pp. 3, 5.
13. *AN* 22, 29/8/1868, *AR*, *AN* 5/9/1868.
14. *AR* 17/10/1868, 21/11/1868, pp. 3, 7.

15. *AR* 8/8/1868, 5/9/1868, *AN* 12/9/1868, *AR* 19/9/1868, *Stalybridge Standard* 2/4/1870.

16. *Brighton Observer* 11/2/1870, p. 3. Holyoake, p. 231.

17. *AH* 12/3/1892. *SS* 2/4/1870. Holyoake, p. 214.

18. Earle–J. R. Stephens 28/2/1870, G. Stephens–J. R. Stephens 1/3/1870. Marriage Certificate 18/5/1870. *AR* 28/5/1870. *AR, AS* 29/4/1871. *AR* 9/3/1872, 26/10/1872, 9/11/1872. B. Harrison, 'Teetotal Chartism', *History* 58.113, June 1973, pp. 193–217. See also the same author's *Drink and the Victorians*, Faber 1971, pp. 267, 271, 276, 391, and his article 'Henry Vincent', *Dictionary of Labour Biography*, p. 332. Harrison contrasted Vincent and Stephens on licensing; in 'Teetotal Chartism' (p. 215) he argued that the Socialist critique of the temperance movement was foreshadowed by Stephens.

19. *Brighton Observer* 11/2/1870, p. 3. *AR* 19/3/1870. Census return 1871. *AR* 16/9/1871, 31/8/1872. R. S. Betts, 'Jonathan Schofield of Stalybridge and Compulsory Elementary Education (1872)' *Looking Back at Stalybridge*, Stalybridge 1989, pp. 92–103.

20. *AR* 2, 16/3/1872, 3/8/1872, 21/12/1872, *SR* 1/3/1873, 6/9/1873.

21. *AR* 30/8/1873, 6/9/1873, 4/10/1873.

22. *SN* 31/1/1874, 7/2/1874.

23. *SS* 20/6/1874.

24. *SS* 26/6/1874, 13/11/1874.

25. *AR, SS* 1, 8/1/1876.

26. *AR, SS* 15/1/1876, 5/2/1876, 11/3/1876, *AR* 18/4/1876, *AS* 13/1/1877.

27. Holyoake, pp. 222–5.

28. *The Academy* 27/12/1881. W. E. A. Axon, *Cheshire Gleanings*, 1884, p. 111. J. T. Ward, *RT*, p. 115. *AH* 11/3/1905. T. Middleham, *Poets, Poems etc.* 1908, pp. 56–8, *AR* 9, 16/8/1879, p. 4.

29. Holyoake, pp. 224–5. Death Certificate, 18/2/1879. *AR* 1/3/1879. *Times, MG, AR* 22/2/1879.

30. *AR* 9, 16/8/1879. R. Storr–S. Stephens 6/8/1879. *The Stephens Memorial Fund* (pamphlet). Holyoake, pp. 237, 13–18. Holyoake omitted the Newcastle speech of January 1838, the Murphy riots, the elections of 1868 and 1874, and details of the School Board election of 1876. A Wesleyan Methodist reviewer noted his 'lofty contemptuousness which betrays insufficient knowledge' in his treatment of the Conference trial of 1834 (*WM Mag.* 1882, p. 77). For J. C. Gill on Holyoake, see *The Ten Hours Parson*, SPCK 1959, p. 186.

31. *SH* 24/5/1888, *AR* 26/5/1888.

32. *AH* 5/11/1892. *AR* 21/1/1906. *AR, AH* 11/3/1906. Henrietta Earle, Marriage and Death Certificates, 1904, 1906. *Bideford Gazette* 15/5/1906, *AR* 12/5/1906. *AR, SR* 18/7/1885. A. C. Stephens, Marriage and Death Certificates, 1887, 1907.

33. S. Stephens, Death Certificate, 1920. *Derby Mercury* 7/1/1921. There was no obituary of Susanna Stephens in the Stalybridge or Ashton press.

10   The Stephenites

1. *AR* 22/2/1879.
2. *CA* 8/5/1837 pp. 148–9 showed John Stephens' fear that circulation had suffered because of the paper's stand on factory reform. For the belief that the Stephenites were political rather than religious, see W. Glover, *History of Ashton under Lyne and District*, 1884, p. 317.
3. *SMM* Oct 1834, p. 194. Stephens upheld this principle; see *SMM* Feb 1840, pp. 38–42. B. Gregory, *Sidelights on the Conflicts* of Methodism 1827–1852, Cassell 1899, p. 150.
4. Stephenite *Plan*, May–July 1839. *Watchman's Lantern* 1835, p. 384 (Ashton), *CA* 22/9/1834 (Stalybridge), *CA* 10/11/1834. *Observer* 30/12/1838.
5. E. Butterworth, *Diary* 18/8/1836, 11/11/1836. *The Watchman's Lantern* 1835, p. 384. *Oldham Circuit Plan* April–July 1835. *MSA* 20/6/1835. *MG* 4/10/1834 (Royton). *CA* 7/12/1835 p. 391.
6. *NS* 6/10/1838, *CA* 22/8/1836.
7. *CA* 22/8/1836, 26/9/1936, Holyoake, p. 56. Compare *NS* 6/10/1838, in which Stephens lost five or six preaching places at a stroke within three months of taking up the factory issue. *CA* suggests it happened five months later, spread over a period of two months in August–September 1836.
8. *CA* 22/8/1836, 17/10/1836. The placards in these two accounts are different, the former relating to the London lobbying in March, the latter to the 'turning off' of Stephens in August–September. *AH* 5/11/1892. *Lancashire Quarter Sessions Dissenting Meeting House Register*, 94A 1834–7, and 3051/43. *WMA Mag.* 1850 p. 247, 1849, p. 464, 1851, pp. 145–8.
9. Information from Mr E. A. Rose. *CA* 10/7/1837, p. 222. E. Butterworth *Diary* 13/8/1836. *MSA* 8/4/1837, p. 3.
10. *CA* 17/10/1836. See also Chapter 5, p. 171.
11. *NS* 6/10/1838. Stephens reminded the Charlestown membership in 1840 of the days 'when we had no other shelter than what the bare heaven afforded us. In cold and heat, by day and night, the wayside or the hill was our only temple' (*SM Mag.* May 1840, pp. 114–6). *Charlestown chapel deeds. NS* 1/9/1838, p. 5. *St Thomas Hyde Diamond Jubilee Souvenir Handbook* and information from Mr E. A. Rose.
12. Charlestown chapel deeds.
13. Holyoake, p. 16, quoting from handbill of 1838. *MSA* 7/7/1838, p. 3. *NS* 4, 18/8/1838, 8, 22/9/1838.
14. *NS* 13/10/1838. Leaflet *Our Champion Stephens. Observer* 30/12/1838. E. A. Rose, *Methodism in Ashton under Lyne 1797–1914*, Ashton 1969, p. 50.

15. Stephenite *Plan*, May–July 1839. *NS* 26/10/1839, p. 6.
16. Goddard, p. 155. *PP 6*, p. 44 (Shepherd and Shepherdess Fields 12/5/1839). *PP 13*, p. 104 (Ashton 3/8/1839).
17. *NS* 24/3/1838, 14/4/1838. However, Stephens' first known contact with the republican freethinker Holyoake was not until July 1848; see *The Reasoner* 1848, pp. 119, 187–8. Charlestown chapel deeds. *CA* 4/8/1834 p. 246. Stephenite *Plans* May–July 1839, April–July 1852. *NS* 5/1/1839 p. 7. *HO 20/10*.
18. Stephenite *Plan* May–July 1839. *Stockport Advertiser* 10/1/1839. *Champion* 6/1/1839, *HO 20/10*. *MT* 21/2/1846. R. Sykes, 'Early Chartism and Trade Unionism in South–East Lancashire', *The Chartist Experience* ed. J. Epstein and D. Thompson, Macmillan 1982, p. 169. C. Godfrey, 'The Chartist Prisoners 1839–41', *International Review of Social History* 24, 1979, pp. 189–228. J. T. Ward, *FM*, pp. 322, 356, 363.
19. *AH* 12/8/1893. Stephenite *Plans* May–July 1839, April–July 1852. *MT* 21/2/1846. Holyoake, p. 237.
20. *Champion* 6/1/1839. Stephenite *Plans* May–July 1839, April–July 1852, 9/10/1853–1/1/1854. *Deed* of the People's School. *AR* 16/9/1871, p. 8.
21. *AH* 12/3/1892, 5/11/1892. Stephenite *Plans* May–July 1839, April–July 1852, 9/10/1853–1/1/1854. Information from Mr E. A. Rose. Holyoake p. 257.
22. *Times* 27/6/1839. *Sun* 1/7/1839. *MSA* 6/7/1839. *Champion* 7/7/1839.
23. *NS* 26/10/1839 p. 6. *SM Mag* Feb. 1840 p. 41, Jan 1840 pp. 5, 9–10, Oct. 1840, p. 232.
24. *SMM* May 1840, pp. 97–104, April 1840, p. 92. For other warnings against sectarianism, see *SM Mag* April 1840, pp. 82–7, 94–5, May, pp. 104–6, July, pp. 145–7, 161–4.
25. *SM Mag* Jan. 1840, p. 4, July 1840, p. 161–4, Feb. 1840, pp. 38–42, July 1840, pp. 145–7, October 1840, pp. 234–41, Jan. 1840, p. 9, May 1840, pp. 97–104, April 1840, p. 93, July 1840, p. 154.
26. *SM Mag* May 1840, pp. 114–6, October 1840, pp. 232–4.
27. *PM* June 1841, p. 192. *Deeds* of the People's School 1838–41. The occupations of the school trustees were: confectioner, shopkeeper (three), cabinet maker, leather cutter, weaver (two), spinner, carter, moulder. J. T. Ward, *RT*, p. 95.
28. *MG* 10, 17/2/1844. Charlestown Chapel deed 22/3/1844.
29. *AC* 7/10/1848, p. 1. Religious Census, 1851.
30. Stephenite *Plans* April–July 1852, 9/10/1853–1/1/1854, *AH* 24/5/1888, 5/11/1892.
31. Charlestown Chapel deed. *AR* 19/4/1856. W. Glover, *History of Ashton-under-Lyne and the Surrounding District*, 1884, p. 317. The George Street Hyde cause is last heard of on the *Plan* for 9/10/1853–1/1/1854. *AWH* 11/7/1857, p. 3; in 1873, King Street worship was still Anglican 'almost to the letter' (*AR* 30/8/1873). *AS* 20/8/1859, p. 3. *AWH* 4/4/1857, p. 2.

32. *AS* 17/4/1858, *AR* 5/9/1868, p. 8.
33. *SR*, *SS* 13/11/1875. *AH* 5/8/1893–28/10/93. Stephenite *Plan* 9/10/1853–1/1/1854. *AH* 18/1/1906, *AR* 20/1/1906. Holyoake, p. 237.
34. *AR* 26/6/1875, 17/7/1875–6/11/1875. Stephens gave no prior warning of his last sermon, so it could not be reported in full. The two brief surviving accounts are in *SR* and *SS* 13/11/1875. 'About thirty persons, comprising the remnant of Mr Stephens's late congregation' are mentioned as having attended their ex-minister's School Board campaign meeting in January 1876; see *SS* 8/1/1876. *AR* 22/2/1879. The People's School was let to the British schools (*AR* 4/10/1862) and became Holy Trinity Mission Hall in 1881.
35. Disestablishment as the motive of the Wesleyan Conference's action in 1875 is strongly implied in the *Methodist Recorder* editorial of 17/8/1875. See also Anon., *Methodism in 1879*, London 1879, pp. 89–114.
36. *SM Mag* April 1840, p. 82. *AC* 3/11/1849, p. 2.

11 Conclusion

1. *Oldham Weekly Chronicle* 22/5/1976. Stephens and Paisley are totally dissimilar in character and message, but both in particular regions founded their own churches which maintained them in independence, both were compelling speakers who held that their politics came from their faith, both could count on unquestioning support in their own strongholds, and both were accused of an ambiguous attitude to violence, while avoiding involvement in it.
2. *Stalybridge Standard* 8/1/1876.
3. H. Butterfield, *Christianity and History*, Fontana 1957, p. 189.
4. Joseph Parker, *A Preacher's Life*, 1899, p. 48. I am indebted to Mr E. A. Rose for knowledge of this source.
5. *Stalybridge Standard* 2/4/1870, p. 7. R. Blake, *The Conservative Party from Peel to Churchill*, Fontana 1972, pp. 22–6.
6. R. Blake, *Disraeli*, University Paperback, Methuen 1969, pp. 549–550, 553–4, 555–6. In a leaflet issued by the committee of the Stephens Memorial Fund, workers were reminded of the 'very active part' Stephens took in old age in the agitation preceding the 1874 Act. *Wakefield Express* 7/11/1863. Stephens–Howell, 11/2/1875.
7. *Observer* 30/12/1838. S. Liveing, *A Nineteenth Century Teacher*, London 1926, p. 102. *AR* 13/4/1867; in this speech he said: 'I have always thought the invention of machinery good.' *AR* 22/6/1872.
8. *The Political Preacher* 6/1/1839, pp. 13–20, from which the quotation is taken, is another general summary of Stephens' message; it was reprinted in the *People's Magazine* and in *Champion* 10/11/1849. *Stalybridge Standard* 13/11/1875. For Professor Butterfield on religion in history, see *Daily Telegraph Magazine* 287, 17/4/1970, p. 26. S. E. Keeble, *Christian Respon-*

sibility for the Social Order, Epworth 1922, p. 132.

9. H. Gollwitzer, *The Christian Faith and the Marxist Criticism of Religion*, 1970, p. 91. I am grateful to Dr J. Pasztor for knowledge of this source.

10. Holyoake, p. 217.

Bibliography

A. Original sources

1. Manuscripts

Ashton Poor Rate Books 1855–60 (Tameside Local Studies Library)

Butterworth, E., *Diary*, (Oldham Reports) 1829–43 (Oldham Local Studies Library)

Census Returns, 1841–71 (Public Records Office)

Certificates of birth, marriage and death

Charlestown Chapel deeds

Egerton, Lord F., Letters (Lancashire Records Office, Preston)

Fielden, J., Papers (JRULM)

Home Office Papers (Public Records Office, Kew)

HO 20/10 (Interviews with Chartist Prisoners, 1840)

40/38 (Letters and Depositions on disturbances implicating J. R. Stephens in 1838)

45/2410 (Letters on disturbances implicating J. R. Stephens in 1848)

45/7523 (Letters on disturbances implicating J. R. Stephens in 1863)

MH 12/5413–5 (Documents of the Ashton Poor Law Union, 1837–48)

TS 11/814 (Treasury Solicitor's Paper on the Stephens case, 1838)

Lancashire Quarter Sessions: Dissenting Meeting House Register (Lancashire Records Office, Preston)

Minutes of the Committee of the Wesleyan Methodist Missionary Society (MCOD archives in SOAS)

Owen, S., Letters (MCOD archives in SOAS)

People's School Deeds (Tameside Borough Council)

Reece, R., Diary (MA in JRULM)

Scott, G., Letters (MCOD archives in SOAS)

Stephens, J., Letters (MA in JRULM)

——— Notes on life (MA in JRULM)

——— Sampler of the family of John and Rebecca Stephens

—— Will, 1841 (Public Records Office)

Stephens, J. R., Letters (MA in JRULM, MCOD archives in SOAS, Bishopsgate Institute, London; other relevant letters of various members of the Stephens family in private hands)

—— Ordination Certificate, 1826 (in private hands)

—— A Prayer – from the German, 1831 (MA in JRULM)

Wesleyan Methodist Ministerial Candidates Book (MA in JRULM)

NB Key to the abbreviations used above:

JRULM John Rylands University Library of Manchester
MA   Methodist Archives
MCOD Methodist Church Overseas Division
SOAS   School of Oriental and African Studies, London

2. *Printed*

The Academy, 1881

Alfred (S. Kydd), *The History of the Factory Movement* Vol. 2, London 1857

Annual Register 1838–9

Anon, Case and Resolutions of the Manchester District Meeting, 1834

Anon, *Copies of the True Bills found against the Rev. J. R. Stephens,* Liverpool 1839

Anon, *Our Champion Stephens,* n.d.

Anon, *The Case of the Rev. J. R. Stephens, Wesleyan Minister, collected from the Christian Advocate Newspaper,* London 1834

Anon, *Trial of the Rev. J. R. Stephens* (from the *Northern Star*), London 1839

Anon, *Wesleyan Takings,* Volume 1, London 1840

Ashton Chronicle, 1848–9

Ashton Herald, 1888–93, 1905

Ashton News, 1868–74

Ashton Reporter, 1856–1912

Ashton Ricker, 1856

Ashton Standard, 1858–1879

Ashton Times, 1851–2

Ashton Weekly Herald, 1857

The Beehive, 1863–4

Bideford Gazette, 1906

Birmingham Journal, 1834, 1838

Blackburn Gazette, 1836

Blackwood's Magazine, 1838

Bradford Herald, 1842

Bradford Observer, 1842

Brighton Observer, 1870

The Champion, 1839

The Champion, 1849–51

The Charter, 1839–40

Chester Chronicle, 1839

Christian Advocate, 1830–1839

Derby Mercury, 1921

Easby, J., *J. R. Stephens Unveiled,* Manchester 1837

Goddard, H. int. Pringle, P., *Memoirs of a Bow Street Runner,* London 1956

Gordon, A., 'Joseph Rayner Stephens', *Dictionary of National Biography* Vol. 54.

Gregory, B., *Autobiographical Reminiscences,* London 1903

—— *Scriptural Church Principles in Wesleyan Methodist Polity and History,* London 1888

—— *Sidelights on the Conflicts of Methodism,* London 1899

Hartley, T. G. (ed.), Hall's *Circuits and Ministers,* London 1912

Hill, W. *An Alphabetical Arrangement of all the Wesleyan Methodist Ministers and Preachers on Trial . . . London, 1838*

Holyoake, G. J., *Life of Joseph Rayner Stephens,* London 1881

—— *Sixty Years of an Agitator's Life,* London 1906

Leeds Intelligencer, 1837, 1864

Leeds Times, 1836–8

Manchester and Salford Advertiser, 1833–46

Manchester Chronicle, 1839

Manchester Courier, 1847–8, 1861, 1874

Manchester Guardian, 1834, 1838, 1844, 1846, 1849, 1861, 1879

Manchester Times, 1832–46, 1854

Methodist Recorder, 1875

Minutes of Wesleyan Methodist Conferences, 1825–34

Newcastle Chronicle, 1838

National Temperance Advocate, 1848

New Moral World, 1841

Norfolk Chronicle, 1838

Norfolk Gazette, 1838

Northern Liberator, 1838–9

Northern Star, 1837–1841, 1846
Nottingham and Newark Mercury, 1839–42
Nottingham Review, 1839–42
Observer, 1838
Oldham Circuit Plan, 1835
Oldham Standard, 1859–63
Oldham Weekly Chronicle, 1976
People's Magazine, 1841–2
Preston Chronicle, 1836
Preston Herald, 1868
The Reasoner, 1848
Robinson, S., *A Letter to Charles Hindley Esq. M.P.*, Ashton 1837
Scott, G., *A Coronet laid at the feet of Jesus*, London 1856
Smith, J. F. (ed.), *Manchester School Register* (Cheetham Society Vol. 93)
Stalybridge Annual, 1927
Stalybridge Herald, 1888
Stalybridge News, 1874
Stalybridge Reporter, 1873
Stalybridge Standard, 1874–7, 1879
Standard, 1839
Stephenite Circuit Plans, 1839, 1852, 1853–4
Stephens, J., *The Advantages which Man derives from Woman*, 3rd edn, London 1828
—— *The Mutual Relations, Claims and Duties of the Rich and the Poor*, Manchester 1819
Stephens, J. R., *A Sermon preached by the Rev. Mr Stephens*, London 1839
—— *A Speech delivered at the Co-operative tea party, Stalybridge*, Stalybridge 1866
—— *Report of a Public Meeting of the Ratepayers of Stalybridge*, Stalybridge 1868
—— *Sketch of the Life and Opinions of Richard Oastler*, (Anon, but by J. R. Stephens), London 1838
—— *Stephens's Vindication*, 1838
—— *The Altar, the Throne and the Cottage*, Stalybridge 1868
—— *The Political Preacher*, Manchester 1839
—— *The Political Pulpit 1–13*, 1839
—— *The Unemployed Operatives of Lancashire and the Lancashire Relief Committees*, Oldham 1863
—— *To the Electors of the Borough of Ashton under Lyne*, 1837

The Stephens Memorial Fund, n.d.

Stephens's Methodist Magazine, 1834

Stephens's Monthly Magazine, 1840

Stockport Advertiser, 1839

Storr, J. S. and Bridges, J. H., *Home Affairs: the Coming Struggle,* n.d.

The Sun, 1839

Swallow, L., *Shameful Treatment, Important Enquiry before the Poor Law Guardians,* 1848

The Times, 1839–79

The True Scotsman, 1838–41

Wakefield Express, 1863

Wakefield Free Press, 1863

Watchman, 1839–41

Watchman's Lantern, 1835

A Wesleyan Methodist, *An apology for Wesleyan Methodism in a letter to the Rev. Thomas Robinson, minister of the Methodist New Connexion,* London 1834

Wesleyan Methodist Magazine, 1826–34, 1846

Wesleyan Methodist Association Magazine, 1849–51

Yorkshire Post, 1868–9

B. Secondary sources

Anon, *Methodism in 1879,* London 1879

Anon, 'Methodism in Sweden' (in *London Quarterly Review,* 1869)

Ashmore, O., 'The Industrial Archeology of Ashton-under-Lyne' (in Harrop and Rose, *Victorian Ashton,* 1974)

Australian Dictionary of Biography 1788–1850, Melbourne 1986

W. E. A. Axon, *Cheshire Gleanings,* Manchester 1884

Battiscombe, G., *Shaftesbury,* London 1974

Baylen, F. J. O. and Gossman, N. J., *Biographical Dictionary of British Radicals,* Vol. 2, Brighton 1984

Beer, M., *A History of British Socialism,* Vol. 2, London 1940

Bellamy, J. H. and Saville, J., *Dictionary of Labour Biography,* London 1982

Betts, R. S., 'Jonathan Schofield of Stalybridge and Compulsory Elementary Education' (in Lock, *Looking Back at Stalybridge,* 1989)

Blackett, J., *History of South Australia,* Adelaide 1911

Blake, R., *The Conservative Party from Peel to Churchill,* London 1972

—— *Disraeli,* London 1969

Bloomfield, Lady G., *Memoir of Benjamin, Lord Bloomfield*, 2 vols, London 1884

Bowman, W. M., *England in Ashton under Lyne*, Ashton 1960

Bowmer, J. C., 'Ordination in Methodism' (in *Proceedings*, 1974)

Briggs, A. (ed.), *Chartist Studies*, London 1959

—— (ed.), *The Nineteenth Century*, London 1985

Bulletin of the Society for the Study of Labour History, Vol. 34, 1977

√ Butterfield, H., *Christianity and History*, London 1957

√ Chadwick, O., *The Victorian Church*, Vol. 1, London 1966

Chalenor, W. H., 'Reminiscences of Thomas Dunning', (in *Transactions* 1947)

Church History, Vol. 42, USA 1973.

Clark, J. N., *English Society 1688–1832*, Cambridge 1985

Cole, G. D. H., *Chartist Portraits*, London 1941

Colley, L., *Britons: Forging the Nation, 1707–1837*, Yale and London 1992

Daily Telegraph Magazine 217, 17/4/1970

Davies, H., 'A Shot in the Dark' (in Harrop and Rose, *Victorian Ashton*, 1974)

√ Davies, R., *Methodism*, London 1963

√ Davies, R., George, A. R. and Rupp, G. (eds), *A History of the Methodist Church in Great Britain*, Vol, 2, London 1978

Driver, C., *Tory Radical*, Oxford, 1946

Driver, F., 'Tory Radicalism?' (in *Northern History*, Vol. 27, 1991)

Edsall, M., *The Anti-Poor Law Movement 1834–41*, Manchester 1971

Edwards, M. S., 'The Resignation of Joseph Rayner Stephens' (in *Proceedings* 1967)

Epstein, J. and Thompson, D. (eds), *The Chartist Experience*, London 1982

Epstein, J., *The Lion of Freedom*, London 1982

Farnie, D. A., 'The Cotton Famine in Great Britain' (in Radcliffe, *Essays*, 1975)

Faulkner, H. U., *Chartism and the Churches*, New York 1916

Follows, J. W., *Antecedents of the International Labour Office*, Oxford 1951

Gammage, R. C., *History of the Chartist Movement*, Newcastle 1894

Gill, J. C., *The Ten Hours Parson*, London 1959

Glover, W., *History of Ashton under Lyne and District*, Ashton 1884

Godfrey, C., 'The Chartist Prisoners 1839–41' (in *International Review* 1979)

Godfrey, C. and Epstein, J., 'HO 20/10: interviews of Chartist Prisoners 1840–1' (in *Bulletin*, 1977)

Gowland, D., *Political Religion and Religious Politics in South-East Lancashire, 1834–5* (unpublished Ph.D thesis)

Hagen, O., *Preludes to Methodism in North Europe*, Oslo 1961

Harrison, B., *Drink and the Victorians*, London 1971

—— 'Teetotal Chartism' (in *History*) 1973)

Harrison, B. and Hollis, P. (eds), *Robert Lowery, Radical and Chartist*, London 1979

Harrop, S. A., '19th Century Housing in Ashton' (in *Victorian Ashton*, 1974)

Harrop, S. A. and Rose, E. A., (eds), *Victorian Ashton*, Ashton 1974

Hempton, D., *Methodism and Politics in British Society*, London 1987

Hill, S., *Bygone Stalybridge*, Leeds 1987 edn.

History, Vol. 58, 1973

Hobsbawm, E. J., The Age of Revolution 1789–1848, New York and London 1962

—— *Labouring Men*, London 1965

Holland, J., 'Hugh Mason' (in Harrop and Rose, *Victorian Ashton* 1974)

International Review of Social History, Vols. 19, 1974 and 24, 1979

Jephson, H., *The Platform*, Vol. 2, London 1892

Johnson, D. A., 'Between Evangelicalism and a Social Gospel: The Case of Joseph Rayner Stephens' (in *Church History*, USA 1973)

Journal of the Northern Branch of the Wesley Historical Society, 1968

Joyce, P., *Work, Society and Politics*, London 1980

Keeble, S. E., *Christian Responsibility for the Social Order*, London 1922

Kemnitz, T. M. and Jacques, F., 'Joseph Rayner Stephens and the Chartist Movement' (in *International Review*, 1974)

Kent, J. H. S., *The Age of Disunity*, London 1966

—— 'The Wesleyan Methodists to 1849' (in Davies, George and Rupp, 1978)

King, H. and D., 'Stalybridge – A New Town' (in Lock, *Looking Back at Stalybridge*, 1989)

Kirk, N., *The Growth of Working Class Reformism in Mid-Victorian England*, London 1985

Knott, J., *Popular Opposition to the 1834 Poor Law*, London 1986

Liveing, S., *A 19th Century Teacher*, London 1926

Lock, A. (ed.), *Looking Back at Stalybridge*, Stalybridge 1989

—— 'The Role of Local Clergy and Ministers in the Stalybridge Riots of 1862' (in Lock, *Looking Back at Stalybridge*, 1989)

London Holborn Quarterly Review, 1943

London Quarterly Review, 1869

Mackintosh, W. H., *Disestablishment and Liberation*, London 1972

Marcroft, A., *Historical Account of the Unitarian Chapel, Oldham*, Oldham 1913

Marx, K., and Engels, F., *The Communist Manifesto*, int. A. J. P. Taylor, London 1967

Mather, F. C., 'The Government and the Chartists' (in Briggs, *Chartist Studies*, 1959)

Mayor, S., *The Churches and the Labour Movement*, London 1967

Micklewright, F. H. A., 'Joseph Rayner Stephens – A Reassessment' (in *London Holborn Quarterly Review*, 1943)

—— 'Joseph Rayner Stephens' (in *Notes and Queries*)

Middleton, T., *Annals of Hyde and District*, Manchester 1899

—— *Poets, Poems and Rhymes of Past Cheshire*, Hyde 1908

Morris, C., *Unyoung, Uncoloured, Unpoor*, London 1969

Murray, A., *A Brief History of the Church in Sweden*, Stockholm 1961

Northern History, 1991

Notes and Queries, 1944

Obelkevich, J., Roper, L. and Samuel, R., *Disciplines of Faith*, London 1987

Parker, J., *A Preacher's Life*, London 1899

Plummer, A., *Bronterre*, London 1971

Pritchard, F. C., *The Story of Woodhouse Grove School*, Apperley Bridge 1978

Proceedings of the Wesley Historical Society, 1967, 1974

Radcliffe, B. M. (ed.), *Essays in Honour of W. O. Henderson, 1750–1914*, Manchester 1975

Rattenbury, O., *Flame of Freedom*, London 1931

Rose, E. A., 'Ashton Churches and Chapels' (in Harrop and Rose, *Victorian Ashton*, 1974)

—— *Methodism in Ashton under Lyne, 1: 1740–1797, 2: 1797–1914*, Ashton 1967, 1969

Rosenblatt, F. F., *The Chartist Movement in its Social and Economic Aspects*, London 1916

Slugg, J. T., *Woodhouse Grove Memorials and Reminiscences*, London 1885

Smith, G., *History of Wesleyan Methodism*, Vol. 3, 6th edn, London 1870

Spence, N. A., 'Joseph Rayner Stephens' (in Lock, *Looking Back at Stalybridge*, 1989

Stevenson, C. J., *Popular Disturbances in England 1700–1870*, London 1979

Style, Vol. 10, 1976

Sykes, R., 'Early Chartism and Trade Unionism in South-East Lancashire' (in Epstein and Thompson, *The Chartist Experience*, 1982)

Taylor, M., *Joseph Rayner Stephens, Political Preacher*, (unpublished Ph.D. thesis), California 1966

Taylor, P. A. M. (ed.), *The Industrial Revolution in Britain*, Lexington, Massachusetts 1970

Thompson, D., *The Chartists*, Aldershot 1986

——— *The Early Chartists*, London and South Carolina, 1971

Thompson, E. P., *The Making of the English Working Class*, London, revd edn 1968

Transactions of the Lancashire and Cheshire Antiquarian Society, Vols. 59, 1947, and 68, 1958

Tylecote, M., *The Mechanics Institutes of Lancashire and Yorkshire before 1851*, Manchester 1957

Vicinius, M., ' "To be Free or Die": the Relationship between Strategy and Style in Chartist speeches, 1838–1839' (in *Style*, 1976)

Waddy, A., *Life of Samuel D. Waddy D.D.*, London 1878

Ward, J. T., *Chartism*, London 1973

——— *The Factory Movement 1830–1855*, London 1962

——— *Popular Movements c. 1830–1850*, London 1983

——— 'Revolutionary Tory' (in *Transactions*, 1958)

Ward, W. R. (ed. and int.), *The Early Correspondence of Jabez Bunting 1820–1829, London 1972*

——— *(ed. and int.) Early Victorian Methodism*, Oxford 1976

——— *Religion and Society in England 1790–1850*, London 1972

Warwick's *Guide to British Labour Periodicals, 1790–1860*, Hassocks 1977

Wearmouth, R. F., *Methodism and the Working Class Movements of England 1800–1850*, London 1937

——— *Some Working Class Movements of the 19th Century*, London 1948

Weaver, S. A., *John Fielden and the Politics of Popular Radicalism 1832–1847*, Oxford 1987

Williams, D., 'Chartism in Wales' (in Briggs, *Chartist Studies* 1959)

Williams, P. M. and D. L., *Extra, Extra, Read all about it*, Ashton n.d.

Wilson, C., 'Prophets in Reverse' (in *Daily Telegraph Magazine*, 1970)

Yeo, E., 'Chartist Religious Belief and the Theology of Liberation' (in Obelkevich, *Disciplines of Faith* 1987)

Index